Fourth Edition

Statistics for Social Workers

Robert W. Weinbach
The University of South Carolina

Richard M. Grinnell, Jr.
The University of Calgary

 LONGMAN

An imprint of Addison Wesley Longman, Inc.

New York • Reading, Massachusetts • Menlo Park, California • Harlow, England
Don Mills, Ontario • Sydney • Mexico City • Madrid • Amsterdam

Acquisitions Editor: Janice E. Wiggins
Project Coordination, Text Design, and Project Management: Interactive Composition
  Corporation
Cover Design: Lili Schwartz
Cover Photograph: PhotoDisc, Inc. © 1997
Art Studio: Interactive Composition Corporation
Full Service Production Manager: Eric Jorgensen
Manufacturing Manager: Hilda Koparanian
Electronic Page Makeup: Interactive Composition Corporation
Printer and Binder: Maple Vail Book Manufacturing Group
Cover Printer: Phoenix Color Corp.

Library of Congress Cataloging-in-Publication Data

Weinbach, Robert W.
    Statistics for social workers / Robert W. Weinbach, Richard M.
  Grinnell, Jr. — 4th ed.
      p.   cm.
    Includes bibliographical references and index.
    ISBN 0–8013–1826–2
    1. Social sciences—Statistical methods. 2. Social service—
  Statistical methods. 3. Statistics. I. Grinnell, Richard M.
  II. Title.
  HA29.W42   1997
  519.5'024'362—dc21   97–14924
                                                  CIP

ISBN 0-8013-1826-2

345678910—MA—009998

Contents

Preface

The favorable reception afforded the preceding three editions of *Statistics for Social Workers* has encouraged us to write a fourth. As before, we continue to believe that professional social workers have a wide range of mathematical backgrounds and varying attitudes toward statistics. They tend to share one common characteristic, however—they are "people oriented." They have selected our profession because they want to work with people, not numbers or abstract concepts. We believe, nonetheless, that if they can see how the use of statistics can be used to help them to become more effective practitioners, they will approach the topic of statistics with less apprehension.

AUDIENCE

As with the previous three editions, this edition is intended for social work students (undergraduate or graduate) and practitioners who are new to statistics. Thus, we assume no prior knowledge of the topic. We have presented the material in the most unintimidating way possible, using a crisp, readable style, and simple language while avoiding difficult words and convoluted phrases. The text is easy to teach from and to learn from. Figures and case examples have been used extensively throughout the book to provide visual representations of the concepts presented.

As with the previous three editions, we continue to stress our belief that statistics is relevant to the development and refinement of those helping skills that professional social workers require. Readers of this book will soon discover that statistical procedures are powerful tools that can help them answer questions about social work practice and can help them to become more effective practitioners.

Bridgette
(7)454-8068

The Impact of Truancy Among
African American Middle School
Students

Implications for SW Practice

Research
Practicum
Autonomous SW Practice
Human Behavior
Policy
Integration of Class Knowledge into Practice

GOAL

The goal of this book is to meet the challenge of introducing today's people-oriented social work students and practitioners to a topic that they might not choose to study. It seeks to explain statistics while keeping in mind social workers' diverse mathematical backgrounds and practice interests. Consequently, it is as "unmathematical" as we dare make it. We do, however, provide enough mathematical explanation to present the core statistical concepts. The book simply contains the language and concepts needed for beginning statistical literacy.

We hope that our modest goal will permit students to make decisions about when a statistical analysis is necessary, to evaluate theoretical or practice-based social work problems, to determine which type of analysis is most appropriate to use in a given research situation, to interpret statistical results, and to communicate the statistical results and interpretations in terms that are meaningful for others. In short, this book is designed to help social workers to appreciate, to interpret, to use, and to integrate statistics within their professional practice. Other, more advanced texts and courses are required for them to become statisticians.

RELIANCE ON COMPUTERS

You have probably heard the slogan "Let your fingers do the walking." Well, our slogan is "Let the computers do the work." We have avoided the inclusion of unnecessary formulas and their derivations while focusing instead on what statistics is all about. Why have we done this? The cost of personal computers and related statistical software packages have continued to decline in price to the point where most students and practitioners can afford them. Many schools and departments of social work throughout the world, as well as most social service agencies, have computer equipment that allows social workers to perform word processing as well as data entry and analyses.

The current state of computer technology suggests an analogy to taking a trip on an airplane. Do we really have to know the laws of aerodynamics to fly in an airplane? Or do we just have to know how to make a reservation and hope that the people who build and fly the planes know those laws well? Do we really need to know how to perform all the mathematical calculations of a statistical test just to use it correctly? Or do we just have to know when to use the correct test and how to program the computer to have it perform the correct statistical analysis on a given data set?

This book will help the reader to choose the correct statistical analysis, although it will offer little to help the reader do the calculations based on statistical probability theory—we now leave that up to the computer. We believe that people have better things to do with their time than trying to compute a statistic mathematically when a computer can do the job in seconds.

The chances of social workers in the late 1990s doing a statistical analysis by hand with a large data set are small. We would rather have them spend their time determining what a particular statistic means and how to use it than have them try to determine the meaning of a formula and to plug in an endless series of numbers to get a statistic that they may not understand.

We are aware of the limitations of not providing formulas for most statistics in this book and of not showing how the formulas are used in their calculations. There is a great deal of truth to the statement that readers may not totally understand and appreciate a statistic unless they are shown how its formula is derived. To return to our earlier analogy, we admit readily that an airplane passenger who knows the laws of aerodynamics will unquestionably have a greater understanding and appreciation of the achievement of flight than a passenger who does not. However, they both will accomplish their mutual goal: Both will arrive at the same destination at the same time.

Very few of us would fly if we were required to know the laws of aerodynamics before we entered an airplane. In the same vein, very few of us would use statistics if we were required to know the laws of probability and statistical theory. Many of us appreciate and use airplanes without knowing the laws of aerodynamics, and we can be taught to appreciate and use statistics without knowing the laws of probability theory. However, if a reader of this book wishes to further develop statistical literacy by studying the formulas upon which a statistical analysis is based, there are many more advanced books and courses that can assist in this undertaking.

CONTENTS

The contents of this edition have been selected and arranged so that the book can be used as a supplementary statistics text for a social work research methods course or as the primary text in an introductory social work statistics course:

- Chapter 1 introduces basic concepts and definitions that are necessary to the understanding of statistics.
- Commonly used descriptive statistics are covered in Chapters 2–4. These three chapters contain the statistical language and procedures of the most basic form of statistical analyses—that which is designed to summarize and display the distribution of a single variable.
- Chapters 5–7 introduce readers to the related topics of inferential statistics and hypothesis testing.
- The five remaining chapters (Chapters 8–12) present a wide array of statistical methods commonly used by social workers to test hypotheses about relationships between and among variables at different measurement levels.

We have used numerous micro– and macro–social work practice examples to illustrate the use of basic statistical concepts. Through these examples, we have tried to demonstrate that statistics can help us answer everyday social work questions. The answers, in turn, can be used to enhance our effectiveness as practitioners.

CHANGES IN THIS EDITION

Over the years, we have received hundreds of comments from students and instructors who used the first three editions. With these comments in mind, we determined the specific topics to cover, the depth of the topics covered, and the sequencing of chapters within the book.

With a tremendous amount of input, this edition has been reorganized to make the book more functional, practical, and manageable for students and instructors alike. As mentioned, we responded to many of the instructors and students who generously critiqued the three earlier editions. We sought to retain what worked and to revise those areas that needed changes. While this edition has kept its unique identity, it also is much more comprehensive than any one of the previous three editions.

A quick glance at the Table of Contents reveals that this edition has undergone some major and minor changes. The most obvious change is the addition of a new chapter on sampling distributions and hypothesis testing (Chapter 6). This edition has been enhanced with new and updated examples, tables, and figures. To make room for all the new content, some topics (those that were judged to require less extensive discussion) were condensed and others combined.

This edition is organized in a way that makes good sense in teaching introductory statistics. Many other chapter sequences that could be followed would make just as much sense, however. The chapters in this book were consciously planned to be independent of one another. They can be read out of the order in which they are presented, or they can be selectively omitted. They will probably make the most sense to students, however, if they are read in the sequence as presented because each builds upon the preceding one.

ACKNOWLEDGMENTS

Many people have contributed to the completion of this book. Hundreds of students, through questions and challenges posed during class sessions over the past 25 years, have served to shape the authors' thoughts about how statistics can be taught in a meaningful and "user-friendly" manner. A number of colleagues have kindly shared their expertise by commenting on earlier drafts of this edition or by commenting on coverage in the earlier editions.

The following people may take partial credit for whatever achievements and improvements this edition represents; we alone must accept responsibility for its shortcomings:

- Hailv Abatena, University of Nevada-Las Vegas
- William E. Berg, University of Wisconsin-Milwaukee
- Joe Crymes, University of Maryland-Baltimore
- Peter A. Gabor, The University of Calgary
- Leon Ginsberg, University of South Carolina
- Arnold L. Greenfield, Michigan State University
- Bud Hanson, University of Windsor
- Kenneth L. Hobby, Harding University
- Walter W. Hudson, Florida State University
- Miriam Johnson, University of South Carolina
- J. M. Kapoor, Indiana University
- Keith M. Kilty, Ohio State University
- Judy L. Krysik, Phoenix, Arizona

- Sally Mason, University of Illinois-Chicago
- Grant McDonald, York University
- Steven L. McMurtry, University of Wisconsin-Milwaukee
- Barbara Morrison-Rodriguez, University of South Carolina
- Cathy Pike, The University of South Carolina
- Paul R. Raffoul, University of Houston
- Cleora Roberts, University of South Florida
- Allen Rubin, The University of Texas at Austin
- Michael J. Sheridan, Virginia Commonwealth University
- Jackie D. Sieppert, The University of Calgary
- Glenn Stone, Indiana University
- Althea J. Truitt, Benedict College
- Yvonne A. Unrau, The University of Calgary
- Roland M. Wagner, San Jose State University
- Alex Westerfelt, University of Kansas

If the material presented in this book helps readers to develop or expand their statistical knowledge base and assists them in preparing for more advanced statistics courses, our efforts will have been more than justified. If it also encourages them to appreciate the place of statistics in professional social work practice, our task will have been fully rewarded.

July 1997

Robert W. Weinbach
Richard M. Grinnell, Jr.

Chapter 1

Introduction

Both the National Association of Social Workers (NASW) and the Council on Social Work Education (CSWE) strongly encourage professional social workers to study statistics. Both professional organizations believe we need a good statistical knowledge base for three highly interrelated reasons:

1. We *produce research findings*. A good statistical knowledge base enhances our ability to design well-thought-out and useful social work research studies.
2. We *consume research findings*. Understanding how to consume statistics (via the professional literature) increases the likelihood that we will use proven effective and efficient practice interventions with our clients.
3. We *evaluate our practice effectiveness*. We evaluate our practice methods and our social service programs that, at times, rely on statistics.

In reference to the first point, professional social workers simply need to know how to do various statistical analyses that are nothing more than using well-established methods to gather, to sort, to organize, and to analyze data. Why is this so? The answer is simple: We contribute to our profession's knowledge base by disseminating knowledge derived from our own research studies. We communicate this knowledge to other social workers so they can use this new knowledge to become more effective practitioners. If the knowledge that we seek to communicate is to be credible, however, we must demonstrate that our data were generated, analyzed, and interpreted according to well-established, accepted methodological and statistical procedures.

Fortunately, as we shall see throughout this entire book, these procedures are based on simple logic that we already use in many practice situations. We apply these procedures in a similar manner whether we collect and analyze data for making a "practice" decision or for interpreting the findings derived from a "research" study.

Let us now turn our attention to the second point. When we consume knowledge, we must be statistically literate if we are to be critical consumers of information contained in professional journal articles and books. Unless we know whether a particular statistical analysis was performed correctly, we cannot know whether the findings derived from the research study that used it are credible.

Highly related to the first two points is the third; we must systematically and objectively evaluate our own practice effectiveness and the social service programs where we work. To do this, we need to rely on more than personal insight, past experiences, intuition, or the feeling that we are (or are not) being effective. At times, we need to employ accepted evaluative methods that rely, at least in part, on statistics.

In short, a statistical analysis neither guarantees the generation of "true knowledge" when doing a research study (Point 1 above), nor does it guarantee "positive client outcomes" when we work with clients (Points 2 and 3 above). Statistics do, however, have the potential to increase the likelihood of these three interrelated events occurring and, at the same time, helps us move toward the goal of becoming knowledge-based professional social work practitioners.

USES OF STATISTICS

Whether we are evaluating our own practice effectiveness or conducting a research study to generate new knowledge, statistical analysis can be very useful. It is of great assistance, for example, when we select, design, evaluate, and fine-tune data collection instruments. It can also help us make decisions about how large a research sample we need to have for a given research study or whether a measurement instrument is likely to provide valid and reliable data.

Once data are collected, statistical analysis can help us

- summarize the characteristics of a specific research sample or population;
- estimate the characteristics of the population from which our sample was drawn;
- determine if any patterns of relationships found within our sample can safely be generalized back to the population from which the sample was drawn.

A statistical analysis produces useful information only when sound methods for data collection have been used. To put it another way, the results of a good statistical analysis are useless (or, worse yet, misleading) if the data that were collected and statistically examined were not accurate.

Now that we know why we need to have a sound grasp of statistics, we now turn our attention to a few methodological (not statistical) terms contained in many social work research methods books. The understanding of these terms is important if we are truly to understand the place of statistics in social work research.

GENERAL METHODOLOGICAL TERMS

Many terms used in the research enterprise have specific meanings. We begin this book by defining eight of them that are central to our study of statistics. These terms are

(1) data (2) information, (3) variables and constants, (4) conceptualization, (5) operationalization, (6) reliability, (7) validity, and (8) research hypotheses.

Data

The astute reader may have noticed in the previous pages that we have already used the terms "data" and "information." These terms are sometimes used interchangeably in everyday conversation. In this book, however, an important distinction is made between them. *Data* refers to what has been collected within a research study **before** they have been analyzed. (Yes, the term *"data"* is plural, derived from the singular *"datum."*) For example, the combined scores obtained when a standardized self-report measuring instrument that measures the variable "self-esteem" is completed by 100 clients generates data. On the other hand, a client's individual score on the same measuring instrument is datum.

We would like to stress once again that data are the starting point for any statistical analysis; therefore, they must be highly accurate when collected. No conclusions based on a research study's findings can be any better than the data that contributed to those conclusions. A statistical analysis of inaccurate or misleading data is worse than no analysis at all—the analysis can lead to wrong conclusions and to recommendations that can negatively affect the work of social work practitioners.

Information

Data produce *information*. Information is the interpretation we give to the collected data **after** we analyze them. The research finding that "Treatment Intervention A is more successful than Treatment Intervention B in reducing substance abuse among our research participants," for example, is called information. In research, data are collected and analyzed in order to produce information. One of the best distinctions between data and information is as follows: Data are facts, in numerical or descriptive form. Information is the interpretation we give to these facts. The outside temperature is 108F (datum), for example, and we interpret this number to be "very hot" (information).

Both social work "practitioners" and "researchers" engage in many types of data-gathering activities. Our profession uses a wide variety of data collection methods. We use in-depth interviews (e.g., individual, group, telephone), content analyses, participant observations, and direct observations of behaviors in natural settings. We also conduct surveys, group experiments, case experiments, meta-analyses, historical research, and so forth. In addition, we do secondary analyses of existing data sets—data already collected for other purposes—such as agency and hospital records or census data. All of these activities yield data that can be examined using statistical analysis.

Variables and Constants

There is always a limit to how much data we realistically can collect and use in any given practice or research situation. Like a social work practitioner conducting an intake interview, a social work researcher does not need to know everything about the people (or objects) studied. Thus, we limit our data collection activities to only those variables that are useful. Now then, what is a variable?

Variables are characteristics that differ in quantity or quality among the people (or objects) studied. Among human beings, examples of variables are "educational level," "gender," "sexual orientation," "race, ethnicity," "motivational level for treatment," "stress level," and "self-esteem level." The list is practically endless.

In contrast to variables, traits or characteristics that do not vary in quantity or quality among people (or objects) are called *constants*. A simple example of a constant among all human beings is mortality.

Unlike the constant "mortality," "life expectancy," is a variable. As mentioned previously, most, if not all, research studies contain variables. We want to learn why variations occur among people (or objects) and what other variables may relate to these variations in some way. We may study, for example, a sample of female adolescents who are addicted to crack-cocaine. In this study we would attempt to learn how some other variables, such as their "education level" and "income level," might relate to their different patterns of drug usage. In this example, adolescent females and crack cocaine addiction are constants, but the different educational and income levels, along with their patterns of drug use, are variables.

Value Categories and Values of Variables.   The different measurements that a variable can assume can be expressed in words (e.g., high, medium, low) or in numbers (e.g., 1, 2, 3). When measurements are expressed in words, they are called *value categories* and they describe simply different forms that the variable takes. The variable "gender," for example, is measured by classifying clients using two value categories that can be expressed in words—male and female.

The different measurements of a variable can be expressed in numbers as well. When they are expressed in numbers, they are technically called *values,* and reflect more precise measurement than value categories. We can measure the variable "age," for example, by using actual numerical values (e.g., 23, 35, 67, and so forth) to reflect the actual ages of people at their last birthdays.

The variable "highest social work degree completed" can be broken down into four values (1, 2, 3, or 4) based on responses to a questionnaire item:

What is your highest social work degree completed?

1. Associate Degree
2. B.S.W.
3. M.S.W.
4. Ph.D./D.S.W.

The main distinction between a value category and a value is that value categories are usually expressed in words and values are usually expressed in actual numbers reflecting different levels of the variable being measured. Generally, value categories are used with nominal or ordinal level variables and values usually are used with interval or ratio level variables. This distinction will become much clearer when the different measurement levels are discussed later in this chapter.

Frequencies of Value Categories and Values.   More often than not, a given value category (or value) occurs more than once in a group of people (or objects). The number of times that it occurs within a group of cases is called its *frequency*. Obviously, frequencies for the different value categories (or values) of variables vary. Within a research sample of 28 agency clients, for example, the frequency for the value category of "female" might be 16 for the variable "gender," while the frequency for the value category of "male" might be 12.

The following simple example summarizes the relationship between a variable, its value categories, and the frequencies of each value category.

What is your highest social work degree completed?

Value Category	Frequencies
Associate Degree	14
B.S.W.	12
M.S.W.	19
Ph.D./D.S.W.	12

In the above example, the variable "highest social work degree completed" has four value categories (i.e., B.S.W., M.S.W., etc.) and each has a frequency (i.e., there are 14 people who have an Associate Degree, 12 people who have a B.S.W., 19 people who have a M.S.W., 12 people who have a Ph.D./D.S.W.).

Conceptualization

Often when a research study begins, the research problem may contain many constants and variables that appear to be complex. The research problem may seem to take many forms and to be related, or possibly related, to many other constants and variables that in themselves may be difficult to understand. We seek to make this tangle manageable by conceptualizing the constants and variables in which we are most interested. This process is an important first step toward good measurement that makes any statistical analysis meaningful. In its most basic form, conceptualization is a three-step process.

1. Selecting the most important constants and variables to include in a research study.
2. Stating exactly what we mean by each constant and variable.
3. Stating the value categories (or values) that each variable can take.

After we have selected what constants and variables to study, defining exactly what we mean by each of them is a critical part of conceptualization. Let us say, for example, that we wish to test the following simple research hypothesis:

Research Hypothesis:
Among three-year-old children who are diagnosed autistic at a specific level, Treatment Intervention A will reduce their autistic behavior more than Treatment Intervention B.

The previous statement implies a conviction that the two different treatment interventions (A and B) affect autistic behavior differently. In order to examine the relationship between the two types of treatment interventions used and their relationship to the rate of decrease in the autistic behavior of three-year-old children, we must clearly state the meaning of both variables we have conceptualized to include in our study (i.e., intervention, autistic behavior) and the value categories (or values) that each can assume (as well as the nature of the relationship that we believe to exist between them).

What exactly is autistic behavior? What exactly constitutes Interventions A and B? What exactly do we mean by the word "reduce." Without first delineating the meaning of all variables within a research study, it would be futile to attempt to establish a relationship between, or among, them. Note that among the three-year-old children in our study their level of autism are constants as their age and level of autism do not vary.

Operationalization

Specifying exactly how we are going to measure the variables that we have conceptualized is called *operationalization.* The specific methods used to measure variables differ from place to place, time to time, person to person, and study to study. In different research situations, for example, measurement of the variable "self-esteem" might entail direct observations of the client's behaviors by a collateral, a subjective diagnosis of the client by the social worker, a subjective self-report from the client, or the client's response on a standardized self-administered measuring instrument that measures the variable "self-esteem."

More often than not, we measure variables that cannot be directly observed. Various methods have been developed for use in these situations. One method is to record the verbal, written, and/or physical responses of research participants to specific stimuli. We may wish, for example, to find out the extent to which computerization in a particular social work agency has affected the job satisfaction levels of the social workers employed there. The variable "job satisfaction level of the social workers" could easily be measured before and after the computerization takes place. Methods of measurement might include asking workers directly or having them complete a standardized self-report job satisfaction measuring instrument. We could also measure a behavioral response such as job absenteeism, which previous research studies have indicated is directly related to job satisfaction. Better yet, we might even wish to use all three of these indicators to contribute to our overall measurement of job satisfaction.

Specifying exactly how a variable is to be operationalized is just as important to good measurement, as conceptualization. If, for example, we want to learn something about the relative effectiveness of two different treatment interventions (e.g., individual treatment, group treatment) for treating people who are depressed, we need to state clearly how we will measure both the two different types of interventions and depression. One way to measure depression levels might be to have staff keep records of their clients' appearances. Of course, we would not choose this measurement method to provide a measurement of depression unless there were strong evidence for a relationship between depression levels and personal appearances. And when used alone to measure depression levels, such a measurement method would not be expected to yield accurate results. Another measurement method might be to use each person's score on a standardized self-report measurement instrument that is believed to measure the variable "depression."

However we decide to operationalize the variable "depression," we might hope that a pattern would emerge from our measurements. Perhaps clients who received individual treatment would appear (as a group) to be less depressed than clients who received group treatment. We would be premature if we concluded, however, on the basis of an apparent pattern of this nature, that treatment effectiveness (i.e., reduction of depression) and treatment methods (i.e., individual, group) are, in fact, really related.

As we shall see throughout this book, a good statistical analysis can take some of the guesswork out of any conclusions we wish to make regarding the relationship between and among variables. For example the results of statistical testing (in the above example) could help us make more informed statements about different treatment interventions and how they may (or may not) be related to depression levels. Whether or not the results of statistical testing ultimately suggest to us that individual treatment is more effective than group treatment depends in part on the accuracy of the measurements. Statistical tests only perform mathematical operations with data; they have no way of knowing whether or not the methods used to measure the variables are good ones.

Reliability

In the simplest of terms, *reliability* is the consistency of a measurement. It answers the question: To what degree does the measuring instrument produce consistent results in measuring a variable? One measuring instrument that proposes to measure a variable (such as depression) may produce very consistent measurements in a wide variety of situations. Therefore, it can be considered reliable. Another measuring instrument that measures depression may be influenced by such factors as who is performing the measuring, what specific group of people are being measured, the time of day or year that the measurement takes place, and so on. Thus, it would be considered less reliable than the first measurement.

Validity

Even if a measuring instrument contains a high degree of reliability, that does not guarantee that the measuring instrument (or the measuring procedure) used to measure the variable is a perfect one. A measuring instrument can be very consistent in producing the same measurements, but the measurements can be consistently wrong. How can this be? The measuring instrument (or the measurement procedure) may be biased or distorted in some way. A measuring instrument believed to measure the variable "depression," for example, may produce consistent results in a variety of research situations. If the measuring instrument really is measuring some other variable than depression (e.g., self-esteem, self-concept, self-worth), however, it is not producing an accurate measurement of depression and is not an appropriate means for measuring that variable.

Similarly, a cloth tape measure (the measuring instrument) might have been an accurate selection for measuring widths and lengths of tables at one time. But, if it has shrunk from being left out in the rain, it will no longer produce valid measurements. It will produce, however, very consistent (reliable) results under a variety of measurement conditions, but all measurements that it produces will suggest that tables measured with it are wider and longer than they really are. The measurements of the tables' widths and lengths will all be consistently wrong—but in a very reliable way.

If measurement of a variable is both reliable (consistent) and accurate, then the measuring instrument is *valid*. There cannot be validity without reliability. There can be reliability without validity, however. The conclusion that a measuring instrument has validity is a conclusion that it truly measures the variable it is supposed to measure, and does it consistently and accurately. It goes without saying that only valid measurement of variables produces data that, when statistically analyzed, can generate valuable knowledge about those variables and the possibility of relationships between and among them.

Research Hypotheses

We have already used the term *research hypothesis* in some of the examples above. Many types of statistical analysis are devoted to the task of hypothesis testing. What then is a research hypothesis? A *research hypothesis* is a statement of a relationship between or among variables. It is stated in the future tense to reflect the fact that we are predicting what will be found when the data derived from the research study are analyzed. A research hypothesis expresses what we believe will be found to be true. It is stated in such a way that it can gain support (or not gain support) through a statistical analysis. We might state a research hypothesis about the two variables "depression" and "sleep patterns," for example, as follows:

> *Research Hypothesis 1:*
> People who are depressed will have different sleep patterns than people who are not depressed.

We can test the above hypothesis by measuring the sleep patterns for people who are diagnosed as depressed (via some kind of measuring instrument) and compare these patterns with those of people who are identified as not depressed. Sleep patterns could be operationalized in relation to sleep phases or simply as number of hours of sleep.

The above research hypothesis proposes a relationship between two variables—"sleep patterns" and "depression"—but it says little about the nature of the relationship between them, only that one variable is related to the other. If we ultimately find statistical support for the research hypothesis that the two variables are related, that relationship may mean that depression may influence sleep patterns, that sleep patterns may influence depression, or neither one. It could mean, simply, that the two variables naturally covary; that is, certain value categories (or values) of one variable tend to be found with certain value categories (or values) of the other. But suppose that we had stated our research hypothesis in a slightly different way:

> *Research Hypothesis 2:*
> Disturbed sleep patterns will cause depression.

To understand the above research hypothesis, we need to discuss two types of variables, independent and dependent. We now turn our attention to independent variables.

Independent Variables.   Unlike Research Hypothesis 1, Research Hypothesis 2 proposes a direct, causative relationship between sleep patterns and depression—disturbed sleep patterns **cause** depression. In other words, one variable (sleep patterns) is predicted to affect the other variable (depression level). The variable that is predicted to do the affecting is known as the *independent variable*. In experimental research designs, the independent variable is either manipulated or introduced. If we wanted to see whether disturbed sleep patterns cause depression, for example, we could (in theory) disturb the sleep patterns of a number of people to see if they became depressed. (In reality, there are ethical reasons why we would do nothing of the sort.) Theoretically, however, sleep patterns would be the independent variable—the one that is manipulated.

Dependent Variables.   The second variable in Research Hypothesis 2, "depression," is called the dependent variable. A *dependent variable* is believed to be dependent upon the independent variable. In Research Hypothesis 2, people's depression levels (dependent variable) depend on their sleep patterns (independent variable). The research hypothesis could be turned around, however, to read:

Research Hypothesis 3:
Depression will cause disturbed sleep patterns.

Here, depression, which does the causing, is regarded as the independent variable. What is being affected—sleep patterns—is the dependent variable. In order for a variable to be labeled as dependent, it only needs to be believed to be affected in some way by an independent variable. Of course, other variables such as drugs taken to treat depression (called *intervening* or *extraneous* variables, or some other related term) may help to cause the variation in the dependent variable that occurs or to affect the relationship between the independent and dependent variables in other, subtle ways.

Independent Variables and Dependent Variables or Predictor Variables and Criterion Variables.   Note that the same variable ("depression" **or** "sleep patterns" in our example) can be considered independent **or** dependent according to the way the research hypothesis is stated. In Research Hypothesis 2, depression was the dependent variable. In Research Hypothesis 3, it was the independent variable. Similarly, sleep patterns was the independent variable in Research Hypothesis 2, whereas it was the dependent variable in Research Hypothesis 3.

The terms "independent variable" and "dependent variable" are nothing more than simple labels to aid in the communication process. They are used to indicate the direction of influence between or among variables, based upon logic. They generally are used in research hypotheses that suggest that one variable is believed to affect the other (more than vice versa). This was not the case in Research Hypothesis 1.

In social work research we often are not seeking to demonstrate that one variable directly influences another variable; we wish only to find support for the belief that two variables, that we have neither introduced nor manipulated in any way, covary. If demonstration of covariance, or prediction, between variables is our study's main goal, two other terms are used to describe the relationship between variables. The variable that is used for prediction is called a *predictor variable*. The variable whose value categories (or values) we hope to predict (based upon the predictor variable) is called a *criterion variable*. To make it easier for the beginning student of statistics, and to be consistent with how other books have used the terms, we use the labels "predictor variable" and "criterion variable" in discussing only those statistical analyses that in no way can be used to imply causality; the focus here is on their covariance (i.e., Chapters 8 and 9). We use the labels "independent variable" and "dependent variable" throughout the rest of the chapters.

LEVELS OF MEASUREMENT

The conceptualization and operationalization processes provide a necessary and orderly method for selecting and measuring variables. Formulation of hypotheses and, when appropriate, selecting variables within them, as either independent, dependent, predictor, or criterion, provide further clarification of the study's focus and purpose. As mentioned previously, valid measurement of variables makes it possible for a statistical analysis to accurately summarize the characteristics of a research sample (or population) and to analyze the relationships that appear to exist between the variables. Before a statistical analysis can occur, however, we must make another determination; we must make a judgment as to just how precisely our variables have been measured.

Some variables, by their very nature, are difficult to measure with a great degree of precision. Others can be measured quite precisely, but, through choice or accident, they are measured in a way that provides less precise data than could have been produced. We generally want to select a measuring instrument that yields the highest level of measurement precision possible. But, sometimes, this is neither desirable nor necessary because of either ethical or practical concerns.

Prior to a data analysis, a judgment must be made in reference to how precisely each variable has been measured. Determination of a variable's level of measurement within a given research study is crucial. It (along with other factors discussed in Chapter 6) provides direction as to the most appropriate type of statistical analysis to use. Let us now turn to the four levels of measurement a variable can assume: (1) nominal, (2) ordinal, (3) interval, and (4) ratio.

Nominal

The first, and least precise, level of measurement is the *nominal level measurement*. Its value categories are discrete, or distinct, from each other. It only categorizes variables into subclasses—nothing more, nothing less. The different value categories it takes reflect only a difference in kind. There is no implication of a quantifiable difference among its value categories; therefore, no rank-ordering of value categories is possible. Variables such as, "gender," "race," "ethnicity," "referral source," "diagnosis," "occupation," "sexual orientation," "marital status," and "political party affiliation," are considered at the nominal level of measurement since the value categories used with them tend to be little more than simple labels reflecting qualitative differences. The following is an example of a question in a research questionnaire that would produce nominal level data:

Do you believe the government should provide national health care insurance?

1. Yes
2. No
3. Undecided

A nominal level variable must have two or more value categories, and they must be "distinct, mutually exclusive, and mutually exhaustive." What does that mean? It means that each case (e.g., a research participant or object studied) must appropriately fit into only one of the value categories and there must be an appropriate value category for each case. There are only two value categories, for example, of the nominal level variable "life status"—living or deceased. These two value categories are clearly exhaustive and mutually exclusive, as every person can be classified into one of the categories (exhaustiveness), but only one (exclusiveness).

In nominal level measurement, numerals (e.g., 1, 2, 3) or letters (e.g., A, B, C) are sometimes assigned for convenience. Suppose we have divided the nominal level variable, "type of treatment intervention," into three value categories: individual treatment, group treatment, and family treatment. We could, for example, assign numbers as value categories to the three types of intervention:

1. Individual treatment
2. Group treatment
3. Family treatment

The numbers used above (i.e., 1, 2, 3) serve only to classify. We could, for example, have assigned a letter to each value category:

A. Individual treatment
B. Group treatment
C. Family treatment

It would be meaningless to say that the value category of 1 (or A) is more or less treatment than a 2 (or B) or a 3 (or C), or to make any other statement that implies that the three value categories have any quantitative meaning. As we noted earlier, usually value categories are used to measure nominal level variables and values are used to measure the other three higher levels of measurement—ordinal, interval, ratio—since they reflect more than just differences in kind.

Ordinal

The second level of measurement is ordinal. In ordinal level measurement, variables not only assume different values but they have some distinct quantitative meaning as well. Unlike nominal level measurement, ordinal measurement can use values for its different measurement categories. With ordinal measurement, it is possible to rank-order the values that the variable assumes from high to low or from most to least. Examples of variables that often are measured at the ordinal level are "social class," "occupational prestige," "educational degrees received," "ratings of client change," "ratings of treatment effectiveness," "ratings of clients' satisfaction with treatment," and "rankings of problem severity." Below are some of the more common values (e.g., 1, 2, 3, 4) and corresponding measurements (e.g., considerable, some, little, none) that usually suggest that a variable is at the ordinal level of measurement:

1. Considerable
2. Some
3. Little
4. None

1. High
2. Moderate
3. Low

1. Very effective
2. Somewhat effective
3. Somewhat ineffective
4. Very ineffective

1. Very severe
2. Severe
3. Mild
4. Very mild

The following are examples of research questions on a questionnaire that would produce ordinal measurement:

How would you rate your social work supervisor? (Circle one number below.)

1. Very good
2. Good
3. Fair
4. Poor
5. Very poor

How satisfied are you in your current job? (Circle one number below.)

1. Very satisfied
2. Somewhat satisfied
3. Somewhat dissatisfied
4. Very dissatisfied

Values used with ordinal level measurement make it possible to identify not only differences between variable subclasses but also their relative positions. It is important to note that ordinal values neither indicate absolute quantities nor assume equal intervals between them. We might, for example, ask all social workers in North America who hold a social work degree to answer the following simple question:

What is your highest social work degree completed?

1. Associate Degree
2. B.S.W.
3. M.S.W.
4. Ph.D./D.S.W.

Since the four values do not (and cannot) represent equal intervals, we cannot say that a person who has an Associate Degree is exactly two units higher than a person with an M.S.W. or that this interval is exactly the same distance as the one that separates a person with a Ph.D./D.S.W. from a person who has a B.S.W. If this were the case, we could claim that the variable "highest social work degree completed" meets the criteria for the next level of measurement, interval level measurement.

Interval

Like ordinal level measurement, *interval level measurement* also classifies and rank-orders properties of variables. It has one important addition, however,—it places the values for a variable on an equally spaced continuum. Thus, unlike ordinal measurement, interval measurement has a uniform unit of measurement, such as one year, one degree of temperature, and so on. Therefore, the values indicate exactly how far apart one value is from another. With an interval level variable, we can say that a research participant (or object) has more or less of a given property than another participant. In addition, we can also specify exactly how many (equal) units more or less of the variable.

With equal distances between the values, a measurement of 1 for a variable will be the same distance from a 4 ($4 - 1 = 3$) as a 6 is from a 9 ($9 - 6 = 3$). On a measuring instrument that is designed to measure intelligence, generally assumed to be an interval level variable, the difference between IQ scores of 100 and 105 ($105 - 100 = 5$) should reflect the same difference in intelligence between IQ scores of 115 and 120 ($120 - 115 = 5$). On another test, two individuals with achievement scores of 60 and 50 respectively should differ from each other in achievement as much as two other individuals with scores of 90 and 80 respectively ($60 - 50 = 10; 90 - 80 = 10$). Below is an example of a question on a research questionnaire that would produce interval level data:

What was your verbal score on your most recent Scholastic Achievement Test (SAT)? _____

Interval level measurement does not have an absolute zero point. This means that we cannot identify a point at which no quantity of the variable exists. Thus, we cannot say that a 2 is twice as much as a 1—only that it is one standard unit more. Since a reading of zero degrees on a Fahrenheit thermometer does not coincide with the absence of heat, a temperature of 60 degrees does not mean that it is twice as hot as a temperature of 30 degrees. Thirty-two degrees Fahrenheit is nothing more than an arbitrarily chosen point to signify the temperature at which water freezes.

Ratio

The existence of a fixed, absolute, and nonarbitrary zero point constitutes the only difference between interval and ratio level measurement. Therefore, values at the ratio level of measurement indicate the actual amounts of the property being measured. With such measurement, we can say not only that one person (or object) has so many units more of a variable than a second person, but that the first person has so many times more or less of the variable. Examples of variables that can be measured at the ratio level of measurement are "birth, death, and divorce rates;" "number of children in a family;" and "number of times that a client attended group treatment over a six-month period."

The absolute zero point in ratio measurement permits all arithmetic operations— addition, subtraction, multiplication, and division. It also allows for the valid use and meaningful interpretation of ratios formed by two or more measurements. It would be correct to say, for example, that a country with an average birth rate of four children per couple has twice as high a birth rate as a country with an average birth rate of two children per couple. Following is an example of a question on a research questionnaire that would produce ratio level data. It should be obvious that a response of "zero" would reflect no personal contact with the social worker.

How many times did you see your social worker during the past month? _____

One way to test for the existence of ratio measurement is to think about the possibility of negative values for the variable being measured. If negative numbers can logically be assigned (e.g., a temperature of $-25°F$), then the measurement of the variable cannot be considered to be more than interval. With ratio measurement, a zero is assigned to the point at which no measurable quantity of the variable exists.

Table 1.1 provides a brief summary of each level of measurement and the requirements that must be met for each level.

OTHER MEASUREMENT CLASSIFICATIONS

Like the levels of measurement discussed above, certain other classifications of variables also guide the selection of the most appropriate statistical analysis to use when analyzing data.

Discrete Variables and Continuous Variables

Discrete variables can only take on a finite number of values, such as the number of correct answers on the Scholastic Achievement Test (SAT) or the number of siblings a person has. In contrast to discrete variables, *continuous variables* can theoretically take

TABLE 1.1 Levels of Measurement and Numerical Values

Level	Numerical Value Requirements
Nominal	None: uses "value categories."
Ordinal	Values must preserve rank order.
Interval	Values must preserve rank order and unit differences.
Ratio	Values must preserve rank order, unit differences, and fixed zero point.

on all numerical values. "Height of social work students" and "grade point averages" are examples of continuous variables. If we were to take any two measurements of either variable, it would be theoretically possible that there could be one or more other measurements between them. The number of different values a continuous variable can take is therefore unlimited, assuming that we can use measuring instruments capable of measuring the values with ever-increasing precision.

Dichotomous, Binary, and Dummy Variables

A *dichotomous variable* is a specific type of discrete variable that only has two value categories. Examples are "gender" (male *or* female) or the "result of an election" (win *or* lose). Of course, we could take a more precisely measured variable—such as one that is interval or ratio level—divide its range of values into two groups (top half and bottom half), and convert it into a dichotomous level variable, with value categories of "older voters" *or* "younger voters." Such an activity would be wasting the precision of measurement that is available for the variable "age."

A special type of dichotomous variable is a *binary variable*. With binary variables, we assign numerical value categories of 1 or 0 to indicate the presence (1) or absence (0) of something. For the variable "car ownership," for example, we could assign a value category of 1 for people who own a car and a value category of 0 for those who do not own a car.

Another special type of dichotomous variable is called a *dummy variable*. Suppose, for example, we wanted to take the variable "gender," a nominal level dichotomous variable, and make it more quantitative in order to perform a different type of statistical analysis. We could take the variable "gender," and convert it into one of two binary variables—either "femaleness" (female = 1; not female = 0) or "maleness" (male = 1; not male = 0). These two newly created variables are called dummy variables—variables created from the data already collected, but in another format.

LEVELS OF MEASUREMENT AND STATISTICAL ANALYSES

Decisions regarding levels of measurement usually entail our judgment regarding the way in which a variable was conceptualized and operationalized. Determining whether a variable is ordinal, interval, or ratio can be difficult. There is an ongoing debate, for example, as to whether certain types of measurement instruments should be regarded as ordinal or interval. A few people suggest that certain types of measurement scales should be regarded as interval for purposes of statistical analyses. Others strongly disagree, insisting that only standardized measuring instruments that have undergone extensive testing and revision have any claim at all to interval level measurement.

Because of the way that some variables are measured, they may appear to be interval or ratio, but they still should be treated as ordinal. Suppose, for example, we are measuring the variable "driving skill." We can operationalize, or measure, "driving skill" by recording the number of traffic accidents that people have had over the past ten years (not a bad indicator of "driving skill"). Should "driving skill" be regarded as ratio? No, even though the number of traffic accidents has a true zero point and equal intervals, the underlying variable that we are measuring, "driving skill," lacks measurement precision.

We cannot say that the difference in driving skill between a person who had four accidents and a person who had three $(4 - 3 = 1)$ is exactly the same as the difference between a third person who had one accident and a fourth person who had none $(1 - 0 = 1)$. When data are analyzed, it might be best to form grouped values for the number of traffic accidents (e.g., 0–2, 3–5), to treat the variable, "driving skill," at the ordinal level of measurement, and to select a type of statistical analysis created for use with ordinal level data.

Making a judgment as to the variable's level of measurement is very important in determining what statistical analysis to use. As discussed in later chapters, sometimes even if we conclude that we have, say, an interval level variable, that in itself may not be enough to justify the use of a certain form of statistical analysis. Most analyses also require other assumptions about variables and the way in which their values are distributed (see Chapter 7). If these assumptions cannot be met, statistical analyses normally designed for higher levels of measurement (interval or ratio) should not be used. Statistical analyses designed for use with ordinal or even nominal data should then be substituted.

While it may be necessary to "drop down" and use a statistical analysis designed for lower level data, we generally cannot move in the other direction. If, for example, a variable is measured in a way that produces only nominal level data, it cannot be treated as if it were at the ordinal level. It would be equally incorrect to use a statistical analysis intended for use with interval or ratio level variables with nominal or ordinal level of measurement unless the nominal or ordinal variables are first converted into one or more dummy variables (p. 15).

CATEGORIES OF STATISTICAL ANALYSIS

Like everything else in life, there are numerous ways in which statistical analysis can be categorized. It can be categorized by the number of variables being analyzed and the purpose for their use.

Number of Variables Analyzed

The first way of grouping statistical analysis relates simply to the number of variables that are involved.

- *univariate*—examining the distribution of value categories (for nominal level data) and values (for ordinal, interval, and ratio level data) for a single variable
- *bivariate*—examining the relationship between two variables
- *multivariate*—simultaneously examining the relationship among three or more variables

Descriptive and Inferential Statistics

A second way of grouping statistical analysis uses two broad categories, descriptive and inferential. These two categories simply reflect the purpose, or use, of the statistical analysis.

Descriptive Analysis. *Descriptive analysis* is used to summarize the characteristics of a data set (Chapters 2, 3, and 8). These data may have been collected from a *population,* that is, all individuals or events with a specified set of characteristics. Such a population, for example, might be "all full-time students currently enrolled in accredited schools of social work of North America." Summaries of the characteristics of these students are called *parameters*. Descriptive analysis also is used to summarize the characteristics of research samples. When samples are used, their characteristics are summarized using *statistics*.

After data on the members of a particular population (or sample) are collected, the original measurements, or scores (called raw data), frequently can be overwhelming. A way must be found to organize and summarize the most important, salient characteristics of the data set. Through the use of descriptive analysis (also known as data reduction), we can derive summaries of information. Sometimes descriptive statistical analyses are preliminary to other types of statistical analyses (inferential). In some types of research studies—surveys and some qualitative research designs, for example—descriptive analysis is the primary focus of the data analysis.

Descriptive analysis is based on actual measurements of variables. In using them, our concern does not extend beyond the particular sample (or population) studied. Descriptive analysis generally consists of the compiling of graphs, tables, and descriptive numbers, such as means and percentages—all of which are easier to comprehend and interpret than a long list of data reporting the results of measurement of each variable for every case. The main purpose of a descriptive statistical analysis is to reduce the whole collection of data to simple and more understandable terms without distorting or losing too much of the valuable information collected. Of course, any summary sacrifices some detail, and a descriptive statistical analysis is no exception.

Inferential Analysis. *Inferential analysis* is used when we have access to only a sample drawn from a population and when we do not have in our possession all the raw scores that exist within the total population. Inferential statistical analysis uses procedures for determining how safe it would be to make generalizations about the characteristics of a population (parameters) based on the characteristics of the population's sample (statistics). Sample statistics are merely estimates of population parameters that are more or less accurate.

Descriptive and inferential statistical analyses are the major focuses of this book. Unless specifically indicated, our discussion of them assumes that the tasks of constructing a study's research design have been performed well and have generated valid and reliable measurements and, thus, have provided useful data to analyze.

CONCLUDING THOUGHTS

This chapter briefly examined the relationship between good measurement and meaningful statistical data analyses. Basic "research methods" terms have been reviewed that are vital to an understanding of the measurement of variables. These terms are discussed more thoroughly in social work research methods texts.

As suggested in this chapter, and demonstrated in the chapters to follow, statistical analyses involve methods for gathering, organizing, summarizing, and evaluating data. They are not, or should not be, some mysterious mathematical process. In fact, a statistical analysis is little more than the application of logic and common sense reasoning to the analysis of data.

STUDY QUESTIONS

1. Discuss why good measurement is essential to a meaningful statistical analysis. Use an original social work example in your discussion.
2. Discuss how a variable differs from a constant. Provide an original example of each in your discussion.
3. In a research hypothesis, what do we call the variable whose variations we are most interested in explaining? What do we call the variable that we believe may affect these variations? Which other terms are substituted if we are primarily interested in just studying their covariance or in predicting the value category (or value) of one variable through knowing the value category (or value) of the other? Provide one common original example to illustrate your understanding of these terms.
4. What additional characteristic does a valid measuring instrument possess that one that is reliable may not?
5. Provide three different ways that we might operationalize the variable "motivation to attend a graduate school of social work."
6. What does the term "value category" mean when referring to a nominal level variable? What does the term "value" mean when referring to an ordinal, interval or ratio level variable? Provide one common original example in your discussion.
7. What additional criterion must be met for a variable to be considered ordinal that is not a requirement for nominal level measurement? Provide an original example in your discussion.
8. What is required for ratio level measurement that is not required for interval level measurement? Provide an original example in your discussion.
9. Operationalize the variable "educational level" so that it would produce nominal level measurement, ordinal level measurement, interval level measurement, and ratio level measurement.
10. In your own words, discuss the differences between descriptive and inferential statistics. Describe some social work situations where the use of each would be appropriate. What do inferential statistics attempt to determine that descriptive statistics do not? What other methods are used to classify different types of statistical analyses?

11. Describe ways we can use statistics in social work practice, in social work education, and in social work research.

12. Discuss the roles that conceptualization and operationalization play in social work practice and research.

13. Construct a research hypothesis with one nominal level independent variable and one nominal level dependent variable. Explain how you would measure the dependent variable to produce the desired level of measurement.

14. Construct a research hypothesis that has one nominal level independent variable and one ordinal level dependent variable. Explain how you would measure the dependent variable to produce the desired level of measurement.

15. Construct a research hypothesis that has one nominal level independent variable and one interval level dependent variable. Explain how you would measure the dependent variable to produce the desired level of measurement.

16. Construct a hypothesis that has one nominal level independent variable and one ratio level dependent variable. Explain how you would measure the dependent variable to produce the desired level of measurement.

17. What level of measurement is the variable "highest social work degree received?" Justify your response. What other ways of operationalizing the variable would produce different levels of measurement? Explain.

18. Find a research-based article in a social work professional journal that is of some interest to you. Answer the following questions in relation to the article:

a. How much of the article is a report of statistical analyses per se (as opposed to theory, ideas, implications, research design, sampling, data collection, and so on)?

b. Was the study conducted using a sample or population? If a sample was used, how was it selected? Do you believe the findings generated by the sample can be generalized to the population from which it was drawn? Why or why not? Discuss.

c. Do you feel the author conceptualized the study's key variables correctly? Why or why not? How could the author have conceptualized them differently? Provide examples.

d. Do you feel the author operationalized the dependent (or criterion) variable correctly? Why or why not? How could the author have operationalized it differently? Provide examples.

e. What were the study's independent (or predictor) and dependent (or criterion) variables? What level of measurement were they? Justify your response.

f. What statistical method/s was/were used in the article? Was it descriptive and/or inferential?

g. Do you think the measurements of the study's key variables were reliable and valid? Why or why not?

h. Did the author use a standardized measuring instrument to measure the dependent (or criterion) variable? If so, which one was used? Do you feel the instrument measured what it was supposed to measure? Why or why not?

Chapter 2

Frequency Distributions and Graphs

After the data have been collected from a research study, they need to be organized and summarized in a systematic way. There are two simple formats that are used for this purpose: (1) frequency distributions and (2) graphs. They are helpful in visualizing the distribution of the value categories of a nominal level variable and the values of an ordinal, interval, or ratio level variable within a research sample (or population). Frequency distributions and graphs may show trends in a data set, which are then analyzed more extensively (discussed in later chapters).

Even when another, more sophisticated, data analysis is used, frequency distributions and graphs may still appear in research reports. They provide clear dramatic evidence of a point made less effectively in words or in other forms of data displays.

FREQUENCY DISTRIBUTIONS

One of the first questions often asked after data have been collected relates to how many persons (or objects) fell into each value for those variables that were measured. For the sake of simplicity, throughout this chapter, the generic term "value" is used to include "value categories." As pointed out in the last chapter, however, the term "value categories" usually is used with nominal level data, and "values" is used with ordinal, interval, and ratio level data.

Notwithstanding a variable's level of measurement, we are curious to know how the research sample, or population, "broke"—that is, we want to know each *frequency* for each value for each variable. *Frequency distribution* tables are designed to help us with this task. They also provide additional information on the distribution of values of variables.

If a variable is at the nominal level of measurement, frequency distributions are constructed directly from the raw data. If data are at the ordinal level of measurement or higher, however, it is necessary to first arrange the data into an array. An *array* is an ordering of every case value that occurred within the raw data set from the lowest (smallest) value that occurred to the highest (largest) value. A hypothetical research example is used in this chapter to show what an array looks like and to illustrate various frequency distributions that can be formed from one.

Suppose that a social work agency administrator, Sharon, wonders whether her agency is truly serving "older" residents of the community as written in the agency's mission statement. (The agency has operationally defined "older residents" as 50 years of age or older.) She decides to record the ages of all new clients who apply for services in October. Twenty clients apply for services during this month, and their ages are obtained from the agency's intake forms. These raw data for the 20 clients are listed in Table 2.1.

As we can see from the data in Table 2.1, the first new client was Rashad, who was 32 years of age; the second client was Rosina, 27 years of age; and so on. The raw data from Table 2.1 can be placed in an array, such as Table 2.2.

Note that the array displays the data set from the lowest value (21) to the highest (69) value. Every one of the clients is represented by a value, or number—his or her

TABLE 2.1 Raw Data: Clients' Names and Ages

Name	Age	Name	Age
Rashad	32	Rosemarie	37
Rosina	27	Marguerite	49
Brad	26	Raquel	31
Chuck	21	Peter	27
Shanti	37	Clarisse	37
Kathy	31	Karen	26
Antoinette	32	Elwin	49
David	69	Tony	21
Herb	26	Leon	27
Vincent	31	Mario	31

TABLE 2.2 Array: Clients' Names and Ages (from Table 2.1)

Name	Age	Name	Age
Chuck	21	Raquel	31
Tony	21	Mario	31
Brad	26	Rashad	32
Herb	26	Antoinette	32
Karen	26	Shanti	37
Rosina	27	Rosemarie	37
Peter	27	Clarisse	37
Leon	27	Marguerite	49
Kathy	31	Elwin	49
Vincent	31	David	69

age. Table 2.2 demonstrates that 2 of the 20 clients were 21 (low) years of age (Chuck and Tony) and only 1 was 69 (high) years of age (David).

The data in Table 2.2 provide a beginning answer to the research question about clients served. Only one client (David) meets the agency's operational definition of "older," since he was the only client over 50 years of age. As we can see, Table 2.2 makes it much easier for us to "eyeball" the data than Table 2.1. If the data had consisted of 250 cases instead of just 20, the data contained within an array would have been even more helpful in this regard.

Having formed an array with the data, it is now possible to construct frequency distribution tables in order to make them even more comprehensible. Frequency distributions do nothing more than consolidate data taken from arrays.

Absolute Frequency Distributions

To construct an *absolute frequency distribution* (also known as a *simple frequency distribution*), we simply count the number of times each value for the variable was found to occur and place it in a table next to that value category. An absolute frequency distribution may be constructed for data at any level of measurement.

Table 2.3 reports that the clients' ages in our example ranged from 21 (Chuck and Tony) to 69 (David) and that the age most frequently reported was 31 (i.e., Kathy, Vincent, Raquel, Mario). The absolute frequency column on the right side of the table indicates the number of times each value occurred. For instance, Chuck and Tony were 21 years of age, and as a group they constitute a frequency of 2—that is, the absolute frequency for the value 21 is 2. Similar data are given for each of the eight ages that occurred. Absolute frequency distributions sometimes are seen in research reports, but, more commonly, they appear as just one column within one of the other frequency distributions discussed next.

Cumulative Frequency Distributions

It is possible to provide an additional description of the distribution of a variable by adding another column to an absolute frequency distribution. A *cumulative frequency distribution* table, such as Table 2.4, can be constructed if the data are at least at the ordinal level of measurement (that is, if an array can be formed as in Table 2.2).

As Table 2.4 shows, 2 clients were 21 years of age and 3 clients were 26. Thus, the cumulative frequency of clients' ages 26 and under is 5 (2 + 3 = 5). We can also see, for example, that 17 clients (2 + 3 + 3 + 4 + 2 + 3 = 17) were 37 years of age and under. In a cumulative frequency distribution, the last number in the cumulative frequency column always is the same as the total number of cases, indicating that all case values have been included.

Percentage Distributions

A third type of frequency distribution table, the *percentage distribution* table, includes other information drawn from the data set. Table 2.5 uses the same data as Table 2.4, but it adds an absolute percentage column (far right-hand side) alongside the cumulative frequency column.

Since there are 20 clients in our sample, each client represents 5 percent of the sample (100%/20 = 5%). The number in the percentage column for each age that occurred within the sample of clients represents the absolute percentage of the entire sample (20 clients) represented by a given age. As Table 2.5 indicates, 2 people (Chuck

TABLE 2.3   Absolute Frequency Distribution Table: Clients' Names and Ages (from Table 2.2)

Name	Age	Absolute Frequency
Chuck + Tony	21	2
Brad + Herb + Karen	26	3
Rosina + Peter + Leon	27	3
Kathy + Vincent + Raquel + Mario	31	4
Rashad + Antoinette	32	2
Shanti + Rosemarie + Clarisse	37	3
Marguerite + Elwin	49	2
David	69	1
Total . . .		20

TABLE 2.4   Cumulative Frequency Distribution Table: Clients' Names and Ages (from Table 2.3)

Name	Age	Absolute Frequency	Cumulative Frequency
Chuck + Tony	21	2	2
Brad + Herb + Karen	26	3	5
Rosina + Peter + Leon	27	3	8
Kathy + Vincent + Raquel + Mario	31	4	12
Rashad + Antoinette	32	2	14
Shanti + Rosemarie + Clarisse	37	3	17
Marguerite + Elwin	49	2	19
David	69	1	20

TABLE 2.5   Percentage Distribution Table: Clients' Names and Ages (from Table 2.4)

Name	Age	Absolute Frequency	Cumulative Frequency	Absolute Percent
Chuck + Tony	21	2	2	10
Brad + Herb + Karen	26	3	5	15
Rosina + Peter + Leon	27	3	8	15
Kathy + Vincent + Raquel + Mario	31	4	12	20
Rashad + Antoinette	32	2	14	10
Shanti + Rosemarie + Clarisse	37	3	17	15
Marguerite + Elwin	49	2	19	10
David	69	1	20	5

TABLE 2.6   Cumulative Percentage Distribution Table:
Clients' Names and Ages (from Table 2.5)

Name	Age	Absolute Frequency	Cumulative Frequency	Absolute Percent	Cumulative Percent
Chuck + Tony	21	2	2	10	10
Brad + Herb + Karen	26	3	5	15	25
Rosina + Peter + Leon	27	3	8	15	40
Kathy + Vincent + Raquel + Mario	31	4	12	20	60
Rashad + Antoinette	32	2	14	10	70
Shanti + Rosemarie + Clarisse	37	3	17	15	85
Marguerite + Elwin	49	2	19	10	95
David	69	1	20	5	100

and Tony) were 21 years of age, and together they represent 10 percent of the total number of clients (5% for Chuck + 5% for Tony). Similarly, Brad, Herb, and Karen together represent 15% of the total sample (5% for Brad + 5% for Herb + 5% for Karen). Of course, the total for all the clients should equal 100 percent.

If the number of cases in a data set is not a number that can be divided "cleanly" into 100 to obtain the percentage that each case represents, the percentages in the row alongside a value may have to be rounded off to either whole numbers or numbers containing decimals. When this is done, the total for all cases may not be exactly 100 percent. It may be slightly more or less than 100. A notation at the bottom of the table is then used to explain why the total is something other than 100 percent.

Cumulative Percentage Distributions

A fourth type of frequency distribution table is the *cumulative percentage distribution* table. It combines features of Tables 2.4 and Table 2.5, but it contains an additional column that reports cumulative percentages for each value for a variable that occurred. In our example, it would tell us, for example, what percentage of all 20 cases were a given age or below.

As can be seen in Table 2.6, 2 clients (Rashad and Antoinette) were 32 years of age. Together they represent 10 percent of all clients (5% for Rashad + 5% for Antoinette). Additionally, 70 percent ($14/20 = .7 = 70\%$) of all clients (including Rashad and Antoinette) were 32 years of age or younger.

GROUPED FREQUENCY DISTRIBUTIONS

Sometimes it is difficult to interpret frequency distribution tables because of the unequal "spread" of values of the variables that occur within a data set. In our example, the variable "age" is distributed in such a way that there are differently sized gaps (e.g., 21 to 26, 27 to 31, 32 to 37, 49 to 69). It is sometimes easier to visualize and to comprehend the meaning of values that are distributed in this way if they are "condensed"

TABLE 2.7 Grouped Cumulative Percentage Distribution Table: Clients' Ages (from Table 2.6)

Ages	Absolute Percentage	Cumulative Percentage
20–29	40	40
30–39	45	85
40–49	10	95
50–59	0	95
60–69	5	100

into a smaller number of groupings (e.g., 20 to 29, 30 to 39, and so on). These groupings could then be displayed using any of the frequency distributions in Tables 2.3 to 2.6, or we might choose to use only those columns from Table 2.6 that are of special interest to us.

In creating grouped frequency distributions we can use the age groupings in the first column of Table 2.7 instead of the clients' actual ages and adjust the numbers in the other columns accordingly. Table 2.7 is a *grouped cumulative percentage distribution* table of the data that we have been using. Note that Table 2.7 does not contain the actual frequency for any one age, but that it nevertheless provides a good overview of how the data were distributed in the data set.

Grouped frequency distributions are especially useful when there are too many different values for a variable to list each of them individually. This often occurs when there are a large number of cases with many different values and when forming frequency distributions for variables that are at the interval or ratio levels of measurement. The number of miles driven to class by students in a school of social work, for example, would make for a lengthy list, especially if miles were measured in fractions or tenths of a mile. Transforming the observations into meaningful groupings may make it easier for the reader to visualize the distribution of the data.

What is a "meaningful" grouping when we refer to grouped data? It is a grouping that reduces the number of values of a variable to a reasonably small number (one that can be easily understood) while not losing any more measurement precision than is necessary. When the values of a variable are fairly evenly distributed, it is desirable to have groupings that each encompass an equal number of potential case values. If this is not the case, the groupings should be set up to reflect homogeneity within the groupings selected. This means that the groupings should use value intervals of a size that allows cases within them to be similar in relation to the variable. In grouping students based on the number of miles they travel to class, for example, five meaningful value groupings might be as follows:

1. 3 miles or less
2. 4–10 miles
3. 11–50 miles
4. 51–100 miles
5. 101 miles or more

What makes the previous value groupings homogeneous? Note that all persons in the "3 miles or less" category share a similar characteristic—they all live relatively close to the university. Those in the 4–10-mile grouping live fairly close, but they probably do not want to walk to class, do not feel a part of the university community, and so forth. Those commuting over 101 miles may likely have been involved in some form of distance education, may have difficulty participating in student activities on campus, and so forth.

There is a logic to the groupings—people within a specific grouping share some similarities with the other members within the group and are likely to be different in some important ways from people in the other groupings. Obviously, they cannot be similar to others in their grouping in all respects. Which characteristics matter the most? Here we must rely on judgment and a review of the literature to suggest areas where homogeneity is most important for our specific research topic.

Of course, every case should fall cleanly into one and only one grouping. In the above five groupings, a consistent method would have to be devised for assigning those students who would be on the edge of the different value groupings (e.g., 10.6 miles) into a group. A customary way to do this, for example, is to consider 11 miles as really representing the interval 10.50 to 11.49 miles. Then the student who drives 10.6 miles would fall into only the 11–50-mile grouping.

USING FREQUENCY DISTRIBUTIONS TO ANALYZE DATA

Frequency distributions are very revealing. Cumulative frequency distributions are especially useful when we are interested in knowing approximately where a particular value fell relative to the other values in a distribution of values. Suppose, for example, that an administrator of a large social service organization, Bob, wants to study the problem of unauthorized staff absenteeism. He would like to identify seasonal patterns that may exist that could possibly be reduced by creating new policies on vacations and annual leave. A cumulative percentage distribution might reveal such patterns.

Table 2.8 reveals that in April, there were 30 instances of absenteeism, or 15 percent of the total amount of absenteeism for the 4-month period (200 instances). Another 40 instances (20%) occurred during May. In all, only 70 instances (35%) occurred

TABLE 2.8 Cumulative Percentage Distribution Table: Staff Days Lost by Month at XYZ Agency (N = 200)

	Monthly Totals	
Month	Absolute Frequency	Cumulative Percentage
April	30	15
May	40	35
June	60	65
July	70	100

during the first two months examined (April and May), while the other 65 percent (100% − 35% = 65%) occurred during the months of June and July. The table would seem to suggest to Bob that there is a seasonal pattern of absenteeism—absenteeism increases as the summer months come around.

Frequency distributions also can be helpful for comparing measurements taken from two different groups, or data sets. If the measurements taken on the groups differ somewhat (e.g., if the actual ages were recorded for one data set and age ranges were recorded for the other one), grouped frequency distributions can be used to make the different data sets comparable.

Example: A State Merit Examination Study Guide

An example will illustrate how frequency distributions can be used to compare two groups of data sets. Sue, a social worker, developed a state merit examination study guide. She wished to get a preliminary indication of whether or not it was effective. (Later we will discuss how more sophisticated forms of statistical analyses could provide more definitive answers about the study guide's effectiveness.) She decided to compare the respective scores of people who used the study guide (experimental group) with those of people who did not use it (control group). Cumulative distribution tables displaying the differences between the results for the two groups are shown in Tables 2.9 and 2.10.

As we can see from Table 2.9, 40 percent of the people in the experimental group scored between 70 and 79 on the examination, and 50 percent scored 79 or lower. In Table 2.10 we note that 40 percent of the people in the control group scored between 70 and 79 on the examination, and 60 percent scored 79 or lower.

We can note that cumulative percentages also make it possible to calculate at least approximate percentile ranks for individuals within the two groups. Percentile ranks indicate the percentage of the cases within a group whose value falls below a particular value. Suppose that Clarice, a member of the experimental group, for example, scored a 90 on the merit examination after using the study guide. A review of Table 2.9 would indicate that she scored higher than at least 80 percent of all people in the experimental group, or that she scored at approximately the 80th percentile. Percentile ranks enable us to put an individual score in perspective relative to the other scores in a group.

TABLE 2.9 Grouped Cumulative Percentage Distribution Table: Experimental Group's Scores (N = 300)

Scores	Absolute Percentage	Cumulative Percentage
50–59	0	0
60–69	10	10
70–79	40	50
80–89	30	80
90–100	20	100

TABLE 2.10 Grouped Cumulative Percentage Distribution Table: Control Group's Scores (N = 200)

Scores	Absolute Percentage	Cumulative Percentage
50–59	5	5
60–69	15	20
70–79	40	60
80–89	35	95
90–100	5	100

Also notice that the two groups contained different numbers of cases (*N*), 300 in the experimental group and 200 in the control group. Using percentages facilitates drawing comparisons between two or more groups of unequal size. It puts groups of different sizes into the same framework; all percentages are based on 100. This is very helpful if two research samples are either of unequal size from the beginning of the study or if they begin equal but become unequal because more people are lost from one group than from the other.

MISREPRESENTATION OF DATA

From a statistical perspective, the two groups of 200 and 300 research participants in the previous illustration were fairly comparable in size. Percentage comparisons drawn from them would be appropriate, since they would make the data easier to interpret. But a word of caution is in order: The practice of drawing comparisons between two groups of **vastly** unequal sizes actually can distort, rather than clarify, the data for the reader. Another example will be used to demonstrate how this can happen.

Example: An Agency's Affirmative Action Plan

Emma, a social agency administrator, proudly reported to the board of directors that the results of her agency's affirmative action plan for the years 1996 and 1997 were "outstanding." She took the data from Table 2.11 and presented them to the board of directors as a glowing endorsement of her agency's efforts to hire women. She noted that in five of the six job classifications (i.e., A, B, C, E, F), she has hired a higher percentage of women than men. Emma was able to make this statement because she was using percentages with value groupings of very different sizes. The actual data she summarized presented a drastically different picture. In fact, as Table 2.11 illustrates, Emma's agency hired 78 percent of all male applicants but only 21 percent of all female applicants.

We all know that it is possible to "lie with statistics," but more often than not the misrepresentation is not deliberate. Emma's report may have been an honest mistake based on an inadequate understanding of the importance of using comparably sized

TABLE 2.11   1996 and 1997 Hiring Data for XYZ Agency Broken Down by Gender

Classification	Males		Females	
	Number	Percent	Number	Percent
A	3 of 6	50	4 of 6	67
B	1 of 3	33	1 of 2	50
C	0 of 1	0	1 of 10	10
D	85 of 100	85	2 of 40	5
E	2 of 3	67	2 of 2	100
F	3 of 7	43	4 of 7	57
Totals . . .	94 of 120	78	14 of 67	21

groups when making comparisons using frequency distributions. There is a way to avoid giving the impression that we are attempting to distort the facts in such situations. The actual numbers on which percentages are based can be reported along with the percentages for all groups.

Percentages are helpful to others in comprehending large numbers, especially when they are used to report research findings based upon odd numbers. For example, "35.5 percent" is more easily understood than "146 out of 411." They are generally meaningless, however, if not misleading, in reporting data from small samples. There is little reason to report, for example, that "60 percent of the graduates of an intensive job training program found work" if the 60 percent really means three of five completed the program and found a job (3/5 = 60%). With a small number of cases, it is best to report just the numbers.

Statements that describe findings based upon small numbers are quite comprehensible by themselves. In our example, it would have been perfectly understandable if we had just reported that "three out of five graduates found work." Reporting findings based upon small numbers as percentages, however, can be misleading. Percentages convey an impression that findings were based upon larger numbers of cases (100 or even more).

GRAPHICAL PRESENTATION OF DATA

Sometimes it is difficult to grasp the "bigger picture" of the distribution of values of a variable using frequency distribution tables. A graphic, however, often can communicate the "bigger picture" almost immediately.

Graphical representations generally sacrifice detail in an effort to improve communication. This sacrifice is justifiable and even desirable in many situations. If the intended audience of a research presentation or report is not research oriented, the audience, along with the presenter, may become impatient or disinterested with tabular presentation of vast amounts of data. Graphs are more likely to hold everyone's interest. Also, if it is essential to get a point across quickly and dramatically, graphs can do the job effectively. They allow readers of reports or participants at presentations of research findings to obtain a comprehensive picture of the distribution of the values of a variable without having to focus on unnecessary detail.

Of course, like all methods of displaying data, graphs can be constructed so as to produce misleading statements. It is possible to "lie with graphs," just as with other types of statistical analyses. This fact should serve to alert us to the dangers inherent in the use of graphs and cause us to ask whether they are communicating the findings of a research study accurately. But it should not preclude their use—they can be very effective communicators.

There are several graphs that commonly are used to display how many cases (persons or objects) were found to have the various measurements (values) of a variable. Both the measurement level of the variable and clarity requirements of data portrayal determine which of the various graphical options is best. Most graphs are drawn (usually with statistical computer software) using x- and y-axes. The vertical line is called the *ordinate*, or *y-axis*, and the horizontal line is called the *abscissa*, or *x-axis*. The point

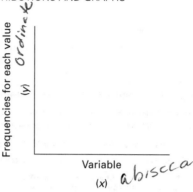

FIGURE 2.1 Basic Outline of a Graph for Depicting Frequencies *(y)* for One Variable *(x)*

where the x-axis and the y-axis meet (see Figure 2.1) is called the *point of origin*. In a graph used to present a description of the values observed for one variable, for example, the y-axis is used to indicate frequencies for each value. The graph may extend along the x-axis to the left of the y-axis if there are negative values of the variable.

Bar Graphs

A basic method for representing the distribution of value categories for a nominal level variable in pictorial form is the *bar graph*, also called a bar chart. Bars of equal width are drawn so that they do not touch. This suggests the qualitative (not quantitative) differences in value categories of the nominal level variable. Figure 2.2a is an example of a simple bar graph.

If lines rather than bars are used, they are drawn so their length reflects the frequencies with which given value categories occur. We refer to this type of graph as a line diagram. Line diagrams may be constructed simply using vertical lines instead of the bars of a bar graph, or they may be constructed so the lines run parallel to the x-axis (i.e., horizontally) with different nominal value categories placed along the y-axis, as in Figure 2.2b. Bar graphs and line diagrams are used pretty much interchangeably.

Pie Charts

At times we may choose to use a *pie chart*, also called a pie graph, to represent the distribution of value categories of a nominal level variable. Pie charts are primarily used with nominal level variables, but they can be used with variables that are measured more precisely as well. The components of a pie chart reflect segments of "the whole." Traditionally, pie charts are constructed as circle graphs divided into wedges representing fractions of the total circle (the pie).

With today's computer software graphic programs, many other pictorial representations of the division of "the whole" are now possible. If we want to show how a client's family budget is divided into sums for food, shelter, clothing, and recreation, for exam-

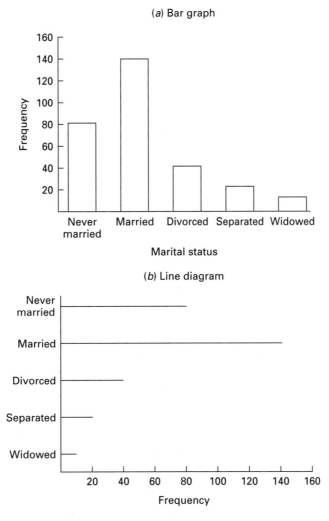

FIGURE 2.2 Two Similar Graphs: Bar Graph and Line Diagram Portraying the Marital Status of Active Clients in XYZ Agency

ple, the total budget could be displayed as a pie. Pieces (areas) of the pie could be sized to reflect the portion of the total budget represented by the various budget items. Or we could portray the family budget as a picture of a cash bag with its areas divided to represent the percent of the budget that is spent for the various budget items.

Figure 2.3 is an example of a pie chart that portrays the percentages of staff who work at XYZ Agency, broken down by their highest postsecondary social work degree obtained. Note, for example, that those staff members whose highest degree completed is an Associate Degree (25% of all staff) occupy one-fourth the total area of the "pie."

Pie charts provide a way to make a rapid visual appraisal of the distribution of value categories. Their main limitation is that they cannot easily accommodate very

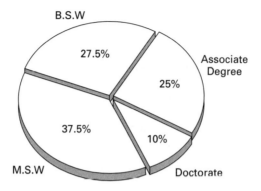

FIGURE 2.3 Distribution of Social Workers at XYZ Agency by Degree (*N* = 100)

many different categories of a variable without becoming too complicated, large, or even illegible. Figure 2.3 is quite comprehensible, but a pie chart that displays, for example, the frequencies for all of the academic majors within a large university would be impractical. There would have to be many different "slices of the pie," some of them so small as to be barely visible.

Histograms

A useful graph for displaying ordinal, interval, or ratio level data is called a *histogram*. Histograms look like bar graphs, except the bars touch each other. The rank order of the variable's values determines the sequence of the values displayed in the graph. The bars of a histogram displaying ordinal data are of equal width, such as those in Figure 2.4, which displays outcome data, via four categories, derived from a review of February case records at XYZ Agency.

A histogram, like a bar graph, uses the height of a bar to display the frequency of a value for a given variable. A comparison of the frequency for different values is implicit. If a bar of one length represents the frequency for one value, for example, a bar twice as long represents a frequency twice that large for another value.

When displaying the frequencies for interval or ratio level data, and when grouped frequencies of unequal value intervals are used, the bars may be constructed so that their different widths correspond to the size of the different intervals. Figure 2.5 illustrates this variation on the usual form of a histogram. Note that the graph accurately portrays frequencies by showing bars of different heights, intervals, and widths. To do this, there must be a degree of measurement precision not present within nominal or ordinal level data.

Frequency Polygons

After constructing a histogram with interval or ratio level data, we can convert the histogram into a frequency polygon. A *frequency polygon* is nothing more than a shape. Frequency polygons are designed to portray the overall shape of a distribution of values. If we were to take a pencil and mark a dot in the middle of the top of each vertical bar

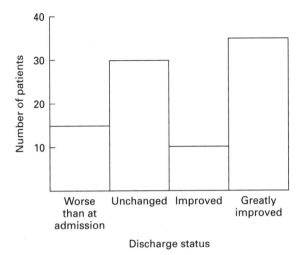

FIGURE 2.4 Histogram: Frequency of Discharge Status at XYZ Agency During February

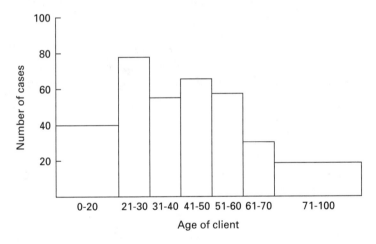

FIGURE 2.5 Histogram: Ages of Clients on Record in XYZ Agency During October

in a histogram and then connect the dots with a straight line, we would have a frequency polygon. Lines usually are drawn at each end of the distribution of values to connect the first and last dot with the horizontal axis, thus completing the polygon. Figure 2.6 is a frequency polygon displaying data that might have been collected at intake and stored in an agency's computer-assisted management information system.

The data in Figure 2.6 probably were collected at the ratio level of measurement (e.g., as actual dollars and cents of income reported on clients' most recent federal income tax returns). When they were grouped into income intervals to reduce the number of value groupings of the variable, some sacrifice of accuracy (measurement

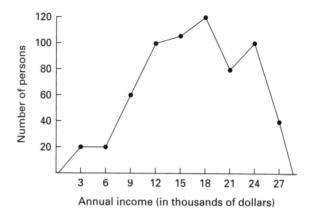

FIGURE 2.6 Frequency Polygon: Annual Income of Families Receiving Family Counseling at XYZ Agency (Rounded to Nearest Category)

precision) occurred. The data became only ordinal. In Figure 2.6, the numbers along the x-axis are the midpoints of the income groupings that were used. As Figure 2.6 demonstrates, it is possible to plot a frequency polygon for data that are only ordinal, but this should be done only when the data are inherently interval or ratio and then only when it serves some useful purpose (such as better communication). Frequency polygons present a more accurate portrayal of the distribution of a variable when used with data that are interval or ratio than with those that are nominal or ordinal.

Pareto Charts

A graph that is gaining in popularity as we rely more and more on computers to create graphics is called a *pareto chart*. It portrays a rank-ordering of values of a variable by frequency (in descending order). It also reflects cumulative frequencies and cumulative percentages of cases at any point where cases with new values are added to the graph.

Figure 2.7 displays the education level of 40 residents of an extended care facility for older adults. In it, we can see that the greatest number of people (11) completed the 12th grade (highest grade completed). The next greatest number (7) completed fourteen years of school. Only one resident (each) completed 4, 5, 6, 7, 10, and 17 years—each value has a frequency of one within the sample. The curved line displays both cumulative frequencies and cumulative percentages. Note that when those residents who completed 11 years of school are added to the group, the residents to the left of the chart represent 30 (75 percent) of the sample and another 10 residents (25 percent) are to their right (the values with lower frequencies).

Stem-and-Leaf Plots

Another graph that is easily generated by computer software packages is the *stem-and-leaf plot*. Like the pareto chart, it makes it possible for the reader to view the actual case values in the distribution of a variable. Figure 2.8 portrays the distribution of

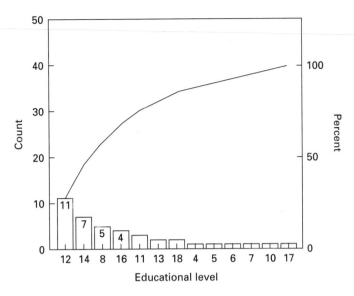

FIGURE 2.7 Pareto Chart: Educational Levels of Residents at XYZ Residential Care Facility (N = 40)

Frequency	Stem & Leaf	
1	5	9
2	6	24
6	6	566889
4	7	1144
16	7	5577777777788999
6	8	014444
3	8	558
1	9	5
1	10	3

FIGURE 2.8 Stem-and-Leaf Plot: Ages of Residents at XYZ Residential Care Facility (N = 40)

the ages of the residents of the extended care facility whose education levels were displayed in Figure 2.7.

In a stem-and-leaf plot such as Figure 2.8, each case value is present. The age of a resident is displayed as a stem in the middle column (in this case, the first digit of his or her age) and a leaf in the right-hand column (in this case, the second digit of his or her age). Thus, a resident who is 77 years of age would be represented by one of the sevens in the row where the seven appears under the leaf column. We also can see that the sample contains 2 residents who are 66 years of age, one who is 80, four who are 84, and so forth. The two oldest residents, are 95 and 103. It is interesting to note that if we were to rotate the graph 90° counter-clockwise onto its side with the frequency column

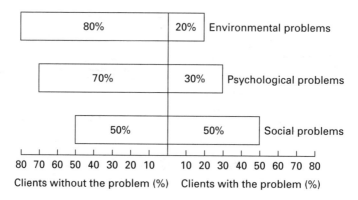

FIGURE 2.9 Bar Graph: Types of Client Problems at XYZ Agency

on the bottom and connect the top of the columns of numbers (case values), we would have a frequency polygon for the variable "age of residents."

A COMMON MISTAKE IN DISPLAYING DATA

As computer graphics become more user-friendly, there is a temptation to display greater and greater amounts of data. Some graphs can become hard to interpret by the reader of a research report.

Even relatively simple ways of displaying data like bar graphs and histograms can easily be made quite complicated. The horizontal bars in bar graphs, for example, may be extended to the left or to the right simultaneously. Figure 2.9 displays data relative to client problems in a social service agency. It illustrates the actual percentage of clients who reported problems within any of three nominal level categories of presenting problems—environmental, psychological, and social.

The graph illustrated in Figure 2.9 portrays a common agency situation. A given client may have reported one, two, or all three types of problems, but it takes quite a bit of study to be able to understand the data presented in it. The x-axis represents the percentage of clients reporting each problem area (right side) and the percentage not reporting the problem area (left side). Thus, the total number of clients either reporting or not reporting each problem must equal 100 percent for each vertical line on the graph. With some study, Figure 2.9 indicates that 30 percent of all clients reported psychological problems and, of course, 70 percent did not; 50 percent reported social problems, while the other 50 percent did not; and so forth.

The data in Figure 2.9 could have been communicated more easily using three simple bar graphs, one for each type of client problem. The computer technology that easily created it is a mixed blessing. It allows us to communicate more information on a single graph, but it sacrifices clarity of communication in the process. As we are tempted to use more complex and creative frequency distributions and graphs, we must always ask ourselves, "Will they really help the reader understand our data?" Or will they have the undesirable effect of confusing the reader? After all, we must remember that communication is the goal of both frequency distributions and graphs. When we end up confusing the person who is trying to understand what our data looked like, we have failed to accomplish this goal.

CONCLUDING THOUGHTS

This chapter briefly examined some of the most basic ways of organizing and displaying the distributions of value categories and values of a variable—frequency distributions and graphs. It examined how we can take simple frequencies and convert them into tables that portray the percent of the whole that a given frequency represents. It also introduced a concept that is examined in more detail in a later chapter, percentile, and how it relates to cumulative frequency distributions.

We examined a few of the most commonly used graphs, in what situations they are appropriate, and how they are constructed. We alluded to some of the dangers inherent in the use of graphs.

STUDY QUESTIONS

1. Discuss how an array differs from raw data. Provide an original example in your discussion.
2. What additional information is conveyed in a cumulative frequency distribution that is not present in an absolute frequency distribution? Provide an original example in your discussion.
3. What type of frequency distribution would tell us what percentage of AFDC clients in a county social service agency have fewer than four children?
4. In a study attempting to relate type of counseling to success in seeking employment, why would it be inadvisable to group the variable "number of interviews" as 1–10, 11–20, and over 20?
5. Why is it misleading to report a 50 percent success rate in a treatment program for alcoholics when there were only eight people in the treatment program? Explain in detail.
6. How does a bar graph differ from a histogram? Provide an example of each.
7. If an agency with an $800,000 annual budget allocates $160,000 for travel expenses, what portion (percentage) of a pie chart would be reserved for the travel segment?
8. Why are frequency polygons an accurate portrayal of data only if data are at the interval or ratio level of measurement?
9. Why is "simpler" usually "better" when selecting a graph to display data?
10. Describe several ways that we could use graphs to display changes in the ethnic composition of an agency's professional staff between 1995 and 1998.
11. What information contained in frequency distributions is graphically portrayed in a pareto chart?
12. What information do pareto charts and stem-and-leaf plots display that the other graphs presented in this chapter do not?
13. At the University of Twin Peaks, the number of males and females in various major fields of study are as follows:

Major	Males	Females
Social Work	20	80
Humanities	40	40
Business	60	50
Education	90	90
Nursing	10	90

a. What percentage of social work majors are female?
b. What percentage of the total student body are male?
c. Construct a five-slice pie chart for the different female majors.
   Do the same for the males.
d. Construct a bar chart like Figure 2.2a for all males broken down by major.
   Do the same for the females.
e. What level of measurement is the variable major? Justify your response.

14. The dean of your school of social work has requested that you organize and present data from a one-question (one-variable) survey to determine students' satisfaction in the social work program. There are a total of 220 students in the program; 55 of them (25 percent) were randomly selected to receive the survey. The research question was stated as: "How satisfied are you with the social work education you are currently receiving?" Possible responses were

1. Very satisfied
2. Satisfied
3. Somewhat satisfied
4. Somewhat dissatisfied
5. Very dissatisfied

a. At what level of measurement is the variable "satisfaction?" Justify your response.
b. Is the variable an independent variable or a dependent variable? Justify your response.
c. The raw data for the variable were as follows:

   1, 4, 5, 3, 2, 1, 4, 5, 5, 4, 2, 5, 1, 1, 2, 3, 4, 3, 3, 3, 3, 4, 5, 4, 3, 3, 2, 2, 1, 3, 4, 2, 2, 2, 4, 2, 1, 1, 2, 3, 4, 5, 4, 3, 2, 1, 1, 2, 2, 3, 2, 2, 1, 1, and 3.

d. How many students completed the survey? Should these students be considered a research sample or a population? Why?
e. Construct an absolute frequency distribution to display these data.
f. Construct a cumulative frequency distribution to display these data.
g. Construct a percentage distribution to display these data.
h. Construct a cumulative percentage distribution to display these data.
i. Do you believe that, overall, the students were satisfied with the social work education they were receiving? Justify your response.
j. The dean took the results to the vice-president and said that the social work students were very pleased with their education. Was the dean correct in saying this given the results of the survey? Why or why not?

Chapter 3

Central Tendency and Variability

Sometimes we need to go beyond displaying data in tables or graphs as presented in the previous chapter. We may simply wish to direct the reader's attention to some specific characteristic of the data set. We may want, for example, to summarize our data by reporting on what was found to be a "typical" attribute of them and/or to what degree the values of a variable differed from the "typical value." The methods for summarizing the characteristics of data are useful for the description of people (or objects) that were studied. As we shall see in later chapters, a knowledge of them also is fundamental to an understanding of more sophisticated forms of data analyses.

CENTRAL TENDENCY

In our everyday language, we tend to use the word "typical" rather loosely. We speak of the "typical" client or the "typical" starting salary for M.S.W. social workers, often without stating exactly what is meant by the term. In statistics, the search for the "typical" represents an attempt to find a single number, or a series of numbers, that is most representative of a whole group of values. In a raw data set (e.g., Table 2.1 in Chapter 2), a "typical case" would be the one that best represents all cases within the data set.

In statistics, three terms are grouped under the general category of *central tendency*. They are the mode, median, and mean. They are used to describe what is meant by "typical" within a data set. These terms are not interchangeable and have specific meanings that differ in important ways. They must be used correctly to avoid confusion and to avoid misrepresenting what a data set looks like.

All three measures of central tendency have two basic uses:

1. *They summarize data.* They report one value (or number or score) that tells us something important about the characteristics of the distribution of a variable.

A social work agency, for example, may state in its annual report that it processed an average of 3 new client intakes a day during the previous year.

2. *They provide a common reference point for comparing two groups of data.* An agency that hires both M.S.W. and B.S.W. beginning social workers may report, for example, an average monthly starting salary of $3,000 for M.S.W. social workers and $2,000 for B.S.W. social workers. This one number, average monthly starting salary, helps communicate the agency's fiscal policy toward hiring beginning M.S.W. and B.S.W. social workers.

The Mode

The *mode* is the value in a distribution of values within a data set that occurs most frequently. In the 15 ages of clients presented in the array below, 42 is the mode because it occurs more frequently than any of the other values—in this case, four times more frequently.

Ages of clients (N = 15):
28, 31, 38, 39, **42, 42, 42, 42**, 43, 47, 51, 54, 55, 56, 60

Sometimes more than one value will occur "most frequently" within a data set. If we were to draw a histogram of the distribution of the values, it would have two distinct "peaks." If this situation occurs, we would report both values as the mode for the data set and would describe the distribution of the variable as *bimodal.* In the following example, the values in the bimodal array of "years of prior social work experience" among 22 social workers in a family service agency contain two modes—0 and 7. Both values occur five times each.

Years of prior social work experience (N = 22):
0, 0, 0, 0, 0, 1, 2, 2, 3, 4, 5, 5, 6, **7, 7, 7, 7, 7,** 8, 9, 11, 14

When data are available in grouped form, the mode can be reported in one of two ways. We may simply report the grouping that had the largest frequency as the mode, or we can report the midpoint of the interval with the highest frequency. Table 3.1 portrays grouped job satisfaction scores of 50 social workers. For these data, the value interval containing the largest frequency is 48–50, which includes the values 48, 49, and 50. This three-number range occurred seven times. The mode could be reported as 49, since the middle value for this interval is 49.

Of the three measures of central tendency, the mode is the most unrestricted— that is, it has the fewest requirements for its use. It can be used with all four levels of measurement (i.e., nominal, ordinal, interval, ratio). The mode, however, is not used as often as the other measures of central tendency, as it lacks less precision than the other measures. When data are at the ordinal, interval, or ratio level of measurement, we usually can obtain more accurate and representative descriptions of them by using one or both of the other two measures of central tendency. As can be seen in Table 3.2, the most common or frequent value of a distribution of scores is not necessarily the most accurate portrayal of a "typical" value. The mode is clearly not in the center of the distribution; rather, it is toward the high end of it (the 57–59 group).

TABLE 3.1 Grouped Cumulative Frequency Distribution: Job Satisfaction Scores for Social Workers

Scores	Absolute Frequency	Cumulative Frequency (High-Low)	Cumulative Frequency (Low-High)
81–83	3	3	50
78–80	1	4	47
75–77	5	9	46
72–74	6	15	41
69–71	1	16	35
66–68	5	21	34
63–65	4	25	29
60–62	1	26	25
57–59	1	27	24
54–56	4	31	23
51–53	3	34	19
48–50	7	41	16
45–47	1	42	9
42–44	4	46	8
39–41	2	48	4
36–38	2	50	2

TABLE 3.2 Grouped Cumulative Frequency Distribution: Job Satisfaction Scores for Social Workers

Scores	Absolute Frequency	Cumulative Frequency (High-Low)	Cumulative Frequency (Low-High)
57–59	10	10	33
54–56	6	16	23
51–53	7	23	17
48–50	3	26	10
45–47	2	28	7
42–44	1	29	5
30–41	4	33	4

The Median

If data can be formed into an array, that is, if they are at least at the ordinal level of measurement, the median can be used. The *median* divides an array of values into two equal halves. The example in Distribution A below presents an array of 21 values for the variable "number of treatment sessions attended." The median is 9 sessions because 9 coincides with the point that divides the 21 values into two identical parts. There are just as many values, or cases (10), above 9 as there are below 9.

Distribution A: Number of treatment sessions attended (N = 21):
2, 2, 2, 3, 3, 4, 5, 5, 7, 8, **9**, 10, 11, 11, 14, 14, 15, 16, 18, 29, 41

If there had been an even number of values, the median might be the average of the two most central values as in Distribution B below. Here the median is 4.5.

Distribution B: Number of treatment sessions attended (N = 24):
1, 1, 1, 1, 1, 1, 2, 2, 3, 3, 3, 4, 5, 6, 6, 7, 8, 11, 11, 13, 14, 15, 17, 20

The median (4.5) in Distribution B does not coincide with any specific value in the distribution. It cannot because with an even number of cases there is no case that falls at exactly the midpoint. This observation underlines a point that is important to our understanding of the median. Contrary to a common misconception, the median is not synonymous with the value of the middle case in an array of data (although it sometimes works out that way, as in Distribution A).

Even when the array contains an odd number of cases, the median is likely to be a fraction that coincides with no actual case value. That happens because the formula used to compute the median takes various conditions into consideration, such as case values with a frequency of zero near the center and others with a frequency greater than one that occur near the center of the array (but are not centered around it). When these conditions exist, computation involves viewing values as intervals, as discussed in Chapter 2 when we discussed assignment of cases within grouped frequency distributions. Hand computation of the median can get quite complicated; fortunately, most computer statistical software packages can compute a median in a matter of seconds once the raw data have been entered.

Of the three most common measures of central tendency, the median is affected the least by the presence of extremely atypical values. If we look at Distribution A, we see that one client had been seen many more times than any other—41 times. This atypical value is known as an *outlier*. If a histogram were created for the variable, this value would lie outside the area where most of the other values are found (in Distribution A, between 2 and 29). Because the median coincides with the midpoint of the values in an array, the one client who was seen 41 times does not distort the median. This client is "canceled out" by the first client, who was seen only 2 times and is the counterpart at the extreme other end of the array. The client seen 29 times similarly was canceled out by the second client seen only 2 times, and so on.

The Mean

When a raw data set is at the interval or ratio level of measurement, the *mean* (also called the arithmetic mean) can be used to represent a typical value of a variable. It is the most easily understood, the best known, and the most useful of the three measures of central tendency. It is nothing more than the sum of all the values in a distribution divided by the total number of values—what we refer to in everyday speech as the "average."

A mean can be computed for any interval or ratio level variable. It should, however, not be used with nominal or ordinal level variables. Because the mean should be used only with interval or ratio level data, it is not appropriate to report the mean for rankings. Rankings use ordinal level data. A student may rank Number 3 in one class, Number 4 in another, and Number 2 in a third class. While a mean ranking could mathematically be obtained (the student's "average" rank would be 3), to report it could be misleading. The reader of a report should be able to assume that a mean was computed using only interval or ratio level data.

Another issue must be considered when deciding if it is appropriate to use the mean. Unlike the median, the mean uses all the values within a data set in its computation, not just some of the values. This characteristic can promote accuracy or distortion, depending on the absence or presence of outliers. Even one or two outliers can easily distort the mean if the total number of cases is small. With larger data sets few outliers cause less distortion.

The Trimmed Mean. A *trimmed mean* is designed to minimize the effect of a few extreme outliers. It combines the best features of both the mean and the median. It still uses most of the actual case values in its computation but, like the median, it allows extreme values on either end to cancel each other out. It works like this: First a small percentage (usually, the top five percent and the bottom five percent) of values in an array are thrown out. Then, the remaining 90 percent of values are averaged. This average is the trimmed mean.

Despite the fact that a mean can be computed, the presence of a few extreme outliers may produce a value that is either too large or too small to be considered "typical" for a variable. Then, the trimmed mean and/or the median and/or the mode should be considered.

The Weighted Mean. There is still another variation of the mean that we can use in social work research. Sometimes, it is necessary to "average" values that are not equally weighted (or of equal importance). Then we must compute a *weighted mean*. Computing a weighted mean entails the "weighting" of numbers in order to arrive at a value that is more representative of the data set than either the arithmetic mean or the trimmed mean.

Example: Discharge Planning. RuthAnn, a social worker working on a case management team in a hospital, wished to compare her team's mean number of successful hospital discharge placements with those of another case management team within the hospital. She hoped to demonstrate that her team was no less successful during the past week than the other team. Unlike RuthAnn's team, all five members of the other team were full-time employees. RuthAnn used the arithmetic mean to determine the other team's mean rate of success. She simply added together all of the workers' successful placements for the previous week and then divided by five to get the mean number of successes (per worker). The other team produced a total of 35 successful placements during the past week, so the mean number for the other team was 7 ($35/5 = 7$).

Computing a comparable indicator for RuthAnn's team was a bit more complicated. Unlike the other team, her team has six workers. Two (including herself) are full-time (five days per week); three work half-time; and one works one-fourth time per week. Their number of successful placements for the week were (respectively): 8, 8, 3, 2, 4, and 2. RuthAnn could not simply add the number of successes together and divide by six. (The result would be 4.5, suggesting an unfair and unfavorable comparison.) Since most of the workers on her team are part-time, she needed to compute a weighted mean in order to get a fair description of their success.

How did RuthAnn compute a weighted mean for her team? She set up her data as follows:

Worker Name	Employment Status	# Placed Successfully	×	Weighting Factor	=	Score
RuthAnn	full	8		1		8
Ralph	full	8		1		8
Joaquim	half	3		2		6
Jerry	half	2		2		4
Ricky	half	4		2		8
Simeon	quarter	2		4		8
Total . . .						42

RuthAnn used a weighting (multiple) for all six team members, based upon the time that each worker actually worked. For those team workers employed full-time, she used the weighting of 1 (really, equivalent to no weighting). For those workers employed half-time, she used the multiple of 2; for the one worker employed one-quarter time, she used the multiple of 4. When she multiplied the workers' actual number of successful placements for the week by their respective weightings, she produced the number of cases that (theoretically) they would have successfully placed if they had been employed full-time and had continued at the same rate of productivity.

RuthAnn then added the scores for all six workers to get a total of 42, the number of placements that (theoretically) would have been made if all six workers had been employed full-time. Dividing by six, the mean worker success rate was seven discharges, exactly the same as that of the other team. By using the weighted mean, a fair comparison was made.

Weighted means have a variety of uses. Teachers use them to compute final grades of students when averaging scores on assignments and examinations that are given different weights. If Joetta, for example, received a 90 on her midterm exam (1/4 of the final grade), 80 on her final exam (1/2 of the final grade), and 100 on her term paper (1/4 of the final grade), her three scores could not simply be added up and divided by 3 (arithmetic mean) to produce a final course grade of 90. A weighted mean needs to be computed as follows:

Exercise	Score × Weighting Factor	= Points
Midterm	90	.25	22.5
Final	80	.50	40.0
Paper	100	.25	25.0
Course grade (weighted mean)			87.5

As the previous two examples clearly demonstrate, a weighted mean can be used in those situations where not all measurements are of equal importance (weight) in calculating the mean.

Which Measure of Central Tendency to Use?

The answer to the question of which measures of central tendency to use when describing a distribution of values is not always easy. With nominal and ordinal level variables, the mode is the only measure to use. If data are at the interval or ratio level, however, the final decision is often more a question of ethics than of rules. Like frequency distributions and graphs, we want to use the measures of central tendency to provide our readers with an accurate mental image of our data set—a shorthand description of what our data really look like. Yet, in some situations no single measure of central tendency would accurately represent a data set. An example using data from records of closed cases in a social service agency will help to illustrate this point.

Example: Short-Term Crisis Intervention. Suppose an agency administrator wishes to see if the agency really is using short-term crisis intervention treatment, as stated in the agency's mission statement. Data are collected and analyzed for cases closed during the month of December (Table 3.3). Figure 3.1 is a frequency polygon that presents these data (from Table 3.3) with the mode, median, and mean indicated.

The variable "number of interviews," is at the ratio level of measurement, and there are a large number of cases ($N = 1290$). These conditions suggest that the mean might be the best measure of central tendency to report, but what about outliers? The shape of the frequency polygon indicates that the presence of outliers may produce a distorted mean.

TABLE 3.3 Frequency Distribution: Number of Interviews for Cases Closed at XYZ Agency During December ($N = 1290$)

Number of Interviews	Number of Cases	Total Number of Interviews (Column 1 × Column 2)
1	55	55
2	35	70
3	55	165
4	40	160
5	25	125
6	15	90
7	10	70
8	20	160
9	5	45
10	35	350
Totals . . .	295	1290

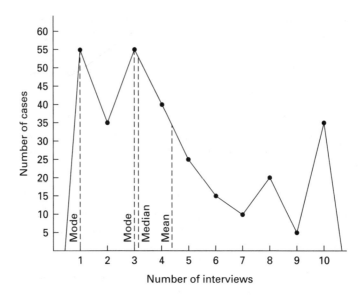

FIGURE 3.1 Frequency Polygon: Number of Interviews for Cases Closed at XYZ Agency During December (from Table 3.3)

The mean number of interviews in Table 3.3 is actually 4.37, primarily because of the fairly large number of cases (outliers) that were seen ten times ($n = 35$). A 10 percent trimmed mean (10 percent off both ends) would be even higher, a little over 5.5. Yet, it is apparent from Figure 3.1 that a client interviewed four or five times (rounding down or up) would not really be a "typical" client within the agency. There are actually four other values (i.e., 1, 2, 3, 10) that occurred as frequently as or more frequently than either 4 or 5. Because three of the values (i.e., 1, 2, 3) are all clustered well to the left of the mean, the mean or trimmed mean appear to be too high to reflect what is a typical value for the distribution.

If the mean or trimmed mean would not be representative portrayals of the data, what about the median? It falls between the values of 3 and 4 and very close to one of the most common values (3). As a choice for a single measure of central tendency to represent the data, it is fairly good. It does not, however, even hint that a fairly sizable group of clients ($n = 35$) were interviewed 10 times, a fact that may be a little surprising and possibly valuable for an agency that is generally believed to engage in short-term crisis intervention. It also does not confirm the more predictable finding that a large number of clients ($n = 55$) were interviewed only once. In short, the median may be better than either the mean or the mode for presenting what is typical, but it is far from perfect for this data set.

The distribution in Table 3.3 is bimodal, with the two modes falling at one and three interviews. But if we were to use only the mode, we would be suggesting that either one or three interviews (both small numbers) is representative of the "typical client" when, in fact, fewer than half of all the clients were seen four times or less. As with the median, the mode alone provides no hint of the possibility that a sizable percentage of crisis intervention cases were interviewed a fairly large number of times. Besides, the mode is really most appropriate for nominal and ordinal level data. It treats different value categories of a variable as if they were differences of kind only. It would not take into account that the value categories in our example reflect quantitative differences, a fact that is critical to an accurate interpretation of the data set.

In our example, as in many data sets, no single measure of central tendency would adequately summarize what the distribution of values for our variable, number of interviews, looked like. Any one measure of central tendency has the potential to mislead. Yet, the mode, the median, and the mean would help to describe how the data looked. The fact that the data set was bimodal, with modes at one and three interviews, indicates that short-term treatment occurs quite often within the agency. Yet, the median best reflects what is typical. It uses some of the available precision of measurement, more than the mode, but less than the mean. It at least suggests that short-term treatment may not be as typical of the agency as one might believe from reading the agency's mission statement. If the mean or the trimmed mean is presented, the fact that either is over four is even stronger evidence that a sizable number of clients clearly are not the recipients of short-term crisis intervention services.

When in doubt about which measure of central tendency to use, report all that would be helpful in visualizing the data set. If the mode, median, and mean (and/or trimmed mean) are all reported, an experienced reader of research reports, or even one with just a good understanding of central tendency, will be able to compare them and piece together a reasonably good picture of how the data were distributed. Any one measure of central tendency alone might mislead; but taken together, they present an accurate communication of the distribution of values of a variable—which, as we have repeatedly emphasized, is the goal of descriptive statistical analysis.

VARIABILITY

As we have seen, one or more measures of central tendency can tell us much about the distribution of the values of a variable. They can fall short, however, of giving us a complete picture of what a data set looks like. They do not, for example, tell us if most values tend to cluster around a typical value or, if not, how widely they vary from the typical value. To get a more accurate description of the distribution of the values, we need to add another summary description called *variability*—one that gives us an indicator of the degree of variation that occurred. Variability is also called *dispersion*.

Why is an understanding of variability so important? Let us take a simple example to answer this question. Suppose that there are two class sections of a graduate social work research course. The ages of the 15 students in both sections are as follows:

Ages: Section 1:
21, 22, 24, 24, 26, 29, 30, 31, 32, 33, 36, 38, 38, 40, 41

Ages: Section 2:
27, 28, 28, 29, 29, 30, 30, 31, 32, 32, 33, 33, 34, 34, 35

If we were to report only the mean and median for the variable "age" for each section, both measures of central tendency would be identical. The mean (31) and median (31) are the same for both sections. Only the sections' modes would give us any hint that the distribution of ages within them are quite different.

If a student who was 23 years of age were to register late for the class, the student might feel more comfortable in Section 1 than in Section 2. A student who is 39 registering late might feel more comfortable in Section 2. Neither student would know this based only on central tendency data. If the two students had one or more measures of variability for the two sections, however, they could anticipate how comfortable they might feel in registering in one section over the other.

If a variable is at the nominal or ordinal level of measurement, variability can be communicated best in a frequency distribution or graph. If a variable is at the interval or ratio level of measurement, however, measures of variability can be helpful in describing the distribution of values of a variable. The five measures of variability are (1) range, (2) interquartile range, (3) mean deviation, (4) variance, and (5) standard deviation.

The Range

The range is the distance that encompasses all values within a data set. Expressed as a formula, the range is computed as follows:

Range = maximum value − minimum value + 1

The formula above differs slightly from the way we use the word "range" in common English usage. Why is the range not simply the difference between the maximum value (the value of the case with the largest value of the variable) and the minimum value (the value of the case with the smallest value of the variable)? We add 1 to the difference so that the range reflects the total number of values of the variable that it encompasses.

In a distribution of the variable "age," for example, with a maximum age of 35 and a minimum age of 30, the range is 6 (35 − 30 + 1 = 6). That is because there are potentially 6 different ages (or values) that are included within the range: 35, 34, 33, 32, 31, and 30. Even if we think of values as reflecting equal intervals (Chapter 1), the range would still be 6 since it would include the distance from the lower limit of the interval for 27 (26.50) and the upper limit of the interval for 35 (35.49).

The range for Section 2 in our previous example is 9 (35 − 27 + 1 = 9). There are potentially 9 different ages included in the data: 27, 28, 29, 30, 31, 32, 33, 34, and 35. The range for Section 1 is 21 (41 − 21 + 1 = 21). The larger range in Section 1, compared with that of Section 2, indicates a greater variation in the students' ages between the two class sections.

The range can be computed quickly and easily. Calculating the range also suggests the number of intervals to employ in creating grouped frequency distributions as well as the most appropriate interval size. Like the mean, however, the range is easily distorted by the presence of outliers. One outlier at either end of an array can greatly increase the range of a data set and suggest much more variability than is actually present. Let us suppose that the student who is 41 years of age in Section 1 drops out of the research seminar and is replaced by a student who is 64 years of age. The distribution of values would now look like this:

Ages: Section 1:
21, 22, 24, 24, 26, 29, 30, 31, 32, 33, 36, 38, 38, 40, 64

While only one value has changed, the range for Section 1 has jumped from 21 to 44 (64 − 21 + 1 = 44). A student considering enrolling in Section 1, upon learning that the range for the students' ages is 44, would mistakenly assume that the ages of the students are much more diverse than they really are.

The vulnerability of the range to the influence of outliers is an undesirable characteristic, especially when comparing the ranges of two distributions of the same variable. The presence of outliers in one distribution and not in the other can give a misleading impression about the degree of similarity of the two distributions.

The Interquartile Range

One way to handle the problem of outliers is to use another measure of variability rather than the range. Instead of using the maximum and minimum values to obtain a range, variability can be reported as the distance between the 75th and 25th percentiles. This distance is known as the *interquartile range.*

As we know, the median falls at the 50th percentile, or midpoint of an array where half the values fall above it and half the values fall below it. In such an array, the 25th percentile would fall at the point where one-fourth of values in the array would have lower or smaller values and three-fourths would have higher values. The 75th percentile would fall at the point where three-fourths of values in the array would have lower or smaller values and one-fourth would have higher values.

Once an array has been formed and the 75th and 25th percentiles have been determined, the interquartile range is found by subtracting the 25th percentile from the 75th percentile. The interquartile range is a more stable measure of variability than the range for the same reason that the median is a more stable measure of central tendency than the mean. Outliers cannot distort the interquartile range as they distort the range because their actual values are used only in the first step in its computation, forming an array. Once an array is formed and the outliers within its first and fourth quartile are located, they are not used any more for computation.

Like the formula for the median, the formula for the interquartile range can be difficult to compute by hand. It is often a decimal or fraction, as it would be with any of the examples of distributions that we have previously used. With the use of computers to analyze data, however, this presents few problems as its computation takes only a few seconds once the data have been entered.

Another, less widely used measure of variability that is a variation of the interquartile range is the *semi-interquartile range*. It is simply the interquartile range divided by 2. Thus, it is a distance that is one-half the distance between the 75th and 25th percentiles.

The Mean Deviation

The range, interquartile range, and semi-interquartile range all can present accurate descriptions of the variability within values of a variable. They are all useful in certain situations. As we know, they do not use every case value in their final calculations. This sometimes results in a distorted picture of the data set. The *mean deviation*, however, is derived from computations involving all the values in a given data set.

The mean deviation is the average amount that the values of a variable differ (or deviate) from the mean. Like other measures of variability, it describes only the amount of variation among values of a variable, not their absolute values. That is the work of frequency distributions and graphs as presented in Chapter 2.

Table 3.4 lists 5 values (i.e., 1, 2, 3, 4, 5), their mean (3), and the deviation score of each (i.e., −2, −1, 0, 1, 2), which is the difference between each respective value (i.e., 1, 2, 3, 4, 5) and their mean (3).

The formula for the mean deviation is:

$$\text{Mean deviation} = \frac{\text{Sum of deviation values (ignoring sign)}}{\text{Number of cases}}$$

To compute the mean deviation for the data in Table 3.4, we would proceed as follows:

$$\text{Mean deviation} = \frac{2 + 1 + 0 + 1 + 2}{5}$$

$$= 1.2$$

While the mean deviation is relatively easy to compute and interpret, it is rarely reported in our professional literature. We have chosen to discuss it because the process of subtracting raw scores (values) from the mean is an important step in computing two other, widely used measures of variability, the variance and the standard deviation.

The Variance

Obtaining the *variance* requires subtracting the mean of the distribution from each value (getting the mean deviation), squaring each difference, and then dividing the sum of the squared differences (called the *sum of squares*) by the total number of values.

TABLE 3.4   Deviations from the Mean

Value	−	Mean	=	Deviation from the Mean
1	−	3	=	−2
2	−	3	=	−1
3	−	3	=	0
4	−	3	=	1
5	−	3	=	2
	Total . . .			0

To compute the variance for the data in Table 3.4, we would proceed as follows:

$$\text{Variance} = \frac{\text{Sum of squared deviations from the mean}}{\text{Number of cases}}$$

Substituting values for letters, we get the following:

$$\text{Variance} = \frac{(-2)^2 + (-1)^2 + (0)^2 + (1)^2 + (2)^2}{5}$$

$$= \frac{4 + 1 + 0 + 1 + 4}{5}$$

$$= 2$$

The variance sometimes is reported as a descriptive statistic within our professional literature. It also is a critical component of some of the statistical computations discussed in later chapters.

The Standard Deviation

The *standard deviation* is simply the square root of the variance. It appears frequently in quantitatively oriented reports. It is useful for describing the variability of data (when certain conditions are met), and it is used in many other types of statistical analyses as well.

The standard deviation requires interval or ratio level data. It also is most appropriately used with fairly large samples and with variables that, if graphed, would produce a frequency polygon that has a particular shape—the normal distribution (discussed in Chapter 4).

Like the mean deviation and the variance, the standard deviation uses all case values in its computation. It tells us to what degree the values cluster around the mean, which makes it extremely useful. As we shall see in Chapter 4, when used with the mean in appropriate situations, it allows us to determine where a given value falls relative to other values and to reconstruct the distribution of all the values of a variable. For the moment, we will concentrate on how the standard deviation is computed from those values.

Computing the standard deviation involves eight simple steps, most of which have already been discussed in relation to the variance:

1. List the values in a distribution in column a.
2. Compute the mean of the values in column a.
3. List the mean in column b.
4. Subtract the mean from each value in column a and place this value into column c.
5. Square each value in column c and place this value into column d.
6. Compute the sum of the squares in column d.
7. Divide the sum of squares in column d by the total number of values in column a.
8. Compute the square root of the number computed in Step 7 (the variance). The result is the standard deviation of the values in column a.

TABLE 3.5   Determining the Standard Deviation
                of Years of Employment for Agency A

Step 1 (a) Value	−	Step 3 (b) Mean	=	Step 4 (c) Deviation from Mean	Step 5 (d) Squared Difference from Mean
5	−	6	=	−1	1
5	−	6	=	−1	1
6	−	6	=	0	0
6	−	6	=	0	0
7	−	6	=	1	1
7	−	6	=	1	1
		Total . . .		0	Step 6 = 4

$$\text{Step 7} = \frac{4}{6}$$

$$= .67 \quad \text{(Variance)}$$

$$\text{Step 8} = \sqrt{.67}$$

$$= .82 \quad \text{(Standard deviation)}$$

The data in the distribution below give the number of years of employment of the six social workers who work in Agency A:

Years of employment: Agency A:
5, 5, 6, 6, 7, 7

Using the data, we can compute the standard deviation using the eight steps described above (see Table 3.5).

Now suppose that Agency B also has six social workers, but their years of employment are as follows:

Years of employment: Agency B:
1, 2, 4, 8, 10, 11

Again, we can compute the standard deviation for the variable "years of employment" (see Table 3.6).

The distribution of years of employment in Agency B shows more variation than does the distribution for Agency A. This is also reflected in their respective standard deviations—3.87 for Agency B and .82 for Agency A. This demonstrates an important point: In comparing two distributions of measurements of the same variable, larger standard deviations reflect more variation and vice versa.

A pictorial representation of the above data will further demonstrate the meaning of standard deviation. Figures 3.2 and 3.3 each show how the data on length of employment in the two agencies would look if displayed as weights on a scale.

TABLE 3.6 Determining the Standard Deviation
of Years of Employment for Agency B

Step 1 (a) Value	−	Step 3 (b) Mean	=	Step 4 (c) Deviation from Mean	Step 5 (d) Squared Difference from Mean
1	−	6	=	−5	25
2	−	6	=	−4	16
4	−	6	=	−2	4
8	−	6	=	2	4
10	−	6	=	4	16
11	−	6	=	5	25

$$\text{Step 6} \ = \ 90$$

$$\text{Step 7} \ = \ \frac{90}{6}$$

$$= \ 15 \quad \text{(Variance)}$$

$$\text{Step 8} \ = \ \sqrt{15}$$

$$= \ 3.87 \quad \text{(Standard deviation)}$$

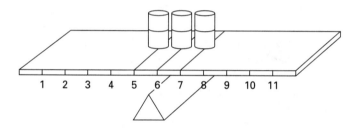

FIGURE 3.2 Variability of Years of Employment for Agency A
(from Table 3.5)

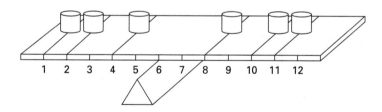

FIGURE 3.3 Variability of Years of Employment for Agency B
(from Table 3.6)

Note that Figures 3.2 and 3.3 both "balance" on 6 years, reflecting the fact that both distributions have a mean of 6 (years of employment). Notice, however, how much more variation is shown in Agency B (Figure 3.3) than in Agency A (Figure 3.2). This is a graphical portrayal of Agency B's greater variability for values of the variable as reflected in its larger standard deviation.

While adding or subtracting a fixed amount to all values of a distribution will affect the mean by increasing or decreasing it by that amount, it will not affect the standard deviation for that distribution. A standard deviation reflects variation, and the amount of variation would not change.

If every employee in the agency in our example above received a $2000 annual raise, for example, the mean annual salary would increase by $2000, but its standard deviation (and its range and interquartile range) would remain exactly the same. Similarly, if we were to repeat our measurement of years of employment one year later with the same employees in either agency, the mean would now be 7 years, but the respective standard deviations would be the same as they were a year earlier.

Reporting Measures of Variability

Like measures of central tendency, different measures of variability are most appropriate for certain situations. Also like measures of central tendency, it often is desirable to report more than one.

The range generally is reported (as a single number) within the narrative text of a research report; interquartile ranges, semi-interquartile ranges, variances, standard deviations, and, when they are reported, mean deviations often are reported in tabular form, especially when there are many to report.

Since the standard deviation represents the distance between the mean and a certain point on a frequency polygon, it is only natural that the mean is commonly reported along with the standard deviation. Where one is appropriate, the other generally is also. Reporting the two together also enables the reader of a research report to get a full picture of how the values of a variable were distributed. This concept is addressed in much more detail in the following chapter.

When the interquartile range or semi-interquartile range are used instead of the standard deviation or variance because of the presence of extreme outliers within an interval or ratio level data set, they are often reported along with the median. Again, this is logical since all three of these measures are designed to counteract the distorting effect of outliers.

To provide an even more complete image of the distribution of the measurements of a variable, we can sometimes report what is referred to as a *five-number summary*. It consists of the minimum value, the 25th percentile, the median, the 75th percentile, and the maximum value.

A graph known as a box plot is also sometimes used to display the central tendency and dispersion of the distribution of a variable. In a box plot such as Figure 3.4 (a representation of the ages of the extended care facility residents described in Chapter 2), we can identify the 25th percentile, the median, the 75th percentile, and outliers. The "box" in the figure contains all cases between the 25th and 75th percentiles (those within the interquartile range). The horizontal line within it is the median. The short horizontal lines outside the box (above and below a vertical line extending from the box) represent the largest values that would not be regarded as outliers. Values above or below these lines would be regarded as outliers. Their case numbers (14 and 30) appear near the top on the graph.

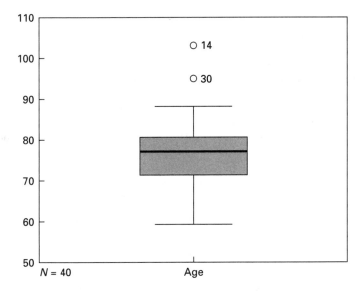

FIGURE 3.4 Box Plot: Ages of Residents at XYZ Residential Care Facility (*N* = 40)

CONCLUDING THOUGHTS

This chapter briefly discussed basic ways for summarizing the distribution of values of variables within any given data set. We looked at one group of measures that is used for describing what was typical of a data set (central tendency) and another group that is used for summarizing how different the values tended to be from each other (variability). We suggested when each measure is most appropriate to use and noted their respective limitations.

As in Chapter 2, this chapter emphasized the importance of honest and clear communication. Frequently a single measure of central tendency, or a single measure of variability, will not accomplish this objective. Thus, we should include as many as are necessary in a research report, or presentation, in order to insure that the distribution of a data set can be fully visualized.

STUDY QUESTIONS

1. What does a frequency polygon look like when its distribution is described as bimodal? Provide an original example in your discussion.
2. Why is the median more likely to be an accurate description of interval level data than the mode? Explain.
3. Discuss why the median is a more stable measure of central tendency than the mean. Provide an original example in your discussion.

4. Why do we generally consider the mean to be a more precise measure of central tendency than either the median or the mode?

5. How does a trimmed mean combine the best features of both the median and the mean?

6. In what situations is it necessary to compute a weighted mean? Provide an example.

7. Why may only one measure of central tendency be an inadequate description of a data set? Provide an original example in your discussion.

8. Discuss why the range is an especially unstable measure of variability and when the interquartile range may be preferable.

9. Which measures of variability consider all values of a variable in their computations? Why is this better than using only some of the values in a distribution? Explain in detail.

10. How would an outlier tend to distort the mean deviation for a data set?

11. How would a data set containing the values of a variable with a mean of 50 and a standard deviation of 3 compare with another data set containing the same variable but a mean of 50 and a standard deviation of 12?

12. How would adding the number 10 to each of the values of a variable affect its mean and standard deviation? Provide an example.

13. Fifteen students are registered in Section 1 and 15 in Section 2 of a research course. They took the same midterm exam, and their exam scores were distributed as follows:

    Section 1: 89, 56, 45, 78, 98, 45, 55, 77, 88, 99, 98, 97, 54, 34, 94
    Section 2: 77, 88, 87, 67, 98, 87, 55, 77, 45, 44, 88, 99, 69, 67, 98

    a. Calculate the mode, median, mean, range, variance, and standard deviation for both sections.
    b. Which section did better overall on the exam, Section 1 or Section 2? Fully justify your answer using the concepts presented in this chapter.

14. Locate an article in a social work professional journal that uses one or more of the measures of central tendency and variability presented in this chapter. Answer the following questions in relation to the article.
    a. Do you feel the author reported the data accurately when referring to the data set used in the research study? Why or why not?
    b. What other measures of central tendency and variability would you have liked the author to report? Why would they have been helpful?

15. Discuss why a mean should not be used with ordinal level variables.

16. For each of the following, indicate the measure of central tendency that would be most appropriate, and indicate why.
    a. An income distribution in which 97 percent of the cases are in a range of $20,000 to $50,000 and a few cases are between 0 and $5,000.
    b. Data reporting the religious preferences of 100 social work students.
    c. A grouped frequency distribution of the variable age that has an open-ended interval of "over 65 years of age."

17. The measures of central tendency have been reported for three different social service agencies for the variable number of years employed in the agency as follows:

    Agency A: mode 16, median 17, mean 16
    Agency B: mode 4, median 7, mean 10
    Agency C: mode 1, median 3, mean 6

    Use the measures of central tendency to describe and compare the staff of the three agencies.

18. What is a box plot and what does it portray? Provide an example of one.

Chapter **4**

Normal Distributions

Chapter 2 presented simple ways of how tables and graphs can be used to portray the distributions of values (and value categories) of a variable within any given data set. Chapter 3 illustrated the various methods that can be used to summarize two important characteristics of a distribution of values within the same data set—central tendency and variability. This chapter demonstrates how frequency polygons can be used to present a more complete description of the distribution of interval or ratio level variables. Let us start our study of distributions with a quick look at skewed distributions.

SKEWED DISTRIBUTIONS

Chapter 2 showed how a frequency polygon can be constructed using interval or ratio level data. The shape of a frequency polygon reflects where the various values of a variable tend to cluster. Some polygons reflect the fact that relatively large numbers of values cluster at the left side where lower values of the variable are displayed; others reflect the opposite pattern.

Suppose, for example, Sue, a hospital administrator, wished to study changes in admission diagnoses over a six-year period. She wanted to substantiate her impression that the hospital was experiencing a decline in some diagnoses and an increase in others. The data might look like those in Table 4.1 for a diagnosis such as emphysema.

Just by glancing at the data in Table 4.1, it is easy to see that the number of emphysema patients admitted to the hospital over the six-year period has declined over time. This trend is even more apparent when the data are placed in a histogram such as the one in Figure 4.1.

The midpoints of the bars in the histogram in Figure 4.1 are connected. The line joining them to form a frequency polygon is called a curve. Distributions like the one

TABLE 4.1 Cumulative
Frequency Distribution:
Emphysema Patients Admitted to
XYZ Hospital by Year (*N* = 210)

Year	Absolute Frequency	Cumulative Frequency
1990	60	60
1991	50	110
1992	40	150
1993	30	180
1994	20	200
1995	10	210

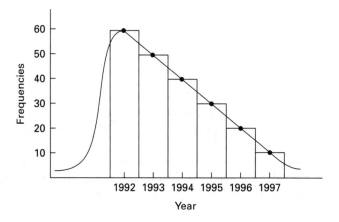

FIGURE 4.1 Positively Skewed Frequency Polygon (from
Table 4.1): Emphysema Patients Admitted to XYZ
Hospital by Year (*N* = 210)

shown in Table 4.1 and reflected in the frequency polygon in Figure 4.1 are referred to as skewed. A *skewed distribution* is asymmetrical—that is, its ends do not taper off in a similar manner in both directions. Note that the frequency polygon in Figure 4.1 has a "tail" on the right side. A curve like the one in Figure 4.1 (which has a tail to the right), is called a *positively skewed distribution*.

Trends in admissions of HIV-positive cases over the six-year period in the same hospital might reflect a very different pattern from those of emphysema admissions. Table 4.2 and Figure 4.2 illustrate this point.

The distribution in Figure 4.2 is also skewed, but this time the tail of the frequency distribution is to the left. A curve that is skewed to the left is called a *negatively skewed distribution*.

TABLE 4.2 Cumulative Frequency Distribution: HIV-Positive Patients Admitted to XYZ Hospital by Year ($N = 210$)

Year	Absolute Frequency	Cumulative Frequency
1990	10	10
1991	20	30
1992	30	60
1993	40	100
1994	50	150
1995	60	210

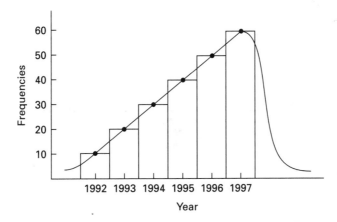

FIGURE 4.2 Negatively Skewed Frequency Polygon (from Table 4.2): HIV-Positive Patients Admitted to XYZ Hospital by Year ($N = 210$)

NORMAL DISTRIBUTIONS

Many interval and ratio level variables can be graphed to form a frequency polygon that is relatively free of skewness and form a symmetrical distribution. There are many different kinds of symmetrical distributions. One of these distributions is of special interest to us when we study statistics—the *normal distribution*. An interval or ratio level variable that is normally distributed can be represented by a "bell-shaped" frequency polygon; the curve thus formed is referred to as the normal curve. One example of a normal curve reflecting a normal distribution is presented in Figure 4.3.

Distributions of all interval or ratio level variables that are normally distributed within any given data set share the same properties. What are the other properties of a

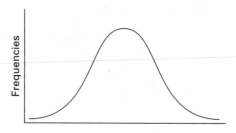

FIGURE 4.3 The Normal Curve

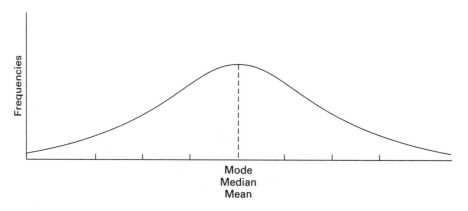

Mode
Median
Mean

FIGURE 4.4 The Normal Distribution

normal curve in addition to being symmetrical and bell-shaped? For one thing, in a normal curve, the mode, median, and mean all occur at the highest point and in the center of the distribution, as in Figure 4.4.

Note that in skewed curves, the mode, median, and mean occur at different points, as in Figures 4.5a and b.

The ends of the normal curve extend toward infinity—they approach the horizontal axis (x-axis) but never quite touch it. This property represents the possibility that, while the curve contains virtually all values of a variable within a population, a small number of values may exist that reflect extremely large or extremely small measurements of the variable (outliers). It also reflects the fact that at a higher level of abstraction, a total population, or universe, is never static because it is always subject to change as cases are added or deleted over time. Thus, populations are always evolving.

The horizontal axis that lies below the normal curve is divided into six equal units—three units between the mean and the place where the curve approaches the axis on the left side, and three units between the mean and the place where it approaches the axis on the right. These six units collectively reflect the amount of variation that exists within virtually all values of a normally distributed interval or ratio level variable. In a normal distribution of any variable, virtually all values (except for .26%)

(a) A positively skewed distribution

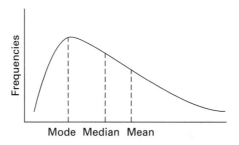

(b) A negatively skewed distribution

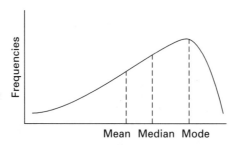

FIGURE 4.5 Skewed Distributions

fall within these six units of variation. The larger the units, the flatter the curve. The smaller the units, the higher the curve.

What exactly are these units of variation and how much variation does each represent? Each unit corresponds to a standard deviation. How much variation it represents within any given normal curve is determined by using the standard deviation formula presented in the previous chapter.

Figure 4.6 shows a typical normal curve with three units of standard deviations to the left of the mean and three units to the right of the mean. Note that the units are labeled to reflect the number of standard deviations (SD) that each falls from the mean. Units to the left of the mean (where values are smaller than the mean) use the minus sign (i.e., $-1SD$, $-2SD$, $-3SD$), and units to the right of the mean (where values are larger than the mean) use the positive sign (i.e., $+1SD$, $+2SD$, $+3SD$).

The term "standard deviation" can be a little misleading. What is "standard" about standard deviation? "Standard" refers to the fact that once the standard deviation for a variable within a data set is computed, it becomes a standard unit which reflects the amount of variation for that variable. Just like means, however, the sizes of standard deviations vary from one data set to another or from one variable to another, based upon the measurements that are used in their computation.

The mean and standard deviation for test scores for males, for example, might be different from the mean and standard deviation for test scores of females who take the same examination. Or the mean and standard deviation computed from people's scores

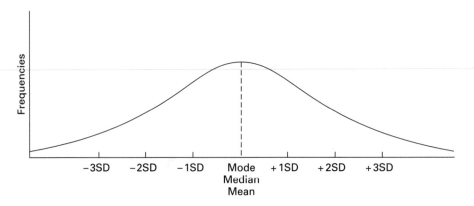

FIGURE 4.6 The Normal Distribution with Standard Deviations Illustrated

who took the examination in 1998 might be different from the mean and standard deviation computed from people's test scores who took the examination in 1997.

Different normal curves, therefore, tend to have different means and different standard deviations. Figures 4.7a, b, and c demonstrate how this occurs by comparing three pairs of normal curves. It also demonstrates the fact that normal curves show variety; that is, they may be high and narrow, low and wide, or anything in between. They are usually drawn to suggest the degree of variation present in the distribution of an interval or ratio level variable; that is, the size of its standard deviation. Flatter curves suggest relatively large standard deviations, and higher ones reflect relatively small standard deviations.

Not surprisingly, 50 percent of the total area of the frequency polygon formed by a normal curve falls below the mean, and 50 percent falls above it. Other segments of the frequency polygon similarly reflect other percentages of its total area. Mathematicians have figured out what percentage of the normal curve falls within its various segments as illustrated in Figure 4.8.

By looking at Figure 4.8, we can see that the area of a normal curve between a point on the horizontal axis (e.g., $-2SD$) and the mean is equivalent to the area of the curve between the comparable point on the other side of the mean (e.g., $+2SD$) and the mean. This makes sense because, as we have already noted, a normal curve is symmetrical. If we were to add up all the percentages within each of the segments of the frequency polygon between $-3SD$ and $+3SD$, they would equal 99.74 percent of the curve.

Thus, almost all of the area of the frequency polygon (99.74%) lies between the points $-3SD$ and $+3SD$. We could also add together other segments of the normal curve to learn that 47.72 percent of it (34.13% + 13.59% = 47.72%) falls between the mean and $+2SD$ and also between the mean and $-2SD$, or that 68.26 percent (34.13% + 34.13% = 68.26%) falls within + or $-1SD$ of the mean.

Now let us look at Figure 4.8 from a different perspective. Up to this point, we have viewed the numbers in the figure as areas or portions of a frequency polygon. But these numbers are also something else. They are the percentage of values (persons, cases, or objects) that fall within the respective distances from the mean of a normally distributed interval or ratio level variable within a given data set. If, for example,

(a) Equal means, unequal standard deviations

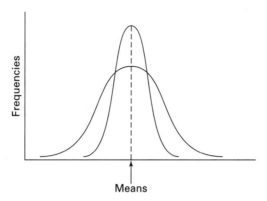

(b) Unequal means, equal standard deviations

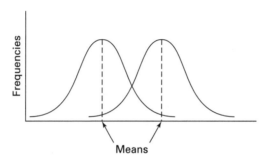

(c) Unequal means, unequal standard deviations

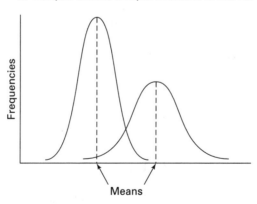

FIGURE 4.7 Variations in Normal Distributions

Figure 4.8 were a frequency distribution of a normally distributed variable, such as "height of female social work students," the figure would tell us that the height of 47.72 percent of all female social work students (34.13% + 13.59% = 47.72%) falls between the mean and $+2SD$; the height of 68.26 percent of them (34.13% + 34.13% = 68.26%) falls between $+1SD$ and $-1SD$ from the mean, and so on.

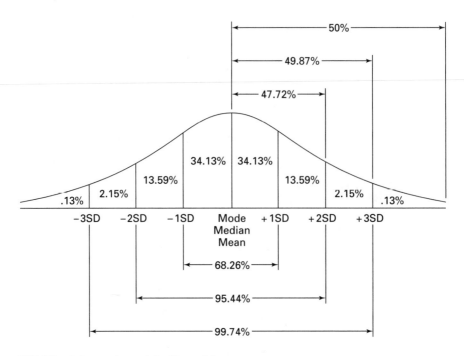

FIGURE 4.8 Proportions of the Normal Curve

If we know, or could compute, exactly what the mean and standard deviation for the height of female social work students is, for example, we could then make very precise statements about the distribution of values of the variable. We could assign actual heights to correspond to the various mean and standard deviation points in Figure 4.8 and make statements like, "68.26 percent of the heights of female social work students fall between ___ inches tall and ___ inches tall." Understanding that the percentage of the area under a normal curve is also the percentage of values that fall within a certain distribution area of a normally distributed interval or ratio level variable is critical to understanding the material in this chapter and other parts of our discussion of statistics that rely on the normal distribution of values.

CONVERTING RAW SCORES TO z SCORES

When we encounter values of an interval or ratio level variable based on measurements taken from two different samples or populations, we are sometimes unable to make direct comparisons between them. Suppose we have two friends, for example, Rita and Miriam who are in two different sections of a social work practice course. Both take their midterm exams. Rita's raw score is 21 and Miriam's is 85. Who did better on her midterm? Without additional information, we would have no way of knowing.

If we could learn the maximum score that each could have received on her respective examination, it would help a great deal. Perhaps, Rita's score of 21 was out of a maximum of 25—that would be 84 percent correct. And Miriam's score of 85 was out of a maximum of 100—85 percent correct. Can we thus assume that Miriam is doing better at midterm than Rita? Maybe, maybe not. Perhaps we would learn that Miriam's 85 percent was the lowest grade in her course section and Rita's 84 percent was the highest grade in her section. That might cause us to rethink our initial assumption.

We could conduct a meaningful comparison of our friends' scores if we had a more comprehensive picture of how each score compares with those of others in the respective course section. In other words, we would have to convert the two scores (i.e., 84, 85) to a common standard.

In order to do this, we would have to assume that the scores in both sections are normally distributed (a pretty big assumption). It is possible to use a common standard to compare values of an interval or ratio level variable taken from two different populations only if the variable is normally distributed within both populations. We do this through the use of z scores.

z scores (also known as standard scores) are raw scores converted to standard deviation units. Every raw score in any normal distribution can be given an equivalent z score that reflects how many standard deviation units it falls above or below the mean. The relative positions of two z scores taken from two different normal distributions can then be compared directly with one another.

When we use the known areas of the frequency polygon formed by the normal curve, z scores can be converted to percentiles. A percentile is a point below which a certain percentage of the distribution of values lies. Thus, each score corresponds to a certain percentile rank. Suppose for a moment, Axel received a score of 75 on a statistics exam. By converting his raw score (i.e., 75) to a z score we could determine that it fell at the 82nd percentile within his course section (82 percent of the class received a grade below his grade). Suppose Durshka's score on a statistics exam in a different section was also 75, but her score fell at the 92nd percentile among students in her section (where 92 percent of students did not receive as high a score as Durshka). It is now possible to compare Axel's and Durshka's scores (using percentiles), even though they took different exams in different course sections.

To convert a raw score into a z score, the following formula is used:

$$z \text{ score} = \frac{\text{raw score} - \text{mean}}{\text{standard deviation}}$$

As mentioned above, a z score reflects the number of standard deviation units that a given raw score falls from the mean of the distribution that contains the score. A raw score above the mean has a corresponding positive z score; a raw score below the mean has a corresponding negative z score. The mean of all the z values of a normally distributed interval or ratio level variable is 0.00. To put it another way, if we were to take all the z scores of a normally distributed interval or ratio level variable and place them into a frequency polygon, that polygon would have a mean of zero and a standard deviation of 1.

As long as we know the mean and the standard deviation of a distribution from which any raw score is obtained, we can compute its z score. As can be expected, z scores usually do not turn out to be whole numbers. More typically, they are fractions or mixed numbers. We express them in the form of decimals such as $z = +2.11$ or $z = -2.24$. A figure such as Figure 4.8 could not be used to determine the percentage of values that would fall between a fractional z score and the mean of the frequency distribution that contains its raw score. We would have to go to a table such as Table 4.3 (or Appendix A) to assist us in converting our fractional z scores into percentiles.

Table 4.3 shows the area of a normal curve (and the corresponding percent of values) within any normal distribution that falls between a whole or fractional z score and the mean. Note that the number alongside 1.0 in the left-hand column is 34.13, the area of the normal curve between the mean and either $+1SD$ or $-1SD$ (see Figure 4.8). Also, the number alongside 2.0 in the left-hand column is 47.72, the sum of the numbers 34.13 and 13.59 in Figure 4.8. The 47.72 represents the percentage of values in any normal distribution that falls between the mean and either $+2SD$ or $-2SD$.

In Table 4.3, the whole number and the first decimal of a z score are found in the left-hand column. The second number to the right of the decimal in the z score is found in the column headings that run across the top of the table. The area of the normal curve between a given z score (obtained by using the z score formula) and the mean would be the number in the body of the table where the appropriate line and column intersect.

To find the area of the curve between a raw score and the mean, for example, when the raw score's z score computes to 1.55, we would first go down the left-hand column in Table 4.3 to 1.5. Then we would move right across the table to the .05 column (to pick up the second decimal). The number 43.94 appears at the intersection of the 1.5 line and the .05 column. That means that the area of the curve between our raw score and the mean would be 43.94 or, viewing it another way, that nearly 44 percent of all values (or cases) fall between that raw score and the mean.

For positive z scores (those to the right of the mean) we would add the area of the curve found in the body of Table 4.3 to 50.00 (corresponding to the area of the curve below the mean) to find the percentile rank where the raw score fell. In our example (using a z score of 1.55), we would add 43.94 to 50.00 to get 93.94. The raw score corresponding to a z score of 1.55 would fall at approximately the 94th percentile. It is logical to add 50.00 to the number found in Table 4.3 since we know that the raw score fell above the mean. All scores below the mean (50 percent of them in a normal distribution), plus the other 43.94 percent between the mean and the score, fell below it.

For negative z scores (those to the left of the mean), we would subtract the area of the curve found in the body of Table 4.3 from 50.00 (the percentile of the mean). If the z score in our example had turned out to be -1.55, we would subtract 43.94 from 50.00 to get 6.06. The raw score corresponding to a z score of -1.55 would fall at approximately the 6th percentile.

Table 4.4 provides additional examples of z scores and their corresponding areas and percentiles as obtained using Table 4.3.

z scores are used appropriately with interval or ratio level variables that form normal distributions or at least approximate the normal curve. When the distribution is skewed, the area between $-1SD$ and the mean is not equal to the area between $+1SD$ and the mean. Then, a z score cannot be used to produce a standardized proportion of the distribution from which it was computed. The distribution in Figure 4.9, for example, is positively skewed. Area A is not equal to Area B, even though each area corresponds to $+1SD$ from the mean.

TABLE 4.3 Areas of the Normal Curve

	Area under the normal curve between mean and z score								
z	.00	.01	.02	.03	.04	.05	.06	.07	.08	.09
0.0	00.00	00.40	00.80	01.20	01.60	01.99	02.39	02.79	03.19	03.59
0.1	03.98	04.38	04.78	05.17	05.57	05.96	06.36	06.75	07.14	07.53
0.2	07.93	08.32	08.71	09.10	09.48	09.87	10.26	10.64	11.03	11.41
0.3	11.79	12.17	12.55	12.93	13.31	13.68	14.06	14.43	14.80	15.17
0.4	15.54	15.91	16.28	16.64	17.00	17.36	17.72	18.08	18.44	18.79
0.5	19.15	19.50	19.85	20.19	20.54	20.88	21.23	21.57	21.90	22.24
0.6	22.57	22.91	23.24	23.57	23.89	24.22	24.54	24.86	25.17	25.49
0.7	25.80	26.11	26.42	26.73	27.04	27.34	27.64	27.94	28.23	28.52
0.8	28.81	29.10	29.39	29.67	29.95	30.23	30.51	30.78	31.06	31.33
0.9	31.59	31.86	32.12	32.38	32.64	32.90	33.15	33.40	33.65	33.89
1.0	34.13	34.38	34.61	34.85	35.08	35.31	35.54	35.77	35.99	36.21
1.1	36.43	36.65	36.86	37.08	37.29	37.49	37.70	37.90	38.10	38.30
1.2	38.49	38.69	38.88	39.07	39.25	39.44	39.62	39.80	39.97	40.15
1.3	40.32	40.49	40.66	40.82	40.99	41.15	41.31	41.47	41.62	41.77
1.4	41.92	42.07	42.22	42.36	42.51	42.65	42.79	42.92	43.06	43.19
1.5	43.32	43.45	43.57	43.70	43.83	43.94	44.06	44.18	44.29	44.41
1.6	44.52	44.63	44.74	44.84	44.95	45.05	45.15	45.25	45.35	45.45
1.7	45.54	45.64	45.73	45.82	45.91	45.99	46.08	46.16	46.25	46.33
1.8	46.41	46.49	46.56	46.64	46.71	46.78	46.86	46.93	46.99	47.06
1.9	47.13	47.19	47.26	47.32	47.38	47.44	47.50	47.56	47.61	47.67
2.0	47.72	47.78	47.83	47.88	47.93	47.98	48.03	48.08	48.12	48.17
2.1	48.21	48.26	48.30	48.34	48.38	48.42	48.46	48.50	48.54	48.57
2.2	48.61	48.64	48.68	48.71	48.75	48.78	48.81	48.84	48.87	48.90
2.3	48.93	48.96	48.98	49.01	49.04	49.06	49.09	49.11	49.13	49.16
2.4	49.18	49.20	49.22	49.25	49.27	49.29	49.31	49.32	49.34	49.36
2.5	49.38	49.40	49.41	49.43	49.45	49.46	49.48	49.49	49.51	49.52
2.6	49.53	49.55	49.56	49.57	49.59	49.60	49.61	49.62	49.63	49.64
2.7	49.65	49.66	49.67	49.68	49.69	49.70	49.71	49.72	49.73	49.74
2.8	49.74	49.75	49.76	49.77	49.77	49.78	49.79	49.79	49.80	49.81
2.9	49.81	49.82	49.82	49.83	49.84	49.84	49.85	49.85	49.86	49.86
3.0	49.87									
3.5	49.98									
4.0	49.997									
5.0	49.99997									

Source: The original data for Table 4.3 came from *Tables for Statisticians and Biometricians*, edited by K. Pearson, published by the Imperial College of Science and Technology, and are used here by permission of the Biometrika trustees. The adaptation of these data is taken from E.L. Lindquist, *A First Course in Statistics* (revised edition), with permission of the publisher, Houghton Mifflin Company.

TABLE 4.4   Examples of z Scores and Their Corresponding Areas
and Percentiles

z Score	Row	Column	Area Included between Mean and z Score	Percentiles
.12	0.1	.02	04.78	54.78
1.78	1.7	.08	46.25	96.25
−2.90	2.9	.00	49.81	.19
1.15	1.1	.05	37.49	87.49
−1.15	1.1	.05	37.49	12.51

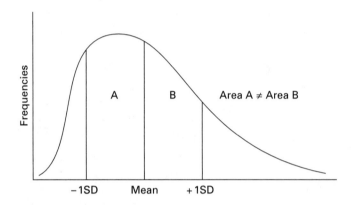

FIGURE 4.9 Comparing Areas of the Curve of a Skewed Distribution

Practical Uses of z Scores

When used with normally distributed distributions, z scores make it possible for us to take any single interval or ratio level raw score from a normally distributed distribution and gain an accurate understanding of where it falls relative to the other scores. By converting raw scores to percentile ranks, we can put raw scores into perspective. A student receiving a raw score of 57 on a first statistics exam, for example, may become quite alarmed, but learning that the score fell at the 96th percentile would be of considerable comfort, especially if the instructor has promised to "curve" the students' grades.

In fact the process of "curving" grades is a dubious one, especially in course sections that are not very large. Scores on statistics exams do not tend to be normally distributed. Because of this and because of the frequent presence of outliers (extremely high or low values), assigning grades based on, essentially, how many standard deviations they fell from the mean can produce grades that may seem unfair.

Treating course grades as if they are normally distributed might lead an instructor to award an A to exam scores that were in the top 16 percent (above +1SD) or an F to all exam scores below the 2nd percentile (below −2SD). But is this fair? What if the class was especially knowledgeable and the 2nd percentile corresponded with a raw score of 97 out of 100? Should an individual who received a 97 on the exam get a letter grade of F, even though mastery of most of the content was demonstrated? Or should a student who received only 35 percent of questions correct get an A on an exam, just because all scores were extremely low and the 35 fell at $+1SD$ for the class?

Curving grades may be desirable if it is unknown whether an exam is too easy or too difficult. It guarantees the distribution of letter grades among class members in a way that not "too many" (whatever that is) will get any one grade, but it is unnecessary if an instructor can create a fair and rigorous exam and knows what constitutes exceptional, average, or poor performance on it.

A common and more statistically justifiable use of normal distributions can be seen in standardized tests, such as IQ tests or Scholastic Achievement Tests (SAT). Over the years, these tests repeatedly have been refined to the point that the scores of the large numbers of persons taking them tend to fall into patterns with consistent means and standard deviations. In other words, their scores now form normal distributions.

SAT scores were originally designed so that combined verbal and math scores for large numbers of students would form a normal curve with a mean of 1000 and a standard deviation of 200. In addition, all scores would fall between $-3SD$ and $+3SD$ from the mean. The lowest possible score would be $3 \times 200 = 600$ below the mean, or 400. (This is the 400 that one is rumored to get for just "showing up" or "signing one's name.")

The highest possible (or perfect) score (the 100th percentile) would be 1600. SAT scores declined considerably during the 1980s and early 1990s, however. Although scores of 400 and 1600 still occured, the mean dropped to around 920. In 1994, a decision was made to adjust future test scores upward so that they would again have a mean of 1000 and would better approximate a normal curve.

The results of various IQ tests tend to form normal distributions. They generally have a mean of 100 and a standard deviation of either 15 or 16, depending on the test. If we understand the principles and characteristics that relate to normal distributions, it is possible, given these data, to convert any raw IQ score to its corresponding z score and then to percentile using Table 4.3. A score with a z score of 1.00 (115 or 116, depending on the test), for example, would fall at about the 84th percentile. It would also be possible to reverse this mathematical process to convert a percentile into a raw score.

Even when we have little or no knowledge of a standardized measurement instrument other than its general mean and standard deviation, we can put a raw score derived from it into a meaningful perspective. Or we can compare a score derived from it with another score on a measuring instrument with which we are more familiar. Let us see how that would work.

Example: Student Anxiety. Deborah is a social worker in a student health center. She leads a treatment group of college students diagnosed as experiencing chronic anxiety. In the past, group members have been selected for treatment on the basis of their scores on Anxiety Scale A, a standardized measuring instrument given to all students as a part of intake screening at the center. The measuring instrument has a mean of 70 and a standard deviation of 10. Only students scoring over 80 on Anxiety Scale A are eligible to join Deborah's group.

A vacancy occurred in the group. Deborah checked the files of active cases and noted that the highest score among potential group members was 78 (Gina). Deborah, however, had just received a referral from a family service agency stating that one of their former clients (Tom) had just enrolled at her university and needed further assistance with his anxiety problems. The referral letter indicated that Tom had received a score of 66 on Anxiety Scale B. The letter further stated that Anxiety Scale B has a mean of 50 and a standard deviation of 12.

Both standardized measuring instruments (Anxiety Scales A and B) are considered to be valid and reliable when used with college students. Based on her knowledge of normal distributions and the information received in the referral letter, Deborah saw no need to retest Tom with Anxiety Scale A. She decided to use z scores to determine whether Gina or Tom was a better candidate for the group vacancy. To simplify her decision, Deborah constructed Table 4.5.

Deborah then computed the z score for both potential group members, which allowed her to compute their percentile rank.

$$z \text{ score (Gina)} = \frac{\text{Raw score} - \text{mean}}{\text{Standard deviation}}$$

Substituting values for letters, we get:

$$= \frac{78 - 70}{10} = 8/10$$

= .80 (corresponds to 28.81, Table 4.3)

Area between raw score and mean = 28.81
Area left of the mean =   +50.00
                                                      ‾‾‾‾‾‾
                                                       78.81

= 79th percentile (Scale A)

$$z \text{ score (Tom)} = \frac{\text{Raw score} - \text{mean}}{\text{Standard deviation}}$$

Substituting values for letters, we get the following:

$$= \frac{66 - 50}{12} = 16/12$$

= 1.33 (corresponds to 40.82, Table 4.3)

Area between raw score and mean = 40.82
Area left of the mean =   +50.00
                                                      ‾‾‾‾‾‾
                                                       90.82

= 91st percentile (Scale B)

Based on her comparative analysis using z scores, Deborah chose Tom for the group. His relatively higher level of anxiety (based on his measuring instrument) made him more appropriate for the group than Gina. Furthermore, Deborah saw no need to relax the group's admittance criteria, which required a score of 80 (84th percentile), in order to admit Gina (79th percentile).

Figures 4.10 and 4.11 illustrate the comparison that Deborah was able to make using z scores. Note that the score of 80 (cutoff point on Scale A) is comparable to a score of 62 on Scale B, because both fall at the point $z = 1$ (the 84th percentile). Tom's score was above this point (Figure 4.11) and Gina's (Figure 4.10) was below it.

TABLE 4.5 Comparative Data:
Two Indices and Clients' Scores

Data	Anxiety Scale A (Gina)	Anxiety Scale B (Tom)
Raw score	78	66
Mean	70	50
Standard deviation	10	12

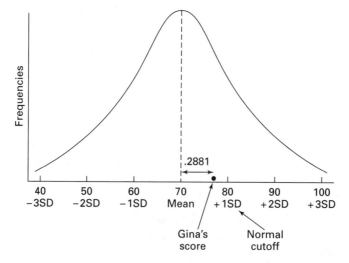

FIGURE 4.10 Distribution of Scores on Anxiety Scale A
(Mean = 70; Standard Deviation = 10)

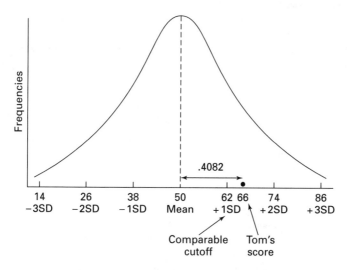

FIGURE 4.11 Distribution of Scores on Anxiety Scale B
(Mean = 50; Standard Deviation = 12)

CONCLUDING THOUGHTS

By converting raw scores from a normal distribution into *z* scores, we can compare individual scores drawn from two different data sets. We can learn each score's percentile rank in order to see how each score compares to others in its own group of scores. Understanding the normal distribution also enables us to visualize where a given score falls relative to others in a large sample or population.

Through the use of percentile ranks, we can determine about what percentage of scores falls above any given score. This can be especially useful to the social worker in evaluating the results of standardized testing performed on clients. Even if all we know about a test are its mean and standard deviation and the fact that it is believed to provide a valid and reliable measurement of an interval or ratio level variable, it is possible to take a raw score on a standardized test and put it into meaningful perspective.

STUDY QUESTIONS

1. How does a positively skewed distribution differ in appearance from a negatively skewed one? Provide examples of social work variables that tend to be positively skewed or negatively skewed.
2. Discuss the characteristics of a normal, or bell-shaped, curve.
3. In a frequency polygon for the variable, "number of times married" within the general population, is the distribution likely to be normal, positively skewed, or negatively skewed? Explain.
4. In a positively skewed distribution, where is the median relative to the mean?
5. With a variable that is normally distributed, approximately what percentage of all scores falls within 1 standard deviation of the mean?
6. What is the *z* score for a score of 79 when the mean score of all persons who complete a depression scale is 89 and the standard deviation is 5? Is this person more or less depressed than most other people who complete the scale?
7. In a normal distribution how frequently would a score occur that is more than three standard deviations above or below the mean?
8. On an IQ test with a mean of 100 and a standard deviation of 16, at approximately what percentile will an IQ of 104 fall?
9. Which *z* score corresponds to a higher value within a distribution of values, −1.04 or 1.00? Explain.
10. If an individual falls at the 16th percentile for weight and the 48th percentile for height, would that individual be considered underweight or overweight? Explain.
11. Discuss several ways in which a social worker can use *z* scores in social work practice.
12. Assume that a distribution has a mean of 12, a median of 14, and a mode of 13. Should a distribution with these central tendencies be considered normally distributed? Why or why not?
13. Use Table 4.3 to find the following:
    a. The area of the normal curve above a *z* score of 1.71.
    b. The area of the normal curve between the mean and a *z* score of −1.34.
    c. The *z* score that marks the lower limit of the 38 percent of the curve immediately below the mean.
    d. The *z* scores that mark the upper and lower limits of the middle 42 percent of the normal curve.

Chapter 5

Introduction to Hypothesis Testing

The previous four chapters presented simple ways to organize, display, and summarize the distribution of the values (and value categories) of a variable. What we have described so far is descriptive statistical analysis. Sometimes this is the only type of analysis that we need to accurately describe a variable. But, more often than not, we want to go further into our data analysis efforts. We may want, for example, to determine if two variables that appear to be related within our research sample are truly related within the population from which the sample was drawn—the topic of this and the next chapter.

The issue of generalizing findings from a sample to the population from which it was drawn brings us to the concept of inference and the use of inferential statistical analysis. *Inferential statistics* are used to assess the degree of confidence we have when we say that a relationship between two variables—that we observed within a given research sample—is a real one; one that probably also exists among cases (or objects) within the entire population from which the sample was drawn.

ALTERNATIVE EXPLANATIONS

Just because the distribution of variables within a sample of cases drawn from a population makes them appear to be related, we cannot be 100 percent certain that they **really are** related anywhere but within the sample. In order to make inferences about the relationship between the same two variables within the population from which our sample was drawn, we have to be reasonably confident that what we found to exist within our sample cannot be attributed to alternative explanations, that is, other reasons (besides a true relationship) that might account for the relationship between the two variables within our sample.

Many alternative explanations can be attributed to potential problems that our study's research design failed to control. Two "likely suspects" are (1) rival hypotheses and (2) design bias.

Because rival hypotheses and design bias are both related to problems of research design, they are best addressed before data are collected. Social work research methods texts generally devote considerable space to discussing strategies designed to minimize their existence. Once data are collected, however, it may be possible to conduct some form of statistical analysis to estimate the amount of effect that they had, or to statistically "control" them in some way. But this is not nearly as desirable as a proactive approach that contains strategies to eliminate their potential effects before data are collected. We now turn our attention to rival hypotheses.

Rival Hypotheses

Rival hypotheses are really theoretical alternatives for explaining the presence of an apparent relationship between variables. They refer to the fact that "some other variable(s)," unknown to us, may have caused the two variables within our sample to appear to be related. Perhaps we hypothesized that an independent variable would be found to influence the dependent variable. But in our literature review, we did not identify one or more other variables that, either individually or in concert, are the real explanation for the variations in the dependent variable.

Through these other variables' variations, they may have caused our proposed independent and dependent variables to appear to be strongly related, even though they were not strongly related at all. Or perhaps two variables that appear to be related within our sample would not appear to be related at all if some other variable(s) had not caused them to co-vary within our sample.

Design Bias

A concept that is closely related to rival hypothesis is the concept of *design bias*. It encompasses a wide range of design problems that also can produce an erroneous impression about the relationship between variables within a sample. Two of the most common and troublesome forms of design bias are (1) measurement bias and (2) sampling bias.

Measurement Bias.   The first form of design bias is *measurement bias*. It is a consistent distortion in the measurement of variables that can negatively affect the quality of data we collect and subsequently analyze. It can produce measurements that, while perhaps reliable, are not valid.

There are many ways in which measurement bias can creep into a research study. It might result from the fact that data were collected at an atypical time, for example, or that the research study was influenced by some outside event or to the conscious or unconscious tendency of the person collecting the data to get a less-than-true perception of what was occurring.

If, for whatever reason(s), the measurement of variables is biased, two variables can appear to be related when, in fact, they are not. Like rival hypotheses, measurement bias is best eliminated, or at least minimized, by using sound measurement practices incorporated into good research designs.

Sampling Bias. The second form of design bias is *sampling bias*—the systematic distortion of a research sample. It can result from such factors as an inappropriate sampling method or the time and place when and where the sample was drawn. A biased sample is characterized by either overrepresentation (or underrepresentation) of some types of cases (relative to the population from which it was drawn) in relation to some important variable(s).

How can we be reasonably certain that sampling bias is not the real explanation for an apparent relationship between variables? Some techniques for selecting a sample (e.g., matching, stratification) are designed to increase a sample's representation of the population from which it is drawn. Selecting a simple random sample that is sufficiently large (discussed in Chapter 6) also increases the likelihood that the sample will be representative of its population. We also can pay special attention to how, when, and where a sample is selected.

A true experimental design provides good control of sampling bias. When experimental groups and control groups are formed, for example, random assignment to them increases the likelihood that both groups will be comparable to each other in relation to a wide variety of potentially biasing variables, even some that our literature review failed to identify.

No matter what sampling method is used, it is sometimes possible to use a statistical analysis to detect the presence of measurement bias within a data set. At the point that data have been collected, however, it may be too late to eliminate the negative effects of sampling bias on the quality of a study's findings.

Chance, or Sampling Error

Even if rival hypotheses and design bias can both be successfully dismissed as alternative explanations for an apparent relationship between variables within a sample, there is still another possible alternative explanation—chance, or sampling error. *Chance* contends that no matter how well a research study is designed, any relationship between variables within the sample is just a "fluke." It exists among only those cases within the sample. Through no fault of rival hypotheses and design bias, the sample is atypical of the population from which it was drawn. The reason for its lack of representativeness is *sampling error*, the natural tendency of any sample to differ from the population from which it was drawn. It is especially likely to occur in small samples. We will discuss how sampling error works and how the extent of its influence can be estimated in the following chapter.

Even if we use the most well thought out research study, the best sampling methods, the best measurement of variables, and the best data analyses techniques, we can never totally rule out chance, or sampling error, as the explanation for an apparent relationship between variables. The only way that we could guarantee that chance, or sampling error, is eliminated is to study an entire population. But then, we would have no group beyond those cases actually studied to make any inferences about. The concept of inference would be irrelevant.

In order to conclude that a relationship between variables within our sample data reflects a real relationship within its respective population, rival hypotheses and design bias must first be ruled out (either by design or statistical control) as alternative explanations. But even if we can rule out these two forms of alternative explanations, we are still left with the possibility that the relationship between the two variables occurred just by chance, or sampling error.

Chance, or sampling error, is usually the final explanation that skeptical consumers of a research report propose as the real reason why the two variables appear to be related. It is commonly referred to as the null hypothesis. Thus, in a sense, the null hypothesis is the final "alternative hypothesis." Some authors even categorize it as such, but we have chosen to give it separate attention in this book. The null hypothesis suggests:

> Whatever you found in the way of a relationship between the two variables within your sample was just a fluke. It is not indicative of a real relationship between the two variables within the population from which your sample was drawn. It existed within your sample only because of chance, or sampling error. Your sample is (naturally) different from your population. If you had studied the whole population, you would *not* have found the same relationship between the two variables.

How do we determine what role sampling error may have played in an apparent relationship between our two variables? Unlike rival hypotheses and design bias (which includes measurement bias and sampling bias), solid research designs are not sufficient to minimize the effects of sampling error (the null hypothesis). It cannot be prevented from occurring when samples are used, but it is possible to assess the likelihood that it could have produced any relationship between variables that existed within a sample. We can do this by using inferential statistical analyses which rely heavily on the laws of probability.

PROBABILITY

Probability theory is nothing more than the mathematical likelihood of an event occurring. It is based on certain laws. One basic law, for example, states that the likelihood of any one event occurring can range from 0 (never) to 1.0 (absolute certainty).

One assumption is central to all probability theory. It is that while certain patterns of events can be seen to exist in many repeated observations over time, individual, or short-term, observations tend to differ somewhat from these overall long-term patterns. If we flip a fair coin in the air, for example, it has a 50:50, or 50 percent, chance of landing on heads.

Obviously, it also has a 50 percent probability of landing on tails. These are only theoretical probabilities. They are the percent of heads (or tails) that would occur in an infinite number of flips of the coin, when the "law of averages" has had an opportunity to take effect. (It is not an accurate prediction of what might occur if we flip a coin only a small number of times.) The law of averages suggests that "in the long run" things will "balance out" and events will unfold as they theoretically should.

In reality, we know that if we flip a coin ten times, we can get a different result from the one that is theoretically expected to occur—that is, five heads. We would not be surprised if we obtained four, six, or even three or seven heads. We would simply blame it on chance and assume that in the long run, if we repeated the coin tossing many more times, the percent of heads would eventually approximate 50 percent.

What if the ten coin flips produced nine or ten heads? At this point, we might suspect that something was wrong. The results seem to be so unlikely that they "defy the laws of probability." How could these results have occurred? Could the coin be defective? Could the way in which the coin was tossed have influenced the results? What is going on here? Another way of stating these questions might be, "Is something else (some other variable) influencing the results (the number of heads)?"

The laws of probability can be applied in many areas of life. They have been developed to determine the theoretical likelihood of an event's occurrence. Some are simple; others are complicated. The probability of a student guessing correctly on a multiple choice question with four alternative answers is 25 percent. That is pretty obvious. One law, the multiplication law, states that the likelihood of guessing correctly on two consecutive questions on a multiple choice exam with four possible responses is .25 × .25 or 6.25 percent (or one out of sixteen). That may seem less plausible. Still another law, the addition law, states that the mathematical probability of getting only one answer correct is 37.5 percent (or six out of sixteen) or of getting one or both correct is 43.75 percent (or seven out of sixteen).

We can use these various laws of probability to determine what should happen in various situations, that is, what would happen in the long run (with an infinite number of events), based upon chance, or sampling error. We are most concerned here with how they relate to the statistical analysis of data. Of course, we know that "in the short run" strange aberrations can and do occur.

On a single examination, for example, a student might guess on two questions and get both or neither one correct. This is the same phenomenon (chance) that causes relatively small samples to differ in characteristics from their respective populations from which they were drawn. An unlikely (but not impossible) event occurred in a single situation (sample), even though most of the time (in the long run) it would not happen that way.

The percentage of all cases with a given measurement of a variable within a population also can be thought of as probability. If 40 percent of cases, for example, all have the same value, there is a 40 percent probability that a score drawn at random from that distribution will have that value.

If the variable is at least at the interval level of measurement, the frequency distribution of the variable could be portrayed using a frequency polygon. If 20 percent of cases in the population have the lowest value of the variable found within the distribution, then the area to the far left of the polygon (the bottom 20 percent of it) would represent those cases. The probability of randomly selecting a case from the distribution with this lowest value would be 20 percent. If 10 percent of cases in the population have the highest measurement value of the variable found within the distribution, then the area to the far right of the polygon (the top 10 percent of it) would represent those cases. The probability of randomly selecting a case from the population with this highest value would be 10 percent. And the probability of randomly selecting a case in the range containing all values would be 100 percent.

Example: Adolescents in an Anger Management Program

Suppose we collect data on the ages of adolescents who are participating in an anger management program. The 14 adolescents in the program consist of two 12-year-olds, three 13-year-olds, four 14-year-olds, three 15-year-olds, and two 16-year-olds. In this instance, the ages of these adolescents is normally distributed; the mean, mode, and median age are all 14.

If we were to randomly draw one case from the group of adolescents, there would be a 100 percent chance of selecting a client who is between the ages of 12 and 16. That is because all adolescents are represented in the distribution (100 percent of a frequency polygon that would represent it). We can also specify the probability of selecting a case from the distribution within a certain age range.

What if we wanted to know the probability of randomly selecting a 13- or a 14-year-old if we were to select one client at random from our sample distribution? The probability would be 21.4 percent (3 chances out of 14) for picking a 13-year-old and 28.6 percent (4 chances out of 14) for choosing a 14-year-old—a total of 50 percent (7 chances out of 14) for randomly selecting either a 13- or a 14-year-old. Thus, we would have a 50 percent chance of randomly selecting a 13- or 14-year-old from our sample.

Like the areas of a normal curve between standard deviation units, intervals encompassing specified scores would correspond to areas of a frequency polygon. Narrow intervals (encompassing fewer cases) would correspond to smaller areas of the frequency polygon and would reflect a lower probability of randomly selecting a case with a value within the specified range. Wider intervals (encompassing more cases) would correspond to larger areas and would reflect a higher probability of randomly selecting a case with a value within the specified range.

Probability theory is an integral component of inferential statistical analyses. No matter which inferential statistical test we choose, probability plays a role in determining whether chance, or sampling error, may have produced an apparent relationship between variables within a sample.

REFUTING CHANCE OR SAMPLING ERROR

There are two general methods for demonstrating that an apparent relationship between variables within a sample was not a fluke—the result of chance, or sampling error. They are (1) replication and (2) statistical analyses. The same example is used to demonstrate how both work to refute chance, or sampling error.

Replication

Suppose that we work in an extremely large state hospital system that employs 1000 medical social workers. We observe among the 8 medical social workers in our particular unit that female workers have higher levels of job satisfaction than male workers. Is our observation conclusive evidence of a relationship between the two variables (i.e., job satisfaction, gender) that exists among all the other medical social workers in the system? Certainly not.

But how can we attempt to demonstrate that the apparent relationship between the two variables is not just a fluke—a relationship that exists only within our small non-random sample? After all, we have no reason to believe that the 8 social workers in our unit (what might be regarded as no more than an "availability" or "convenience" sample) are typical of the other medical social workers elsewhere within the system.

In an ideal world with unlimited research resources, we could use replication to determine if the relationship within our sample was more than just a fluke. *Replication* entails repeating the research study one or more times using the same methods to see if the same findings result when different samples are used. To use replication, we could simply use another group (sample) of medical social workers (the staff of another unit) and see if the same relationship between job satisfaction and gender was present.

But even if it was, that might not be enough evidence to dismiss chance, or sampling error, as the reason for the apparent relationship. Perhaps we could study 100 different units (samples) of medical social workers and see how many times out of 100 the same relationship occurred. Then if, for example, the relationship occurred at least 95 times out of 100, we might conclude that the relationship probably is a real one.

Of course, in the real world, repeated replication is impractical. Obtaining resources and access to data even once is often difficult, so how could we ever be able to conduct our research study 100 times? Some replication occurs in social work research, however. It usually is used to see if a relationship between variables that was identified in a previous research study will be found to still exist at a different time or with a different sample of research participants. It is used far less to demonstrate initial support for the existence of a relationship between variables.

While the cost of repeated replication makes it impractical, other methods for determining if an apparent relationship exists between variables employ some of the principles of replication. Later in this chapter we shall see how the concept of "95 times out of 100" is applied in making decisions while statistically analyzing data collected within a single research study.

Statistical Analyses

There is another, less expensive way, that we can gain logical support for the inference that there is a true relationship between job satisfaction and gender—statistical analyses of data drawn from a single study. Suppose we had made an educated guess (prediction) that we would find a relationship between job satisfaction and gender among our sample of 8 medical social workers.

Suppose that we had arrived at this prediction through the process of synthesizing existing qualitative and quantitative knowledge on gender differences and job satisfaction among medical social workers. We did it by using our own observations and experiences in working with medical social workers, as well as the writings of scholars in the profession and many other sources, such as unpublished documents and interviews with persons who "ought to know." We synthesized the knowledge thus found. We even learned enough about the characteristics of medical social workers, as a group (their demographic characteristics), to conclude that the 8 social workers in our convenience sample do not appear to be unusual in any obvious or important way. Based upon what we learned, we hypothesized the following research hypothesis:

Research Hypothesis:
Female medical social workers will have higher levels of job satisfaction than
male medical social workers.

The fact that the two variables appeared to be related within our sample, exactly as
we predicted they would be, would not be enough evidence to claim support for our
prediction. It would help, but we would need to do more. First we would have to rule
out the alternative explanations for an apparent relationship (rival hypotheses and
design bias). Even if we were satisfied that they did not produce the apparent relationship between job satisfaction and gender that existed within our sample, it still might
have been produced by chance, or sampling error (the null hypothesis).

Our small sample of 8 medical social workers may have differed from the population of all medical social workers within the system in some important ways just
because of the phenomenon of chance, or sampling error. So, we would have to more
rigorously "test" our hypothesis. We would have to demonstrate that the data we examined are so "impressive," so clearly and strongly in support of it, that the apparent relationship is unlikely to have been the work of chance, or sampling error—it is most likely a real one that exists within the system's population of medical social workers.

RESEARCH HYPOTHESES

This is a good point in our discussion to examine in more detail what we first alluded to
in Chapter 1—the importance of hypotheses to statistical analyses. There are many different definitions of hypotheses, but they all suggest the same idea: A hypothesis is a
tentative answer to a research question. In its simplest form, it is a statement of a proposed relationship between variables.

As has been suggested in the previous example, hypotheses are generated in many
different ways. They may evolve as the product of someone else's research study. This
occurs most frequently following qualitative research studies in which we inductively
identified and labeled variables and then suggested possible relationships between
them for subsequent studies to examine.

Hypotheses may also evolve from our own observations and from our own reviews
of the professional literature. Among other things, we use the literature to narrow or
refine a general research question. Frequently, as the evidence in the literature starts
to accumulate, we think we may have an answer to that question. We then try to express
our tentative impressions, or our conclusions, in the form of a hypothesis.

A *research hypothesis*, also called a substantive hypothesis, experimental hypothesis, or alternative hypothesis, is a statement that expresses what we believe to be the
relationship between two variables. It is the hypothesis that we set out to test using a
suitable research design. A research hypothesis can take on three different forms:

1. It can state that two variables are related and predict the direction of their relationship (a directional, or "one-tailed," research hypothesis).
2. It can state that two variables are related but does not predict the direction of
   their relationship (a non-directional, or "two-tailed," research hypothesis).
3. It can state that two variables are unrelated (a "null" research hypothesis).

The One-Tailed Research Hypothesis

A *one-tailed research hypothesis* states that there is a specific relationship between variables. It also predicts which values of one variable are to be found with, or associated with, which values of another variable. Continuing with our previous example, a one-tailed research hypothesis might be as follows:

One-Tailed Research Hypothesis:
Female medical social workers will have higher levels of job satisfaction than male medical social workers.

It is important to note that a one-tailed research hypothesis predicts the direction of a relationship between variables, which is why it is sometimes called a directional hypothesis.

The Two-Tailed Research Hypothesis

A *two-tailed research hypothesis* (also referred to as a nondirectional hypothesis) states only that there is a relationship between variables. Unlike the one-tailed research hypothesis, it does not predict which values of one variable will be associated with which values of the other variable. The following is a two-tailed research hypothesis for our example:

Two-Tailed Research Hypothesis:
Gender is related to job satisfaction levels.

Note that the above two-tailed research hypothesis does not predict whether males or females will be found to have higher levels of job satisfaction, as the one-tailed research hypothesis did.

The Null Research Hypothesis

The third form of research hypotheses states that there is no relationship between variables. In our example it would be this:

The Null Research Hypothesis:
There is no relationship between gender and job satisfaction.

It is important to note that it is, in a sense, the opposite of either a one-tailed or a two-tailed research hypothesis. Null research hypotheses are rare. They are used to try to dispel false beliefs when we wish to gain support for our belief that two variables, generally believed to be related, really are unrelated. In the past, for example, we sought to disprove the sexist stereotype that one gender is intellectually superior to another. We did so by finding statistical support for the null research hypothesis that gender and intelligence are not related. Similarly, we sought to demonstrate that women are just as effective as fire fighters as men. We set out to find support for the null research hypothesis that there is no relationship between gender and fire-fighting competence.

TESTING THE NULL HYPOTHESIS

We never refer to a one- or two-tailed research hypothesis as proven or disproven; we state that we found support for it or that we did not. This conclusion is based upon whether or not, using our knowledge of research design and statistics, we feel that all other explanations for an apparent relationship between variables (besides a true one) can be discounted.

One- and two-tailed research hypothesis testing is a "process of elimination." To gain support for a one- or two-tailed research hypothesis that two variables are related, we must first be reasonably certain that **nothing else** caused the variables to appear to be related within our sample.

As suggested earlier, we would try to eliminate rival hypotheses and design bias as possible explanations by utilizing good research designs. But that still leaves us with chance, or sampling error. Before we can claim support for a one- or two-tailed research hypothesis, we also have to demonstrate, using statistics, that chance, or sampling error, is a highly unlikely explanation for a relationship between the two variables we are studying. If we can accomplish this we are left with only one other explanation—a true relationship exists between the two variables within the population from which the sample was drawn. We would then be able to claim support for our one- or two-tailed research hypothesis.

What would we have to do to demonstrate support for a null research hypothesis of "no relationship" between variables? Let us assume that rival hypotheses and design bias have been adequately controlled by utilizing a sound research design. There might still appear, however, to be a relationship between the two variables within our sample. Does that mean our null research hypothesis was incorrect?

Not necessarily. We could still gain support for it through utilizing statistical procedures. We could attempt to demonstrate that the relationship between the two variables within our sample is really quite small or weak—that it is fairly likely to have been produced by chance, or sampling error. In other words, we would hope to show that the evidence is not strong enough to reject sampling error as the explanation for the apparent relationship between the two variables.

Let us now return to our previous example to illustrate how the logic of hypothesis testing can be applied. Remember that after a thorough literature review, we decided that we had justification for stating the following one-tailed research hypothesis:

One-Tailed Research Hypothesis:
Female medical social workers will have higher levels of job satisfaction than male medical social workers.

In statistical analysis it is the null form of the research hypothesis that actually is tested. Thus, it is helpful to restate our one-tailed research hypothesis in its null form. Its null hypothesis would be as follows:

Null (Form of the Research) Hypothesis:
There is no relationship between the gender of medical social workers and their levels of job satisfaction.

If we were really testing our one-tailed research hypothesis, we probably would not just trust our impressions of the job satisfaction levels of the 8 medical social workers in our sample. We would collect data from them. We might note, for example, each social worker's gender and administer a standardized measuring instrument that measures job satisfaction to each worker. A person's score on the measuring instrument can range from a maximum of 100 (very high job satisfaction) to a minimum of 0 (very low job satisfaction).

As we analyzed our data, frequencies might seem to provide a reason to reject (or not to reject) the null hypothesis, particularly since the number of social workers was small and it would be easy to identify any differences in the distribution of the dependent variable (job satisfaction) between the two genders. If, for example, we observed that the two groups (females and males) both had a mean job satisfaction level of 60, we would obviously not reject the null hypothesis since, even within our sample, there is no difference between the mean job satisfaction levels for males and females. However, what if the females were found to have a mean job satisfaction level of 90 and the males had a mean job satisfaction level of 10? We would feel that we had pretty strong support for the rejection of the null hypothesis.

Such a clear pattern of a relationship between variables is rare. If it exists, we probably already know about it. But what if there was a difference in the mean job satisfaction levels between the two groups (males and females), but it was not so dramatic? What if the mean job satisfaction level was, say, 62 for females and 56 for males? How likely is it that our observed relationship is a real one that represents a relationship between the two variables within the larger population?

Could we infer, based on these central tendency data alone, that as a group, female medical social workers including those not in our sample possess a higher mean level of job satisfaction than males? Such a conclusion would seem a little premature, even if we had carefully designed and implemented our research study so that we were fairly certain that rival hypotheses and design bias could be ruled out as alternative explanations for the apparent relationship. But what about chance, or sampling error? After all, 8 research participants is a small sample. Any relationship between the two variables found in our small sample could be a fluke. Is the evidence in support of our one-tailed research hypothesis so strong that it is unlikely to be the work of chance, or sampling error?

Inferential statistical analysis tells us the likelihood that chance, or sampling error, might have produced the difference in the mean job satisfaction levels between the female and male social workers. In short, it determines the likelihood that a relationship between variables within our sample data could have occurred as a result of chance, or sampling error. Thus, it can help us to determine if an apparent relationship between variables within our sample data is a real one, that is, one that exists in the population from which our sample was drawn.

In attempting to gain support for a research hypothesis, we can never totally eliminate chance, or sampling error, as the explanation for an apparent relationship between variables. After all, even if females did have a mean job satisfaction level of 90 and males had a mean job satisfaction level of 10, we theoretically could have used that one sample out of a million in which females might differ by that much from males, even if the two variables really are unrelated within the population from which our sample was drawn. While we never can be 100 percent certain that what we found was not the work of chance, or sampling error, we generally are convinced if we can be reasonably certain that what we observed was not a fluke occurrence caused by chance, or sampling error.

We do not want to report a relationship between variables that appears to be real when it is not. At the same time, we do not want to be so rigid or so unreasonable that we will not claim support for a relationship between variables just because there is a remote possibility that chance, or sampling error, may have produced it. If we did that, few, if any, research findings would ever see the light of day. Thus, we need guidelines to help us to know when to reject (and when not to reject) the null hypothesis. Fortunately, they are available. We will discuss tham later in this chapter.

ERRORS IN DRAWING CONCLUSIONS ABOUT RELATIONSHIPS

Ultimately, we must make a "judgment call" and decide whether we should reject (or not reject), the null hypothesis. Whatever we decide, we run the risk of making an error. The two possible errors that we can make are referred to as Type I and Type II errors.

A Type I error occurs when we reject the null hypothesis and conclude that a relationship between variables within a sample exists within the population from which it was drawn, when, in fact, it really does not. On the other hand, a Type II error occurs when we fail to reject the null hypothesis and conclude that a relationship between variables does not exist within the population from which it was drawn, when, in fact, it really does exist. Neither type of error is inherently better than the other. Either one can mislead and misinform social work practitioners and researchers.

Type I and Type II errors can result from the use of inappropriate analyses of data. If, for example, we incorrectly use a statistical test that requires certain conditions that are not present, or we use a statistical test that lacks the capacity to detect a true relationship between variables, errors can occur. If the appropriate statistical test is not used within the conditions for which it was designed, we can either falsely conclude that a true relationship between variables exists (Type I error) or a true relationship may remain unidentified (Type II error). Chapter 7 discusses the issues to be considered in selecting the most appropriate statistical test for any given data set.

TABLE 5.1 Type I and Type II Errors

Real World	Our Decision	
	Reject Null Hypothesis	Do Not Reject Null Hypothesis
Null hypothesis false	No error	Type II error
Null hypothesis true	Type I error	No error

No matter what we ultimately decide about whether (or not) to reject the null hypothesis, we can never totally eliminate the possibility of committing an error. In fact, if we are overly careful not to commit a Type I error (mistakenly rejecting the null hypothesis), we increase the likelihood of committing a Type II error (mistakenly failing to reject the null hypothesis).

Conversely, if we are overly careful to avoid committing a Type II error, we increase the likelihood of committing a Type I error. We must ultimately decide which error, Type I or Type II, would be more acceptable to us, should it occur. This is, in part, an ethical decision that requires a knowledge of social work practice and the consequences of committing one error over the other. Fortunately, as we shall see, there are also statistical conventions to help guide us in this decision-making process.

In some research studies, the consequences of making a Type I or Type II error can be potentially grave. A Type I error, however, is not always less desirable than a Type II error. When we apply research findings to social work practice situations, for example, both Type I and Type II errors have the potential to harm our clients or to result in a wasteful expenditure of limited agency resources.

If social work practitioners do not recognize that an error was committed in a statistical analysis, for example, they may mistakenly believe that there is a true relationship between a particular treatment method (independent variable) and an increased rate of client success (dependent variable). They may adjust their treatment interventions based on this result. They may also respond to other research findings in which, for some reason, a Type II error was committed and discard a treatment intervention that really was effective but appeared not to be related to client success.

Usually, the consequences of making an error in deciding whether (or not) to reject the null hypothesis in social work research are not grave. The possibility of committing either a Type I or a Type II error should not preclude us from taking reasonable risks in interpreting research findings and drawing conclusions and implications from them. This is how we make progress in becoming knowledge-based social work practitioners.

STATISTICAL SIGNIFICANCE

In our example of looking at job satisfaction levels between male and female medical social workers, it would be nice if it had been possible to repeat our research study with 100 different samples of medical social workers within the hospital system (replication). We could then have seen if females showed somewhat higher levels of job satisfaction than males in most of the samples (say, in at least 95 percent of them). We typically get, however, only "one shot" at doing a research study. Within a single research study and with only one research sample, we need some comparable evidence (to the 95 samples out of 100) that a relationship between variables is a real one. Statistical analysis can provide it.

At what point can we be sufficiently certain that whatever relationship between variables we find in our sample cannot reasonably be dismissed as the work of chance, or sampling error? When using statistics, we rely on mathematics, the laws of probability, common sense, and convention. We also use two very important and related concepts: p-values and rejection levels.

p-Values

The statistical tests of inference that we will discuss later in this book (and many more that we will not be discussing) have something in common. They produce a *p*-value. A *p-value* is the mathematical probability that a relationship between variables found within a sample may have been produced by chance, or sampling error. (It is important to note that it tells us nothing about the likelihood that rival hypothesis, or design bias might have produced it.) A *p*-value can range from 0.00 (would never occur by chance) to 1.00 (definitely the work of chance). All *p*-values fall somewhere in between these two theoretical extremes.

In a sense, a *p*-value is the "bottom line" in an inferential statistical analysis. (In fact, it often is found on the last line in the computer printout of the data analysis.) Different statistical analyses use different formulas, but the *p*-value that each produces is interpreted exactly the same way. Thus, it is possible to know the likelihood that chance, or sampling error, produced a relationship between variables within a sample (the *p*-value) even if we do not fully understand the statistical analysis that produced the *p*-value. However, this can be dangerous. Unless we have a good understanding of the general way in which a specific form of statistical analysis works, and know when it should or should not be used, it is possible to misread the importance of any given *p*-value.

Rejection Levels

As noted earlier, the decision to reject the null hypothesis does not totally rule out chance, or sampling error, as the explanation of an apparent relationship between variables. (It also does not address the possibility that some other variable[s] or an unidentified research design problem may still have caused the variables to appear to be related when, in fact, they were not.) However, if we can demonstrate that there is a small likelihood that chance, or sampling error, caused the relationship between the variables within a sample, we generally reject the null hypothesis. Rejecting, (or not rejecting), the null hypothesis involves risk (of a Type I or Type II error respectively), but the risk is supposed to be a small one. But how small is small?

Over the years, we have settled on the 95 percent certainty level as the point at which we are sufficiently confident to be able to reject the null hypothesis. Expressed another way, we feel safe in rejecting the null hypothesis if a statistical analysis suggests that there is less than a 5 percent probability that chance, or sampling error, may have produced an apparent relationship between the two variables (the *p*-value produced by a statistical analysis is less than .05). That much risk of committing a Type I error is considered acceptable in most research situations. This is referred to as the .05 *rejection level*. Rejection levels also are called *alpha levels*, or *significance levels*.

There is nothing sacred about the .05 rejection level. While it is the most widely used cutoff point for rejecting null hypotheses, other rejection levels also can be used. The decision to use rejection levels other than .05 is based on our assessment of the possible consequences of either mistakenly rejecting the null hypothesis or failing to reject it (Type I or Type II errors).

A more demanding proof of a relationship between variables, such as a .025 or .01 rejection level, might be used when we wish to allow only a very small possibility that we might erroneously reject the null hypothesis and conclude that a relationship exists between variables (a Type I error). These more stringent rejection levels allow for even less likelihood that chance, or sampling error, is the reason for an apparent relationship between the two variables than does the conventional .05 level.

If the application of the research findings might be a matter of "life and death," such as in some forms of medical research, an even more demanding threshold for rejection of the null hypothesis might be used, such as .001. The .001 rejection level means that the probability of erroneously rejecting the null hypothesis is less than 1 out of 1000.

In research studies in which the consequences of mistakenly rejecting the null hypothesis (a Type I error) are less likely to be fatal or traumatic, we occasionally consider a .10 rejection level as acceptable. A .10 rejection level allows for twice the possibility of committing a Type I error because of chance, or sampling error, than does a .05 level. Of course, it also reduces the likelihood of committing a Type II error. Sometimes a less demanding rejection level, such as a .10, is used as evidence of a relationship between variables if the research design includes at least one replication. While achieving one .10 rejection level may be viewed as inconclusive support for a relationship between variables, achieving it two or more times in succession may lead us to the conclusion that the null hypothesis can be rejected. Why? Because achieving two or more successive .10 levels seems to "defy the laws of probability."

While some flexibility is allowed in selecting the threshold at which chance, or sampling error, is reasonably eliminated as the explanation for an apparent relationship between variables, the choice of a rejection level should not be viewed as casual. Convention states that the .05 rejection level should be used unless we develop and state a convincing rationale for the use of another rejection level. The selection of a rejection level must always be made before data are collected. It would be unethical to change the level afterward, because the decision could be construed as an effort to manipulate the study's findings, generally to gain support for the study' s one- or two-tailed research hypothesis.

When reporting the findings of a statistical analysis, the rejection level that was used as a "cutoff" to reject the null hypothesis is always reported. Usually, this is done using wording like, "The mean job satisfaction level for females was 85 and for males 65. This 20-point mean difference is statistically significant at the .05 level." This can also be reported as: "$p < .05$." The p is in lowercase italics and stands for probability. It usually is followed by a "less than" sign ($<$); however, if statistical significance is not achieved, the "greater than" sign ($>$) is substituted in front of the rejection level that was used. What we would be reporting is that there is less than a five percent probability that the higher mean level of job satisfaction of women (i.e., 85) than men (i.e., 65) in our sample could have occurred by chance, or sampling error.

STATISTICALLY SIGNIFICANT VERSUS MEANINGFUL FINDINGS

The word "significant" is widely and loosely used in our profession and elsewhere to emphasize the importance of something, such as when we refer to a social worker's "significant contribution" to the passage of some social legislation or the role of a "significant other" in the development of a client' s self-esteem. As with many other words that we use daily (e.g., value, relationship), it is best to set aside the everyday meaning of statistical significance in order to understand its specific meaning in the field of statistics.

Statistical significance is the demonstration, through the use of statistical testing, that the relationship between variables within a sample is unlikely to have been produced by chance, or sampling error. A relationship that is declared to be statistically significant is one in which the p-value (mathematical probability that chance, or sampling error, produced the relationship) is less than the selected rejection level. For us, this is the only relevant meaning of the words "statistically significant" or "significant;" we must be careful to use the terms in this sense, and only in this sense.

The presence of a statistically significant relationship between variables, of course, still may be dismissed as just the result of rival hypotheses and/or design bias (which includes measurement bias and sampling bias). The results of inferential statistics, as we have suggested earlier, are useful only if the effects of other variables were controlled in some way, if the data that produced them are valid and reliable, and if those data were obtained from a representative sample correctly drawn from a population.

What if the other alternative explanations (for the existence of a real relationship between variables) can be successfully dismissed? In that case, does the presence of a statistically significant relationship demonstrate that chance, or sampling error, is a very unlikely explanation for the apparent relationship between the two variables?

Yes! The relationship probably is real; the variables probably really are related within the population from which the sample was drawn. But is the relationship between them necessarily a meaningful one? Maybe, maybe not. We must be careful to evaluate every statistically significant relationship between variables in the context of the question, "So what?" In social work practice, every statistically significant relationship is not a meaningful finding that cries out for immediate implementation.

In fact, in an absolute sense, some statistically significant relationships are meaningless. Relationships between variables, for example, can be real, but very weak. Virtually all variables, to some degree, are related to all other variables. Some forms of statistical analyses can identify relationships that are so weak that they are worthless in a practical sense, even though the relationship is statistically significant (probably not the work of chance, or sampling error).

Other relationships are already so well known, or are just so logical, that the "discovery" of them within a research study is of little or no value. How valuable would it be to learn, for example, that among people there is a statistically significant relationship between people's physical health and longevity? We would be surprised if it were otherwise.

Example: Marital Adjustment

An example may help to illustrate a more subtle distinction between statistical significance and a substantive or a meaningful relationship between variables. Suppose that Angie, an administrator of a family service agency, conducts a research study using a large sample of clients in an attempt to determine which type of marital treatment intervention (A or B) produces better marital satisfaction when used with couples in marital counseling. She does not feel comfortable in predicting which intervention will be more effective, so she uses a two-tailed research hypothesis:

Two-Tailed Research Hypothesis:
There will be a difference in marital satisfaction between clients in Treatment Intervention A and clients in Treatment Intervention B.

Angie believes that her measurement of all variables (including marital satisfaction) is valid and reliable and that her research design has adequately controlled for the effects of rival hypotheses and other forms of design bias. Using a standardized self-report marital satisfaction measuring instrument, she finds a mean marital satisfaction level of 51 among couples who received Treatment Intervention A and a mean marital satisfaction level of 54 among couples who received Treatment Intervention B. (Higher scores indicate better marital satisfaction.)

Using the appropriate statistical analysis, Angie concludes that the difference between the two groups' marital satisfaction means is statistically significant. Thus, she rejects the null hypothesis. The relationship between type of treatment intervention (independent variable) and level of marital satisfaction (dependent variable) is apparently a real one. Despite the finding of statistical support for her two-tailed research hypothesis, however, Angie concludes that the relationship between the two variables is not very meaningful, especially given her current budget constraints.

A mean difference of three points $(54 - 51 = 3)$ on the marital satisfaction measuring instrument is really quite small in the absolute sense. It is not large enough to justify sending her staff members to an expensive staff development workshop to get the knowledge and skills necessary to learn to use the "better" treatment intervention. Based on the lack of what can be viewed as a meaningful difference in the results of the two types of treatment interventions (at least for Angie in her current situation), she decides that no action is indicated.

The existence of a statistically significant relationship between variables can be determined by statistical testing, which is based on the laws of probability. The determination of whether a finding is meaningful or not, however, requires judgment; it entails the use of insight into many different aspects of the social work practice milieu.

CONCLUDING THOUGHTS

This chapter briefly examined the underlying logic of statistical testing for relationships between variables. It stressed that research designs are the primary means to eliminate two possible explanations of apparent relationships between variables within a research sample (rival hypotheses and design bias). However, statistical analysis tells us the probability that an apparent relationship between variables may have been produced by chance, or sampling error. We noted that statistical testing really tests a null hypothesis and, only indirectly, a one- or two-tailed research hypothesis.

Throughout this chapter, we have discussed the roles that rival hypotheses, design bias, and chance, or sampling error, have in causing two variables to be related within a research sample when the relationship does not really exist within the population from which the sample was drawn. We have focused primarily on one result of the effect of alternative explanations on research findings—"false positives." Of course, they can lead us to erroneous conclusions in the opposite direction as well. Any or all of them can make two variables appear to be unrelated when in fact they are related within the population from which a sample was drawn. Thus, they can obscure a true relationship between the variables that may be quite strong.

In deciding whether (or not) to reject the null form of a research hypothesis, we must consider the ethical implications of making an error. If we reject it and conclude that the two variables probably are related within the population from which a sample was drawn, we still must address the issue of the meaningfulness of such a finding. Even if we have statistical support for the likelihood of a true relationship between variables (in the form of statistical significance), the relationship may be a very weak, well-known, or otherwise meaningless one. Decisions about the value of a relationship between variables must always be made with reference to their potential to benefit or to harm those served, our clients.

STUDY QUESTIONS

1. Before we can claim a true relationship between variables, what competing explanations for an apparent relationship must be eliminated?
2. Which one of the competing explanations do statistical procedures seek to discredit?
3. What competing explanations are controlled primarily by the design of a research study?
4. What are some other terms for chance that are sometimes used?
5. What is the difference between a Type I and a Type II error? How does reducing the likelihood of committing one affect the likelihood of committing the other?
6. What is the null form of a statement (null hypothesis) for a relationship between the variables "age" and "political party preference?"
7. What is the relationship between the null hypothesis and chance in hypothesis testing?
8. Does a "statistically significant" relationship between variables mean that there is no possibility that the variables are unrelated? Explain.
9. When might we use a rejection level other than the conventional .05 to conclude whether statistical support exists for a research hypothesis? Provide examples from potential social work research studies.
10. Which rejection level, .01 or .10, suggests a greater likelihood of a true relationship between variables? Explain.
11. Discuss the advantages and disadvantages of implementing the results of a study that found a statistically significant, 10 percent mean difference in job performance level between the female and male social workers who work for an Employee Assistance Program (EAP). Discuss what additional information you would want before taking action on the study's results. Justify any assumptions or recommendations.
12. Discuss what you would do with a research study's finding that there was a significant difference ($p < .05$) between the mean client hospital readmission rate for those workers who used Treatment A and those who used Treatment B. How would you use the fact that Treatment A had a mean client readmission rate of 15 percent and Treatment B had a mean client readmission rate of 17 percent? Or the fact that Treatment B requires 25 percent more staff than Treatment A? Justify your answer. Does statistics help us to make an ethical decision in this situation? Why or why not?

13. As an administrator of your local United Way agency, your job is to allocate funds for agencies that request them. Two agencies (A and B) require money from you so that they can stay in operation next year. Both offer the same services, but you have enough money to fund only one. Agency A states that its clients had a mean treatment success score of 42 on a standardized measuring instrument that measures client functioning ($N = 1000$). Agency B, using the same measuring instrument, states that its mean treatment success score was 44 for the same period. Agency B also had 1000 clients. You take these data and calculate the appropriate statistic to determine if chance played any role in the difference in scores. Your statistical analysis produces a finding of $p < .25$. Will you be able to use your statistical analysis to decide which agency to fund? Why or why not? Discuss what additional information you would want before taking action on the study's results. Justify your answer.

14. You are an administrator in a very large family service agency. There are two treatment techniques (A and B) that your workers use to help parents whose children have school truancy problems. Half your workers use Treatment A and the other half Treatment B. You conduct a research study to determine which treatment is more effective in reducing truancy. When they first applied for services, all children in the study were truant a mean of five times per month. After treatment, the parents who received Treatment A reported a mean of two instances of truancy per month, while the parents who received Treatment B reported a mean of three instances of truancy per month. The difference of one is statistically significant at the .05 rejection level. How could you use these findings?

Chapter 6

Sampling Distributions and Hypothesis Testing

$\mathbf{A}$s we have seen from the previous chapter, in order to infer that any relationship between variables within a sample is present within the population from which it was drawn, we need to have some idea of how well the sample matches its population. In short, simply drawing a random sample from a population in no way guarantees that it is truly 100 percent representative of its population. Thus, as all samples tend to differ from their respective populations, we need to be able to estimate **how much** sampling error is contained within the sample. When using interval or ratio level variables, and when inference is concerned, the difference between a sample's mean (and SD) and its population's mean (and SD) is its sampling error. Thus, a sample's mean (and SD) only provides an *estimate* of its population's mean (and SD). A population mean sometimes is called the "true mean."

This chapter continues our discussion of hypothesis testing by presenting a few ways of determining the degree of sampling error that a sample contains. Before this is done, however, we need to briefly discuss how the amount of sampling error a sample contains is directly related to the size of the sample.

SAMPLE SIZE AND SAMPLING ERROR

As should be evident by now, smaller samples tend to differ more from their populations than larger samples. The way that sample size relates to sampling error can be demonstrated through the use of a simple example. Imagine a research class of 30 students. As presented in Chapter 3, we could collect data on each student's overall grade point average (GPA) and compute an overall mean GPA for the entire group of students ($N = 30$). Let us say the mean GPA for the entire class of 30 students is 3.0 ($SD = .5$).

Now, if we draw a random sample of three students ($n = 3$) from the entire class of 30 students and determine this sample's mean GPA (and *SD*), we would not expect it to be exactly 3.0 (*SD* = .5). Even if we draw repeated samples of three students from the class of 30 hundreds of times, rarely—if ever—would the mean GPAs (and *SDs*) for these smaller samples be exactly 3.0 (*SDs* = .5). The smaller samples' mean GPAs (and *SDs*) simply differ from their population's mean GPA (and *SD*). They will differ from each other as well.

With the above in mind, now suppose this time we once again randomly draw hundreds of random samples of 10 students—instead of 3 as used above—from the same class of 30 students (the population, once again). We still would not expect the samples' mean GPAs (and *SDs*) to be exactly 3.0 (*SD* = .5). We would expect, however, that most of the samples' means (and *SDs*) to be closer to the population's mean (and *SD*) than the 3-student samples. Why? The answer is simple: Sample sizes of 10 are closer to "the long run" (see Chapter 5) than sample sizes of 3. Larger samples randomly drawn from a particular population contain less sampling errors than smaller ones randomly drawn from the same population. Therefore, we might expect that fewer flukes might occur.

The "law of averages" is more than likely to take over with larger samples than with smaller ones. What do we mean by this? If we had drawn random samples of 29 students each, for example, we would once again expect the samples' mean GPAs (and *SDs*) to vary somewhat from the population's mean GPA of 3.0 (*SD* = .5), but not by very much when compared to sample sizes of 3 and 10.

Of course, we would be highly unlikely to study a sample of 29 students out of 30. At that point, we might as well use the entire population of all 30 students. When an entire population is used, there is simply no sampling error as there is no sample. Simple as that! The thing we need to remember at this point is that smaller samples have larger sampling errors than larger samples. And larger samples have smaller sampling errors than smaller samples.

SAMPLING DISTRIBUTIONS AND INFERENCE

Because of sampling error, samples are not a perfect 100 percent indicator of the characteristics of the populations from which they were drawn. All samples vary from their populations—we can never assume that a sample's characteristics (statistics) are the same as those of its population (parameters). We can assume, however, that there is some degree of similarity between a sample and its population. If we cannot assume this, then why would we use a sample in the first place?

How would a good estimate of the amount of sampling error within a sample be helpful for looking at the issue of inference? There are several ways. Let us say, for example, that we observe a relationship between age and some other variable within a sample of cases. It would be helpful to know how good the mean age of the people in our sample is as an estimate of the mean age of people within the population. Or, how closely its mode, median, interquartile range, or standard deviation approximate their counterparts within the population. This is why we need *sampling distributions* (estimates of sample statistics) and how much they may differ from their respective population parameters.

They are a third, hypothetical distribution (along with the distribution of a variable within a sample and the distribution of that variable within its population). They are the necessary link between the other two that makes inference possible.

Comparing an Experimental Sample with Its Population

We could randomly draw people from a specific population, for example, and offer a treatment intervention to increase their self-esteem. This intervention would not be offered to the rest of the population. We could then compare these people with the population from which they were drawn in relation to the dependent variable, "self-esteem." In this case, our sample is called an experimental group. We could then test a simple one-tailed research hypothesis where higher values indicate higher levels of self-esteem, such as the following:

> *One-Tailed Research Hypothesis*:
> The experimental group will have a higher mean self-esteem level than those people in the population.

Or to put it another way:

> *One-Tailed Research Hypothesis*:
> The difference between the experimental group's mean self-esteem level and the population's mean self-esteem level is unlikely to be the result of chance, or sampling error.

As we know, we accept (or reject) the one-tailed research hypothesis by testing its null form:

> *Null Hypothesis:*
> There is no difference between the experimental group's mean self-esteem level and the population's mean self-esteem level. Any difference between the two means is due to chance, or sampling error.

An estimate of the similarity of a sample to its population helps us to gage to what degree a drawn sample is sufficiently representative of its population in relation to one or more variables—usually dependent variables. If we can determine that our sample is sufficiently representative of its population, for example, we can then use this sample to introduce some independent variable and observe its effect on a dependent variable. Because our sample was assumed to be representative of its population, we can then infer (within limits, that is) that whatever effect occurred on the dependent variable for our sample would also have occurred on that dependent variable if we had introduced the independent variable to the entire population.

Comparing a Nonexperimental Sample with Its Population

Unlike samples that are manipulated in some way (usually called an experimental group), we may not wish to introduce, or manipulate, an independent variable at all. We may simply wish to study a specific type, or category, of people (a sample), contained within a population to see if they differ from the general population in some way. We could identify a group (sample) of people who know they are are HIV positive, for example, and have them complete a standardized self-report measuring instrument that measures the variable "self-esteem." We could then compare our HIV-positive sample's mean self-esteem level with the general population's mean self-esteem level. In this instance, we could test the following one-tailed research hypothesis:

One-Tailed Research Hypothesis:
People who know that they are HIV positive have a lower mean self-esteem level than people who are not HIV positive.

We accept (or reject) the above one-tailed research hypothesis by testing its null form:

Null Hypothesis:
People who know that they are HIV positive have the same mean self-esteem level as the general population.

The null hypothesis takes the position that any differences in self-esteem levels between people who know that they are HIV positive and the general population are due to chance, or sampling error. In attempting to reject the null hypothesis, we would have to know how frequently a sample (of a specific size) would likely differ from its population by the amount observed in the sample, just based upon chance, or sampling error.

SAMPLING DISTRIBUTION OF MEANS

A *sampling distribution* (of means) is a social construct. It does not exist and is only theoretical—that is, it is based on the theoretical results of drawing an infinite number of samples from a population. We could, for example, theoretically create a sampling distribution of means for the variable "SAT scores" for all B.S.W. students enrolled in accredited departments and schools of social work in North America in the current year (a specific population at a specific time). To create a sampling distribution of means for this group of students, at this specific time, for this specific variable, we would randomly draw an infinite number of samples (of a certain size) from this population, replacing cases each time before the next sample is drawn.

We could then compute the mean (and *SD*) SAT score for each sample drawn from this particular population. The means of these samples create a theoretical frequency polygon, which simply represents the distribution of the samples' means. If we knew how much the various means differed from each other in an infinite number of samples drawn from the same population, we could estimate—with some degree of accuracy—that a given sample's mean was a certain distance (on the frequency polygon) from its true population's mean. We would do this by determining the likelihood of drawing a sample (of a given size) with a given mean by using *z* scores and the areas within a normal curve (i.e., Table 4.3 or Appendix A).

There are as many different sampling distributions of means as there are different sample sizes. Theoretically, their means (and *SDs*) are identical—the same as the population's mean. Why? Means of individual samples vary from the population's mean and from each other. But since our sampling distribution is based on an infinite number of samples of SAT scores, the "law of averages" (the long run) eventually prevails. Samples with lower means and those with higher means "cancel each other out" when they are averaged together. This concept is called "the mean of the means."

Obviously, the standard deviation of different size sampling distributions of means varies. This (as is true of much of statistical inference) is a function of one of the laws of probability theory. Remember our earlier example of drawing random samples of 3, 10, and then 29 students out of a research class of 30? Let us apply this law here. As we know (now using our SAT score example), if we draw an infinite number of samples of 3 students and compute the mean SAT score for each individual sample, the means of all samples will vary widely from one another. Why? Some samples might consist of three very high scores, which produce high means. Other samples might consist of three very low scores, which produce low means.

What if, instead, we had drawn an infinite number of samples of 29 students? The means of most of these samples would be closer to the population mean and to each other than those of samples of only 3. Why would there be less variability among the sample means with larger samples? We would be much less likely to get all high scores or all low scores in a sample of 29 than in a sample of only 3. In a random sample of 29 there will probably be some low scores to "balance out" any high scores that might be present and vice versa. So, the means of the samples would be closer (as a group) to the true mean. Thus, the standard deviation for the means of these samples (an indicator of variability) will be smaller than that of samples of only three cases.

There are two other factors (besides sample size) that determine what a theoretical sampling distribution for a given variable might look like—the shape of the distribution of the population and whether its true mean and distribution are known. However, as we shall see, these factors are not as important as it might be logical to assume. Now, let us look a little more at how sampling distributions can relate to hypothesis testing.

Samples Drawn from Normal Distributions

If our variable of interest, usually the dependent variable, is normally distributed within in a given population, it is possible to use our knowledge of normal curves, acquired in the previous chapter, and combine it with the contents of this chapter to test one- and two-tailed research hypotheses. Frequently, we wish to conduct a research study to see if a treatment intervention "makes a difference." We may wish to know, for example, if a particular type of group treatment seems to improve our clients' self-esteem levels.

Let us say that client self-esteem levels on a particular standardized measuring instrument have been found to be normally distributed among 1000 clients in an agency with a known mean of 50 (*SD* = 5). As before, higher values indicate higher self-esteem levels than lower values. We then randomly select a sample of 16 clients from the population of 1000, provide a group treatment intervention to this sample (an experimental group), and calculate the experimental group's mean self-esteem level (e.g., 60) to see if it was significantly higher than its population's mean self-esteem level of 50 ($SD = 5$). We could write this assumption as a one-tailed research hypothesis as follows:

One-Tailed Research Hypothesis:
The experimental group will have a higher mean self-esteem level than the population's mean self-esteem level.

Once again, it is important to note that higher values mean higher levels of self-esteem and lower values mean lower levels of self-esteem. A person with a self-esteem level of 70, for example, has higher self-esteem than a person with a level of 60.

To test our one-tailed research hypothesis, we need to compare data drawn from our 16-member sample with a standard normal sampling distribution table (i.e., Table 4.3 or Appendix A). We thus compare our sample's mean self-esteem level with the level that we might expect to get from simply drawing a random sample (of a given size) from a population (and doing nothing to those clients).

By using the concepts of *rejection regions* and *standard error of the mean*, we can determine just how typical, or atypical, our experimental group (or sample) is in relation to how self-esteem levels are distributed within the population. The term "rejection region" refers to a specific region(s) of a normal curve that, when it contains a measurement from a sample, suggests it is safe to reject the null hypothesis. In order to understand the concept of rejection regions, we rely heavily on the use of normal distributions and z scores as presented in Chapter 4.

Rejection Regions for Two-Tailed Research Hypotheses.   As we know from Chapter 5, the rejection region for statistical tests that test research hypotheses depends on (1) the rejection level selected and (2) whether the research hypothesis is one- or two-tailed.

In the above example, we hypothesized that our group treatment intervention would increase the self-esteem of experimental group members (a one-tailed research hypothesis). In a two-tailed research hypothesis, however, we just say that our group treatment will affect the self-esteem of our experimental group but do not say if it would raise or lower it, for example:

Two-Tailed Research Hypothesis:
The experimental group's mean self-esteem level will be different than the population's mean self-esteem level.

For two-tailed research hypotheses, the z values of the two rejection regions are located using procedures similar to those discussed in Chapter 4 (and the same table) that are used to locate a raw score's corresponding standardized z score. The steps for locating the two rejection regions for two-tailed research hypotheses are:

1. Divide the selected rejection level by 2.
2. Subtract the derived value from .50 and multiply by 100.
3. Locate the derived proportion in the body of a normal distribution table (i.e., Table 4.3 or Appendix A).
4. Determine the z score that corresponds to that proportion.

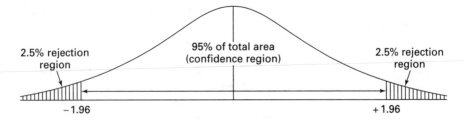

FIGURE 6.1 The Normal Distribution Showing the 95% Confidence Region and Two 2.5% Rejection Regions for Two-Tailed Research Hypotheses

If we are using the conventional .05 rejection level, for example, the calculations for the preceding four steps would look like this:

1. $.05/2 = .025$
2. $(.50 - .025) \times 100 = 47.50$ (1/2 of 95.00)
3. Find 47.50 in the body of a normal distribution table (i.e., Table 4.3 or Appendix A).
4. The z score corresponding to 47.50 is $+1.96$ or -1.96.

How do we interpret the results of the above calculations? When a rejection level of .05 is used, the rejection regions for a two-tailed research hypothesis are the areas at, or above, $z = +1.96$ and at, or below, $z = -1.96$. Such a result must be achieved in order to reject the null hypothesis for a two-tailed research hypothesis. Figure 6.1 provides a graphical illustration of this concept.

In our two-tailed research hypothesis, the experimental group's mean self-esteem level would have to be at least $+1.96$ standard deviations higher than, or at least -1.96 standard deviations lower than, the population's mean self-esteem level of 50. As we know, the standard deviation of the sampling distribution of the means (more correctly referred to as the "standard error of the mean" or just "standard error") that we use to test this two-tailed research hypothesis is not simply the standard deviation for the population. The standard deviation that we use must be specific to the size of the sample, in our example 16. It is computed by using the formula for the standard error of the mean, which is equal to the standard deviation of the parent population (in this case 5) divided by the square root of the sample size (in this case 4). In our example, 5 divided by 4 equals 1.25.

Thus, to feel reasonably safe in rejecting the null hypothesis for our two-tailed research hypothesis, our experimental group's mean self-esteem level would have to be

- at least $+1.96 \times 1.25$, or $+2.45$ points, **higher** than 50, or at least 52.45;

or

- at least -1.96×1.25, or -2.45 points, **lower** than 50, or less than 47.55.

It should be noted that $+1.96$ or -1.96 is the required z value for all two-tailed research hypotheses that use the .05 rejection level, not just the one in our example. Only the standard deviation for the sample (the standard error of the mean) will vary, based on the sample's size.

Rejection Regions for One-Tailed Research Hypotheses.   What if we had hypothesized that our intervention with the experimental group would produce a higher mean level of self-esteem than the level found within the general population (i.e., mean = 50, *SD* = 5)? A one-tailed research hypothesis could be written as follows:

One-Tailed Research Hypothesis:
The experimental group will have a higher mean self-esteem level than the mean self-esteem level found within the population.

Where would this rejection region lie? Since a one-tailed research hypothesis predicts the direction of a relationship between variables, there is only one variation in the above procedure for obtaining its appropriate rejection region—the selected rejection level is not divided by 2. Thus, the .05 rejection region for a one-tailed research hypothesis is derived as follows:

1. $(.50 - .05) \times 100 = 45.00$.
2. Find 45.00 in the body of a normal distribution table (i.e., Table 4.3 or Appendix A).
3. The z score corresponding to 45.00 is $+1.65$ or -1.65.

How do we interpret the results of this calculation? When using a one-tailed research hypothesis and a rejection level of .05, the calculated z must be at least $+1.65$ or -1.65 in order to reject the null hypothesis. Which cutoff point would we use—the $+1.65$ or the -1.65? In our hypothetical study, in order to claim support for our one-tailed research hypothesis, the experimental group's mean self-esteem level would have to be at least $+1.65$ standard deviations higher than the population's mean level of 50. Why? Because we hypothesized that our experimental group would have a higher mean self-esteem level than is found within the population from which it was drawn.

If we had hypothesized, for example, that our experimental group's mean self-esteem level would be lower than found within the population, we would have used the $z = -1.65$ cutoff point. Since our sample size is still 16, the standard error of the mean for our sampling distribution would be the same as when we had a two-tailed research hypothesis, 1.25. With a one-tailed research hypothesis, however, the experimental group's mean self-esteem level would have to be at least $+1.65 \times 1.25 = +2.0625$, rounded off to $+2$ points, higher than 50 for us to reject the null hypothesis.

Thus, our experimental group's mean self-esteem level would have to be at least 52 for us to be reasonably certain (95 percent) that there really is an association between our treatment intervention and the experimental group's relatively higher levels of self-esteem (when compared to the population, that is).

Figure 6.2 graphically portrays the rejection region (z = at least $+1.65$) for a one-tailed research hypothesis where the upper tail is specified as the rejection region.

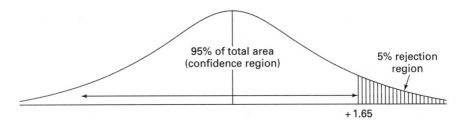

FIGURE 6.2 The Normal Distribution Showing the 95% Confidence Region and the One 5% Rejection Region for an Upper One-Tailed Research Hypothesis

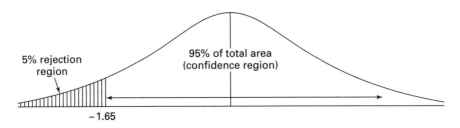

FIGURE 6.3 The Normal Distribution Showing the 95% Confidence Region and the One 5% Rejection Region for a lower One-Tailed Research Hypothesis

Likewise, Figure 6.3 provides an illustration of the rejection region (z = at least -1.65) for a one-tailed research hypothesis where the lower tail is specified. Unlike Figure 6.1, Figures 6.2, and 6.3 contain only one rejection region, the one that reflects the direction of the one-tailed research hypothesis.

When using a normal distribution to test a one-tailed research hypothesis, only z scores that fall within the specified rejection region allow us to reject the null hypothesis. This region suggests that the probability of chance, or sampling error, producing the relationship between the two variables in our sample is less than .05. We could conclude that by just selecting an infinite number of samples of 16 (and offering no intervention), we could expect to draw a sample with a mean self-esteem level that differs from the mean of its population by at least 1.65 standard deviations in the predicted direction less than five times out of 100. So, we would be able to claim that chance, or sampling error, is unlikely to explain the relationship between our intervention and self-esteem levels. We could state that the relationship between the variables was found to be statistically significant.

By glancing at Figures 6.1, 6.2, and 6.3, it can be observed that a one-tailed research hypothesis has certain advantages. As can be seen, it moves the critical rejection regions closer to the mean of the sampling distribution, thus improving the probability of rejecting the null hypothesis. This is only logical, as when we predict the direction of a relationship using a one-tailed research hypothesis, we should get a little "extra credit" if support for the relationship between variables **and** the predicted direction of the relationship is found. As noted earlier, a specific predicted relationship found to exist is less likely to be the work of chance, or sampling error, than one that is not specified in advance.

Note, however, that if the wrong direction has been specified in a one-tailed research hypothesis—that is, if we incorrectly predicted the direction of the relationship—the probability of the rejection of the null hypothesis is zero. There simply is no rejection region on the other side of the distribution. We are given no prediction "credit" for results that were the exact opposite of what we predicted. Thus one-tailed research hypotheses should not be used unless the direction of a relationship can be confidently predicted or we are interested only in those sample outcomes that fall in one tail (direction) of a sampling distribution of a variable.

Samples Drawn from Skewed Distributions

While many variables are normally distributed within a population, other variables are not, as illustrated in Figure 4.5. What would the sampling distribution of the means look like for a variable when a sampling distribution is skewed? In other words, what would be the shape of a frequency polygon of means from an infinite number of samples randomly drawn from a population in which the variable is **not** normally distributed? Actually, it will approximate a normal distribution if the size of the sample is fairly large! This fact is based on what is called the *central limit theorem*. It states that if the size of the sample is large, the sampling distribution of means created from a variable that is skewed within its population will be the same as its population. Its standard deviation (standard error) is computed the same way as with normally distributed variables.

How large is large? It depends upon the shape of the distribution. In some skewed distributions, however, a sample as small as 30 is sufficiently large to produce a sampling distribution that is essentially a normal (or bell-shaped) one as portrayed in Figures 4.3, 4.4, and 4.6. Let us see the importance of the central limit theorem. We will use an example to which we all can relate.

Example: M.S.W. Students' Scores on a Statistics Test.   The scores on a standardized statistics test administered to all M.S.W. students in North America would not form a normal distribution. For the sake of simplicity, let us say that the variable "scores on the statistics test" is negatively skewed within the M.S.W. student population. What does the central limit theorem tell us about a sampling distribution of our variable? Theoretically, we could take the scores of all M.S.W. students and randomly draw an infinite number of samples of 30 students, replacing each student's score drawn before each subsequent sample is drawn.

We could then compute the mean for each sample. We could take all of the sample means and create a frequency polygon as described in Chapter 2. According to the central limit theorem, the frequency polygon created from these samples would approximate a normal curve, even though the scores within the population create a negatively skewed frequency polygon. The frequency polygon's mean and standard error would be the same as if the scores on the statistics test had been normally distributed among all the M.S.W. students.

ESTIMATING PARAMETERS FROM STATISTICS

We can easily estimate a variable's parameter (characteristic of a population) from the variable's statistic (a measurement of a variable taken on a sample). In this situation, we want to make a determination about the characteristics of a population based upon what we learn from a sample. This procedure is called *parameter estimation*.

To understand parameter estimation, we need to introduce two related terms, confidence interval and confidence level. A *confidence interval* is a range into which we would estimate a population parameter to fall based on a sample statistic. A *confidence level* is an estimate of the probability that the true population parameter lies within the confidence interval. Together, a confidence level and its confidence interval form an estimate of the true parameter based on a statistic. Thus, in conducting a parameter estimation, we seek to fill in the three blanks in the following statement:

Based on measurement of variable X within our sample (a statistic), there is a ____ percent probability that the true mean of variable X within the population from which it was drawn (a parameter) is between ____ and ____.

In the above statement, the first blank is the confidence level. The second and third blanks are the lower and upper limits of the confidence interval. But how would we arrive at the correct numbers to fill in these blanks? We set the first blank's number to reflect how confident we wish to be that the true population mean falls within our confidence interval (2nd and 3rd blanks). If we want to be 95 percent confident that it will, we use the 95 percent confidence level; if we want to be 99 percent confident, we can use the 99 percent confidence level, and so on.

What about the other two remaining blanks in the above statement that deal with the confidence interval? How do we arrive at the correct numbers to place in them? By applying a bit of logic, we can see that finding the lower and upper limits of a confidence interval is easier than we might think. Suppose we want to estimate the self-esteem levels of all 1000 active clients within a large public social service agency. It is impractical to administer the standardized self-esteem measuring instrument to all active clients within the agency. We can estimate the population's mean self-esteem level, however, by simply asking 100 randomly selected clients to complete the measuring instrument and then computing this sample's mean self-esteem level.

Let us say that our sample's mean self-esteem level is 40. Perhaps we believe that the variable, "self-esteem," is normally distributed in the population from which it was drawn. But whether it is, or is not, is not important since our sample is considered sufficiently large (over 30). Thus, the standard error of the mean will be the same either way (a conclusion based upon the central limit theorem). This fact is important to an understanding of how we arrive at a confidence interval.

It should be obvious, but worth stating anyway, that the true parameter (the population mean) can be thought of as the mean of the sample, plus or minus some amount of sampling error. We can never exactly determine how large this error is, but there are some things that we can determine. First, we can determine the probability distribution of all possible errors in an infinite number of samples of 100 cases—the sampling distribution of these errors. Because the sample is fairly large, we already know that the distribution will be normally distributed.

Second, we can determine its standard deviation. Remember that the standardized self-esteem measuring instrument has a known mean of 50 and a standard deviation of 5. Using the formula presented earlier, the standard deviation of the sampling distribution (standard error of the mean) is the standard deviation of the population (5) divided by the square root of the sample size ($N = 100$) ($5/10 = .5$). We know that a probability distribution of the sampling errors in an infinite number of random samples of 100 drawn from a population would form a normal distribution with a standard error of .5.

Constructing a 95 Percent Confidence Interval

Suppose we want to be 95 percent confident that the true self-esteem level of all active clients falls between two levels (the confidence interval) of our sample's mean of 40—10 points lower than the usual mean of 50. Remember that 95 percent of a normal distribution lies between the points $z = +1.96$ and $z = -1.96$ (see Figure 5.1). We now can arrive at our confidence interval as presented below:

Lower limit (N = 100):

$$
\begin{array}{rl}
& = \;\; 40.00 \text{ (sample mean)} \\
-1.96 \times .5 \text{ (standard error)} = & \underline{\;\; -.98} \\
& = \;\; 39.02
\end{array}
$$

Upper limit (N = 100):

$$
\begin{array}{rl}
& = \;\; 40.00 \text{ (sample mean)} \\
+1.96 \times .5 \text{ (standard error)} = & \underline{\;\; +.98} \\
& = \;\; 40.98
\end{array}
$$

Now we can state the following:

Based on measurement of self-esteem within our sample ($N = 100$), there is a 95 percent probability that the true mean of self-esteem among clients in the agency is between 39.02 and 40.98.

Constructing a 99 Percent Confidence Interval

Using the same data, we also could have produced a confidence interval reflecting a 99 percent confidence level. Once again, using Table 4.3 or Appendix A, we could learn that 99 percent of the distribution would fall between the z scores $+2.58$ and -2.58. Instead of using $z = +1.96$ or -1.96, as we did to find the confidence interval for a 95 percent confidence level, we would now use $z = +2.58$ or -2.58 instead:

Lower limit (N = 100):

$$
\begin{array}{rl}
& = \;\; 40.00 \text{ (sample mean)} \\
-2.58 \times .5 \text{ (standard error)} = & \underline{\;\; -1.29} \\
& = \;\; 38.71
\end{array}
$$

Upper limit (N = 100):

$$
\begin{array}{rl}
& = \;\; 40.00 \text{ (sample mean)} \\
+2.58 \times .5 \text{ (standard error)} = & \underline{\;\; +1.29} \\
& = \;\; 41.29
\end{array}
$$

Now we can state the following:

Based on measurement of self-esteem within the sample ($N = 100$), there is a 99 percent probability that the true mean of self-esteem among clients in the agency is between 38.71 and 41.29.

Note that whether we use the 95 or 99 percent confidence levels, the confidence interval each one contains may seem quite small—they encompass just a few points. Why? Because a sample of 100 cases is quite large in the absolute sense. We would expect that any sample of 100 would have relatively little sampling error, since a sample of 100 would begin to approximate "the long run."

Let us take the same example used above to illustrate how decreasing the size of a sample affects the upper and lower limits of a 95% confidence interval. We will use a sample size of 25—not 100. Remember, the square root of 25 is 5 so the standard error for this example becomes 1 (5/5 = 1).

Lower limit (N = 25):
$$
\begin{aligned}
&= 40.00 \text{ (sample mean)} \\
-1.96 \times 1 \text{ (standard error)} \ &= \ \underline{-1.96} \\
&= 38.04
\end{aligned}
$$

Upper limit (N = 25):
$$
\begin{aligned}
&= 40.00 \text{ (sample mean)} \\
+1.96 \times 1 \text{ (standard error)} \ &= \ \underline{+1.96} \\
&= 41.96
\end{aligned}
$$

Now we can state the following:

Based on measurement of self-esteem within our sample ($N = 25$), there is a 95 percent probability that the true mean of self-esteem among clients in the agency is between 38.04 and 41.96.

The 95 percent confidence interval using a sample size of 100 ranges from 39.02 to 40.98 (a range of 1.96 points). The sampling interval for a sample size of 25 ranges from 38.04 to 41.96 (a range of 3.92 points). Thus, the smaller the sample, the larger the range of the confidence interval—the larger the sample, the smaller the range of the confidence interval. We assume that a sample of 100 has a smaller sampling error than a sample of 25, since larger samples begin to approximate "the long run."

SMALL SAMPLE DISTRIBUTIONS

As the converse to the central limit theorem suggests, when sample sizes are small (i.e., < 30), sampling distributions may be quite inaccurate as estimates of the population. The standard deviation of the sample means (standard error) is unlikely to be a good estimate of the population's standard deviation. Still another distribution, a student's t distribution, however, allows us to compute exact confidence intervals when a variable is normally distributed, but we do not know its population standard deviation.

Actually, t distributions are similar to a normal distribution. But they are a group of curves (distributions) which vary based upon the number of cases in the sample(s). When using t distributions, as the size of a sample approaches 30, the distributions actually are quite close to a normal distribution. They are central to many statistical significance tests such as those presented in Chapter 11.

CONCLUDING THOUGHTS

This chapter expanded on the previous one by presenting an introduction to inference and hypothesis testing. The theoretical underpinning of sampling distributions was presented. The chapter examined how our knowledge of the normal distribution (Chapter 4), when integrated with the concept of sampling distributions, is used to answer two related questions that are integral to inference: (1) How well does the sample serve as an estimate of the population? and (2) How confident can we be that the true mean of the population falls within a certain range of values? The first question is answered through the use of rejection regions. The latter question is answered through the use of confidence levels and confidence intervals.

The statistical methods presented in Chapters 8–12 rely heavily on the concepts and ideas presented in this and the previous chapter.

STUDY QUESTIONS

1. Discuss how sample size is directly related to sampling error. Use a social work example in your discussion.
2. Discuss how sampling distributions are used for inferential purposes.
3. What is a sampling distribution of means? Explain in detail how a sampling distribution of means is used in constructing the rejection regions for one- and two-tailed research hypotheses.
4. Discuss how a sampling distribution of means derived from numerous large samples drawn from a skewed population will form a normal distribution.
5. Discuss the concept of parameter estimation. How is it useful for social workers?
6. What is a rejection region? What is a confidence level? What is a confidence interval? Discuss how the three concepts are related to each other. Provide a social work example throughout your discussion.
7. Discuss how the standard error of the mean is calculated.

Chapter 7

Selecting Statistical Tests

The two previous chapters presented a discussion of how statistical analysis is used to test one- and two-tailed research hypotheses. They described how, using the laws of probability, it is possible to determine the likelihood that chance, or sampling error, may have produced an apparent relationship between variables within a sample that was drawn from a population. Assuming that rival hypotheses and design bias (e.g., measurement bias and sampling bias) have been adequately controlled, we can now estimate how safe it would be if we were to conclude that the relationship between variables contained within our sample is a real one and really exists within the population from which it was drawn.

As should be obvious by now, there are many different forms of statistical analyses that are used to test one- and two-tailed research hypotheses. They rely on the principles presented in the previous two chapters. This chapter completes our discussion on hypothesis testing by presenting a few of the basic issues that need to be addressed when selecting the best statistical test from the many that exist.

THE IMPORTANCE OF SELECTING THE CORRECT TEST

The many decisions that need to be made during the course of a research study have the potential to enhance—or to harm—the credibility of the study's findings. For example, a biased literature review, the selection of a measuring instrument that lacks validity, the use of a biased data collection method, or the use of a sampling method that produces a sample that is not representative of its population in relation to some important variable can cause readers to doubt a study's findings.

Even if a study was well designed and implemented, the credibility of its findings still can be jeopardized by an additional error—the use of the wrong statistical test. A critical reader of a research report always asks, "Was an appropriate statistical analysis used to test the study's research hypothesis?" If not, the study's findings are likely to produce only skepticism.

Why are inappropriate statistical tests sometimes chosen when appropriate ones are available for almost any type of data analysis? One reason may be the principle ♯ 3 referred to as the "rule of the instrument." It suggests that some of us have a tendency to see the solution to any problem as requiring what we know and/or do best—that is, that with which we are most comfortable and familiar. There are many examples of this principle in action. Marriage counselors, for example, may see the solution to a social problem, such as child abuse, as requiring more marriage counseling services. Family therapists may see a need for more family treatment. Or lawyers may see improved legal services as the solution; politicians might think the problem could best be addressed through legislation.

Many of us, particularly those of us who received our formal social work education quite some time ago, did not receive extensive statistical training. Our knowledge is often confined to a passing familiarity with only one or two statistical tests. Facing the necessity of choosing a statistical test to analyze the relationship between variables, we can easily fall prey to the "rule of the instrument." We turn to an "old friend," the test with which we are most familiar, rather than explore the possibility of using a lesser-known, more appropriate test.

There also is a widely held misconception that because statistical tests have so much in common, it makes little difference which one is used. After all, as discussed in the previous two chapters, they all rely on the same principles and the same laws of probability. So, why not just use a test that is widely used and understood by potential consumers of a study's findings? Why bother to seek out one that may be more appropriate but is less widely known or would require additional study?

There are two responses to these questions. First, as suggested earlier, using an inappropriate statistical test will result in a loss of credibility for a study's findings among those who are knowledgeable about statistics. Second, and most importantly, those who are not knowledgeable about statistics may fail to question a study's findings when the findings should have been challenged in the first place. Assuming that a study's findings represent new knowledge, they may apply the findings in a manner that has the potential to harm our clients.

There are literally hundreds of statistical tests available. How do we determine which one(s) to use? This decision is a relatively complicated one as several factors must be considered. This chapter examines some of these factors and presents a few general guidelines to help in the selection process.

FACTORS TO CONSIDER WHEN SELECTING A STATISTICAL TEST

Planning for the analysis of data ideally should begin early in the research process, at about the same time that decisions are made about what data collection instrument(s) will be used to measure certain variables of interest—that is, when the variables are operationalized. Questions about how variables are measured and statistically analyzed are closely related. The way variables are measured helps determine which statistical test(s) should, and should not, be used to test the research hypothesis.

Are such decisions "final"? Generally, yes—it is customary to select and specify the statistical test(s) to be used, prior to data collection. Sometimes, no—it is not unusual to encounter problems in a research study that may change either the way data are collected and/or the level of precision with which variables realistically can be measured. When this occurs, it is considered ethical and, in some cases, absolutely essential to select statistical tests different from those that were specified within the original research design.

Whenever the final choice of a statistical test(s) is made, five considerations most directly influence that choice:

1. the sampling method(s) used
2. the distribution of the dependent variable (and sometimes the independent variable as well) within the population
3. the level of measurement of the independent and dependent variables
4. the statistical power of a test
5. the robustness of a test

Sampling Method

The characteristics of a sample and the way that it is drawn from a population influence the choice of a statistical test. Certain statistical tests require the use of certain sampling methods.

The topic of sampling is usually covered in detail in most social work research methods texts. We must be fully aware of the kind of sampling method we used within the research study if we want to select the most appropriate statistical test to test our research hypotheses. Below are some of the questions that need to be addressed:

1. Did the sampling method use a single sample or more than one sample? If so, how many?
2. If more than one sample was used, were the samples independent of each other or were they related in any way? For example, were they "matched" in regard to certain variables to assure that they were comparable?
3. Were the cases within the sample drawn "independently"? Did the selection of one case in any way, for example, increase or decrease the likelihood that any other case within the population would also be selected?
4. Was a probability sampling method used? If so, was the probability of being selected (for the sample) the same for every case?

Answering the above four questions allows us to narrow our search for the appropriate statistical test. It eliminates a majority of the existing tests because of their inappropriateness for the particular sampling method that was employed. It is only one step, however, in the "process of elimination" that is used in selecting a test for use in a statistical analysis of data.

The Distribution of the Dependent Variable

A second major consideration in selecting a statistical test is the way in which the variable of interest (usually the dependent variable) is distributed within the population from which the sample was drawn. Is the dependent variable normally distributed? Some of the most common statistical tests require that this assumption is met.

As seen in Chapter 3, a skewed distribution of an interval or ratio level variable usually precludes the use of the mean as a measure of central tendency, or the standard deviation as a measure of variability. Unless the dependent variable is normally distributed, many potentially useful tests that contain the mean and/or standard deviation in their formulas must be eliminated from consideration for hypothesis testing.

As noted in Chapter 4, normal distributions are rarely perfect in their symmetry; their data may only approximate bell-shaped curves. Many times, full descriptive data on a given dependent variable within a population do not exist. So, how do we know if the distribution is a normal one?

The decision about whether the distribution of a dependent variable within a population is normally distributed is often a judgment call. It requires, among other things, a knowledge of the robustness of a test, a concept that we shall discuss later in this chapter. Generally, a dependent variable whose values at least approximate a bell-shaped curve within the population would justify the use of certain statistical tests that require a normal distribution of the variable. Judgments of this type are common and necessary.

We make a similar judgment, for example when we decide (1) when enough literature has been reviewed, (2) that our sample is sufficiently large and representative of the population from which it was drawn, (3) that we can, or cannot, justify the use of a one-tailed research hypothesis, or (4) what we believe to be the most appropriate rejection level for rejecting the null hypothesis.

Level of Measurement of Variables

A third factor to consider in selecting a statistical test is the level of measurement of the variables of interest. Were they measured in a way that they can be considered nominal, ordinal, interval, or ratio? Well-planned construction and use of measuring instruments help us to generate the highest possible level of measurement for any given variable (as well as ethical and practical). Through carelessness, however, we also can throw away data precision. We may permit, for example, a variable that could have been measured at the interval or ratio level to be measured at only the nominal or ordinal level. As noted in Chapter 1, once measurements have been made, it is usually impossible to achieve the higher level of measurement precision than was initially possible.

Why is loss of measurement precision important? After all, are there not different statistical tests designed for use with different levels of measurement? There are. So what difference does it make what level of measurement is used? In fact, the distinction between interval and ratio level measurement is relatively unimportant in the selection of statistical tests. Many statistics books simply use the term "interval/ratio" to note the presence of either level of measurement, or they use the label "interval" to denote either. But measuring a variable in a way that it produces only nominal or ordinal level measurement when interval or ratio levels were possible can result in a real loss.

The use of a measurement that yields a lower level of measurement (i.e., nominal, ordinal) automatically precludes the use of all statistical tests that require interval or ratio level variables. This would not be problematic except, as we shall see, those tests that require interval or ratio measurement of one or more variables are some of the best statistical tests developed for identifying true relationships between variables (avoiding Type II errors). They are simply some of the most powerful tests.

Statistical Power of a Test

The fourth factor to consider in selecting a statistical test, is the concept of statistical power. *Statistical power* is the ability of a test to correctly reject the null hypothesis; that is, its ability to correctly detect a true relationship between variables. Another way to think of the power of a statistical test is its ability to avoid committing a Type II error.

Based on their mathematical computations, some statistical tests are inherently more powerful than others; that is, some tests are better than others at detecting a true relationship between variables. Some may allow us to justify the rejection of the null hypothesis, while other, less powerful tests applied to the same data set would not allow us to reject the null hypothesis. The more powerful tests have demanding conditions for their use. These conditions must be met in order for the tests to be used correctly.

As presented in Chapter 3, the standard deviation, where appropriate, is preferable to the range as an indicator of variability and the mean, where appropriate, is a more precise indicator of central tendency than is the median or mode. Why? Both the mean and the standard deviation require computations using every case value within the variable's distribution. Less precise descriptive statistics such as the trimmed mean, interquartile range, or range do not.

The same principle applies in understanding the concept of statistical power. All other factors being equal, more powerful tests tend to be those that use all the values for all cases in their computations (directly or indirectly) rather than, for example, the ranks assigned to cases or the frequencies for different nominal level value categories of a variable. Thus, they take full advantage of the greater precision in measurement that is available. Not surprisingly, the formulas for more powerful statistical tests also tend to be more complex than the formulas for less powerful ones.

Before selecting a statistical test, we need to determine how much power is desirable (and appropriate) for examining the predicted relationship between variables. In statistics, "more powerful" is not always better, since a test that is "too powerful" can identify relationships between variables that may be statistically significant but too weak to be substantive or valuable. Using logic, we need to determine what would constitute "not powerful enough" or "too powerful" for our specific data analysis situation.

Having decided what we need in a test, we can explore available alternatives. We may find a test that appears to be about what we need, but it may not seem quite powerful enough or a little too powerful for our needs. While all tests possess a certain inherent power based upon their mathematical formulas, any test can be made more or less powerful by conditions related to its use.

Factors That Affect Statistical Power.   What makes a statistical test more or less able to detect a true relationship between variables within a given data set? Four conditions affect the statistical power of a given test:

1. the strength of the actual relationship between variables that exists within the population (effect size)
2. the predetermined statistical rejection level (e.g., .05, .01, .001) that is used with the test as well as whether a one- or two-tailed research hypothesis was used
3. the likely amount of chance, or sampling error (not to be confused with sampling bias) within sample data—a factor based upon the amount of variability of a variable within a population
4. the size of the research sample used

How does each of these factors relate to the power of a statistical test? How does each affect the likelihood of making a Type II error? If the actual relationship between variables is strong within a population, many tests (even those that are less powerful) will detect it and the null hypothesis will be correctly rejected. But if it is weak, some tests may not be powerful enough to detect it. Unfortunately, we cannot influence the strength of the actual relationship between variables; it generally is regarded as a "given" that we would like to know more about.

At the beginning of a study, we can select either a higher or lower rejection level than the conventional .05. As noted in Chapter 5, however, there must be justification for doing this (usually within the literature). If, for example, we decide to use the rejection level of .10 as the cutoff point at which we will reject the null hypothesis, we can increase the likelihood of not "missing" a true relationship between variables that exists in the population and, thus, of not committing a Type II error. As noted in Chapter 5, however, this will increase the likelihood of committing a Type I error.

On the other hand, if we were to go in the opposite direction and use the .01 level, we would make any given statistical test less powerful and increase the likelihood of committing a Type II error. But we would decrease the likelihood of concluding that two variables are related when they really are not (a Type I error).

In which direction, if either, should we go? It depends on the consequences of making either error and which would be the more tolerable from an ethical and practice perspective. We would want to make a test either more powerful or less powerful only after a careful assessment of the practice implications of implementing research findings that might result from such a decision.

The use of a one-tailed research hypothesis, when justifiable, will decrease the likelihood of committing a Type II error, if the relationship identified is in the direction specified in the one-tailed research hypothesis. Thus, it will make a test more powerful. The logic behind this is that a one-tailed research hypothesis has a larger rejection region (see Figures 6.2 and 6.3) than either of the two rejection regions present when a two-tailed research hypothesis is used (see Figure 6.1). But, as we will recall from Chapter 6, there is no rejection region (critical value) at all if the relationship is found to be in the direction opposite to that expressed in the one-tailed research hypothesis. If that is the case, we can only fail to find support for the research hypothesis.

In examining the relationship between variables with larger standard deviations among their variables, we are more likely to commit a Type II error than when examining relationships between variables with smaller standard deviations. That is because with larger variation within a population, sampling error is likely to be greater—all samples simply vary from their populations (see Chapter 6).

With less variation in a variable within the population, samples selected will be closer to the population in relation to the variable (less sampling error). If sampling error is more likely to be present (because variables have more variation among their values), we will probably not reject the null hypothesis, and thus run a high risk of committing a Type II error.

The first and third of the factors that influence the power of statistical tests are beyond our control. We cannot, and do not wish to, adjust the actual strength of a relationship between variables. We also cannot, and do not wish to, affect the variation that exists between variables. In relation to the second factor, while we have the capacity to adjust the rejection level used or to choose either a one- or a two-tailed research hypothesis, the literature usually dictates our choices in these matters. That brings us to the fourth factor—sample size. It is the factor that affects power, over which we generally have the greatest control.

Selection of a sample size, although sometimes constrained by various ethical and practice considerations, allows us to conduct a statistical analysis using a test that will generate the optimal amount of statistical power. There is a sample size that is considered ideal for use with a given statistical test. It is specified in many advanced statistics books that discuss various tests and their appropriate usage.

Selecting a larger sample than recommended will make any statistical test more powerful, and selecting a smaller sample will make any test less powerful. The reason for this is related to the contents of the previous chapter. Remember that when larger samples are used, "the long run" is approximated. The "law of averages" states that larger samples contain smaller sampling errors than smaller samples. Thus, with larger samples we are more likely to dismiss chance, or sampling error, as the cause for an apparent relationship between variables within a sample and to reject the null hypothesis. With larger samples we are unlikely to miss a true relationship (commit a Type II error).

The fact that the inherent statistical power of a test can be adjusted through sample size is an important point to remember. Selecting a wrong sample size may result in a statistical analysis that is not powerful enough to identify a true relationship between variables. However, it can also produce, an analysis that is too powerful, one which would result in conclusions about relationships that can become dangerously misleading. As suggested earlier, an overly powerful statistical analysis can detect relationships between variables that may be real but are so weak in the absolute sense that they are best left undiscovered and unreported. Generally, if we adhere to the recommended sample size for a given test, we can avoid the problems often associated with an overly powerful statistical analysis.

Let us now summarize the factors that affect the power of a test and how each affects it. A statistical test is less likely to produce a Type II error (it is regarded as "more powerful") if

1. the true relationship between variables is strong rather than weak;
2. a higher (e.g., .10 rather than .05) rejection level is used and, in case of a one-tailed research hypothesis, if the direction of the relationship between the two variables is correctly predicted;
3. the variation in the values of a variable is small rather than large;
4. the sample used is large rather than small.

Robustness of a Statistical Test

The fifth concept to consider in selecting a statistical test is its robustness. In everyday English, power and robustness mean something very similar. They do, however, have very different meanings when used in statistical analyses. As we know, the power of a statistical test is its ability to detect a true relationship between variables. Not to be confused with power, *robustness* is the degree to which a specific statistical test produces accurate findings when one or more of its assumptions is not met. Thus, robustness of a test is relative—every test is more or less robust.

As noted earlier, all statistical tests have certain assumptions (conditions) for their use. Generally, these relate to sampling methods used, the shape of the distribution of one or more variables within the population, and level of measurement of one or more variables as well as other possible assumptions specific to that test. The optimum sample size often also is specified. A relatively robust test, therefore, is one that still produces reasonably accurate results even if one or more of its assumptions for its use cannot be fully met.

The *t* tests described in Chapter 11 are good examples of robust tests. Two of their assumptions, for example, are that the dependent variables used in the tests are at the interval or ratio level of measurement and the dependent variable is normally distributed within the population. When used with variables that are somewhat skewed, however, the results are not too distorted. A certain amount of flexibility about the usual assumption of a normal distribution is quite common among many other tests that are regarded as relatively robust.

Other Factors to Consider

The five main factors above are just the major considerations in selecting a statistical test. They apply to all test selection decisions. There are other factors to consider in the decision-making process, however. A research hypothesis, for example, may indicate that we need to examine more than just the relationship between two variables (*bivariate analysis*). We may need to examine the relationship among three or more variables (*multivariate analysis*).

In a multivariate analysis, if one of our variables is at the nominal level of measurement, we need to determine the number of value categories represented within the variable. If the variable is only dichotomous (e.g., yes, no), some tests are appropriate. But if there are three or more value categories for the variable (e.g., yes, no, undecided), other tests must be used.

PARAMETRIC AND NONPARAMETRIC TESTS

There are two general categories of statistical tests—parametric and nonparametric. *Parametric tests* require:

1. at least one variable (usually the dependent) is either at the interval or ratio level of measurement;
2. the dependent variable is normally distributed (within the population); if samples are drawn from different populations and then compared, the distributions of the variable within these different populations are required to have near equal variances;
3. cases have been selected independently, that is, they are randomly selected or, if an experimental design was used, randomly assigned to experimental and control groups.

Some additional requirements apply to different parametric tests. Other tests allow us to "waive" one or more of the above requirements. A test's special requirements are listed in more advanced statistics books, often along with a statement about its robustness, that is, what assumption of the test, if any, can be waived (and to what degree).

Generally, it is helpful to remember that if the mean and the standard deviation are appropriate descriptive statistics for summarizing a study's findings, parametric statistics may be appropriate for examining the relationships between variables.

Nonparametric tests are designed for research situations in which one or more conditions for the use of parametric tests do not exist, that is, their assumptions are not met. They do not require a normal distribution of the dependent variable within the population from which the sample was drawn. Some are intended for independently drawn samples; others are not. The number of samples, the number of cases within each sample, and the presence or absence of "ties" (cases with the same value of a variable) also are important factors in selecting one specific test from the many that exist.

Most nonparametric tests require only nominal or ordinal level data, but some are more demanding, requiring greater measurement precision. As a group, and on a general level, nonparametric tests are less powerful than parametric tests. That is, they are more likely to result in Type II errors.

Because nonparametric tests generally are designed for the analysis of nominal or ordinal level data (or interval and ratio level data that are not normally distributed), they are often ideally suited to use in social work research situations. As noted earlier, many dependent variables are not at the interval or ratio levels of measurement. Many are dichotomous (e.g., success, failure; rehospitalization, nonrehospitalization; passage, nonpassage of legislation; employment, unemployment of clients).

Nonparametric tests are more than just a second best choice designed for situations in which criteria for parametric statistics cannot be met. They have some distinct advantages over parametric tests and often are the best tests for addressing some of our statistical needs. A nonparametric statistic, for example, is especially useful when one or more of the following three conditions exist:

1. Samples have been compiled from different populations (and we wish to compare the distribution of a single variable within each of them).
2. Variables are at the nominal level of measurement, or value categories of the variables allow for just the rank ordering of responses.
3. Very small samples (e.g., as small as 6 or 7) are all that are available for study.

Fortunately, the relative lack of power of nonparametric tests can be compensated for, at least in part. As noted above, increasing sample size increases the power of any statistical analysis. Many nonparametric tests can be made just about as powerful as their parametric counterparts with the use of sufficiently large samples.

In many situations where nonparametric tests are appropriate, two or more tests could potentially be used, but they are likely to have different sample size requirements. As a general rule, the test that uses the larger sample size is likely to be the more powerful one. If we anticipate the need for more power in testing (such as when we anticipate that a relationship between variables may be weak, but it would be valuable to document its existence anyway), we should consider the possibility of using a larger sample.

MULTIVARIATE STATISTICAL TESTS

Another grouping of statistical tests examines the relationship among three or more variables. As noted earlier, they are collectively referred to as multivariate tests. There are dangers in using a series of bivariate statistical analyses to test the relationship between a number of independent variables and a single dependent variable. This procedure can easily result in a Type I error by causing us to stumble onto a spurious (not real) "relationship" only because so many possible combinations of variables have been examined. That is one reason why we need to understand the principles behind a multivariate analysis and to have a familiarity with some of its more common usages.

There are certain situations where a form of multivariate analysis is the preferred choice for a particular data analysis. A multivariate analysis is consistent with the multiple causation and systems theories of human behavior that dominate much of the social work literature. Like these theories, multivariate analyses allow us to attempt to sort out the complex interaction of variables that exist within our practice and research milieus.

Multivariate analyses differ from bivariate analyses in two important ways. First, as already stated, they examine the relationship among three or more variables (that is why they are called *multi*variate). Second, and more importantly, they examine the relationship among the variables **simultaneously**. What is meant by simultaneously as it relates to a statistical analysis?

Suppose we wished to examine the relationship among the independent variables "per capita income" and "rates of alcoholism" and the dependent variable "incidence of child abuse within various cities." A bivariate analysis might first look at the relationship between income and abuse and then the relationship between alcoholism and abuse. In contrast to these two bivariate analyses, a single multivariate analysis, using a single procedure, would look at the "total picture," including how income and alcoholism might be related and how all three variables (the two independent variables and the dependent variable) might be related and how they interact.

Since multivariate analyses are far more complicated to understand than bivariate analyses, they are the subject of many advanced statistics books and courses. An in-depth examination of them is well beyond the scope of this introductory book. While the brief descriptions of several multivariate tests we mention will not enable readers to perform multivariate analyses, we hope that they provide both an appreciation of the richness of this important area and an impetus to gain more knowledge about them.

GENERAL GUIDELINES FOR TEST SELECTION

Generally, we should use the most powerful test that can be justified in any given data analysis situation. Data are wasted if a less powerful test is used when the assumptions for a more powerful test can be met. As we know, a test should only be used under the conditions for which it was intended. Figure 7.1 presents a general guide for selecting the most appropriate statistical test when the relationship between one independent variable and one dependent variable is examined (bivariate analysis). The figure focuses on only one factor in test selection, the level of measurement of the dependent variable and the independent variable(s). More specifically, Figure 7.1 displays the names of several commonly used parametric tests and their corresponding nonparametric alternatives. We will discuss these tests in later chapters of this book.

Of course, as we have indicated, other assumptions relating to sampling methods or the shape of the distribution of a variable must also be considered. Figure 7.1 is just a beginning point for selecting the most appropriate statistical test.

Although parametric tests traditionally are believed to require interval or ratio level measurement of the dependent variable, some people argue that ordinal level data can be used when the intervals on the ordinal measurement are approximately equal. The decision to use ordinal level data with parametric statistics involves a close review of the data and others' opinions regarding the robustness of a specific parametric test.

What is certain is that a nominal level dependent variable can only be assessed using nonparametric statistical tests. That is why there are no parametric counterparts for Chi-square, Fisher's exact test, and McNemar's tests. Nonparametric tests are most frequently used when the sample size is small, the sample distribution for the dependent variable is heavily skewed, or the data do not meet other assumptions of parametric tests.

There are a number of comprehensive source books on statistical test selection, many of which are available in most college and university libraries. Some present highly detailed flow charts for use in selecting statistical tests given various assumptions about a study's research design and the level of measurement of variables. To use such reference books, it always is necessary to know:

Parametric Statistical Tests			Nonparametric Statistical Tests		
Test	Dependent (Criterion) Variable	Independent (Predictor) Variable	Test	Dependent (Criterion) Variable	Independent (Predictor) Variable
—	—	—	Chi-square test	Nominal (2 or more categories)	Nominal (2 or more categories)
—	—	—	Fisher's exact test	Nominal (2 categories)	Nominal (2 categories)
—	—	—	McNemar's test	Nominal (2 categories)	Nominal (2 repeated measures)
Independent t test	Interval/ratio	Nominal (2 categories)	Mann-Whitney U test	Ordinal	Nominal (2 categories)
Dependent t test	Interval/ratio	Nominal (2 repeated measures)	Wilcoxon Sign test	Ordinal	Nominal (2 repeated measures)
One-way ANOVA	Interval/ratio	Nominal (3 or more categories)	Kruskal-Wallis test	Ordinal	Nominal (3 or more categories)
Pearson's r	Interval/ratio	Interval/ratio	Spearman rho test	Ordinal	Ordinal
			Kendall's tau test	Ordinal	Ordinal
Simple linear regression	Interval/ratio	Interval/ratio	—	—	—

FIGURE 7.1 Using Level of Measurement to Determine the Appropriate Statistical Test to Examine the Relationship between Two Variables

- the level of measurement of the dependent variable(s);
- the level of measurement of the independent variable(s);
- exactly how the research sample was obtained and its size;
- how the dependent variable(s) (and independent variable[s], if appropriate) is (are) distributed within the population from which it (they) was (were) drawn.

GETTING HELP WITH DATA ANALYSES

This chapter has focused on the process involved in selecting a statistical test(s) to analyze the relationship between variables. It has introduced the complicated task of selecting the most appropriate statistical test(s) for hypothesis testing and noted some of the many different factors that need to be considered when selecting a test from the many that exist. We have definitely not provided the answer to the question, "What statistical test should I use given my specific research situation?"

While Figure 7.1 along with the books listed in the References and Further Readings section located at the end of this book can be helpful in test selection, current computer technology has made it even easier for us to select a test.

Computer statistical software programs are now available that use the information provided by the researcher—the level of measurement of the independent and dependent variables, the shape of their distributions, and the sampling method used—to suggest which statistical test(s) is (are) most appropriate for use. As these programs become more widely available, decision-making charts such as Figure 7.1 will no longer be necessary. (In fact, the authors of one of the most comprehensive test selection reference books now have a computer version of their book.)

Computers cannot tell us what meaningful research problems to pursue or what hypotheses to test (not yet, anyway). They cannot tell us how to conceptualize, operationalize, design, implement, and gather data to test our research hypotheses. For now, these tasks are left up to us.

Computers can, however, quickly produce descriptive statistics, frequency distributions, and graphs that accurately describe our sample or population. They can also tell us the likelihood (based upon probability) that chance, or sampling error, may have produced a relationship between two or more variables within the data set. But even with their assisted statistical test selection and their high-powered number crunching, we still need to know how to interpret the findings they derive and decide if the findings are truly meaningful. If the findings are meaningful, we need to determine how to relate them to social work practice.

For those who lack access to either computer software packages for computer-assisted statistical test selection and/or to the most up-to-date reference books, consultation with experts is available to assist us in the task of research design and statistical analyses. In schools and departments of social work, and in many social service organizations throughout North America, there are people who know a lot about statistical analyses. But they can help us only if we know what questions to ask, how to ask them, and can comprehend and respond appropriately to the questions they ask.

Because so many statistical tests are available, even the experts cannot be knowledgeable about all of them. In fact, probably fewer than one or two dozen tests are commonly used in social work research, another group is seen occasionally in the literature, and a third group consists of a large number of relatively obscure tests. Widespread computerization of data analyses has made some tests popular and widely used that previously were avoided because of their long, complicated formulas.

Multivariate statistical tests, for example, are used much more frequently than they were 10 or 20 years ago. Other tests that were very popular (primarily because of their ease of hand calculation) prior to computer data analyses (e.g., some of the nonparametric tests) are now less popular, since computers have made the use of better alternatives feasible. New tests are also continuing to be developed.

CONCLUDING THOUGHTS

This chapter, along with Chapters 5 and 6, discussed various aspects of two related activities that are a central focus of most social work research—inference and hypothesis testing. Understanding their theoretical underpinnings and knowing just how they work make it possible for us to comprehend why a statistical analysis is far more than just number crunching. We can now summarize the process of hypothesis testing as a series of seven steps as contained in this chapter and the previous two:

Step 1. *State the research hypothesis(es).* Is it one-tailed, two-tailed, or in the null form? Label the independent and dependent variables. How is each variable conceptualized and operationalized?

Remember: The research hypothesis guides the entire conceptualization and operationalization process. In addition, it helps to determine the best research design to use in an effort to rule out alternative explanations that could explain an apparent relationship between variables. Research hypotheses, if appropriate, should be supported by theoretical assumptions derived from a literature review.

A research hypothesis can be one- or two-tailed (and sometimes it can be in the null form). The research hypothesis is not statistically tested; it is either indirectly supported or not supported by directly testing the null hypothesis.

Step 2. *For any research hypothesis, state the corresponding null hypothesis.* Conceptualize how the data would look if the null hypothesis were, in fact, correct.

Remember: The null hypothesis states that there is no relationship between the variables in the research hypothesis. It covers all outcome possibilities that are not explicit in the research hypothesis. If a one-tailed research hypothesis, for example, states that the level of job satisfaction for medical social workers has increased significantly over the last four years, the null hypothesis must include the possibilities that it has either decreased or that it has not changed.

If the null hypothesis can be rejected, support is present for the one-tailed or two-tailed research hypothesis. Hypothesis testing is a process of indirect proof. We never directly prove that the research hypothesis is correct; rather, if the null hypothesis can be rejected, the research hypothesis (the alternative hypothesis) is supported only indirectly.

Step 3. *Specify the statistical rejection level to be used.* If any level other than .05 is to be used, specify the justification for its use. Which type of error, Type I or Type II, are we seeking to avoid and why?

Remember: This step entails determining the consequences of erroneously rejecting the null hypothesis. Most of us prefer to take a conservative position by setting a low rejection level (e.g., .01, .025, .05) rather than a higher one (e.g., .10, .15). We would rather commit a Type II error than a Type I error.

Step 4. *State all assumptions about the data and how they were collected.* What levels of measurement are assumed to exist? Which variables are assumed to be normally distributed? What specific sampling methods were employed? How large are the samples?

Remember: We must know the level of measurement for each of the variables to be analyzed. The method by which the sample is drawn, sample size, and the way our variables are distributed in the population also affect the choice of which statistical test to use.

Step 5. *Conduct a descriptive statistical analysis to describe the most relevant characteristics of the sample and/or population. Select and compute one or more statistical tests to test the research hypothesis.* Is each test used appropriate for the conditions described in Step 4? Is a computer package or consultant to be used in the selection of the tests? Is computation of the test to be computer assisted? If so, what statistical software package will be used? Conceptually, how will each test generate a p-value?

Remember: The statistical test used does not determine the degree to which rival hypotheses or design bias (e.g., measurement bias and sampling bias) may have helped to create an apparent relationship between variables. It only determines the likelihood that chance, or sampling error, played a role in the study's findings.

Step 6. *Determine whether the relationship between variables is statistically significant.* Is the probability (p-value) smaller than the predetermined rejection level? If a one-tailed research hypothesis was used, is the direction of the relationship that was found the same as stated in the hypothesis? If so, are we reasonably certain that some other factors (e.g., rival hypotheses, design bias) besides chance, or sampling error, did not produce the relationship between the variables within the sample? If so, it probably is safe to reject the null hypothesis and to conclude that a true relationship between the variables exists within the population.

Remember: We can never be totally certain that chance, or sampling error, did not produce an apparent relationship between variables. When we reject the null hypothesis, we are saying only that we are reasonably certain that the apparent relationship is a real one—but we might still be wrong.

Step 7. *Determine if each statistically significant relationship is meaningful.* To what degree did sample size contribute to statistical significance? How strong is the absolute relationship between the variables? How useful are the study's findings to the social work practitioner, educator, or researcher? To what extent would we feel safe in generalizing the findings beyond our sample and the population from which it was drawn (external validity)?

Remember: These decisions require a thoughtful combination of ethics, common sense, convention, and practice expertise. They must be addressed before a study's findings are implemented in the social work practice milieu.

The chapters that follow present a description of a few statistical tests that have been widely used in social work research for many years and promise to remain popular. They are both versatile and suitable for many types of data analysis situations found in our profession. The emphasis will be on understanding what they do and what their results mean rather than on the mathematics of their computations. In today's professional environment, we usually can leave that job to the computers.

STUDY QUESTIONS

1. How can the use of an inappropriate statistical test harm the credibility of the research study?
2. How might a researcher's use of an inappropriate test ultimately have a negative effect on services to clients? Discuss. Provide an original practice example in your discussion.
3. How does the "rule of the instrument" sometimes lead to the selection of an inappropriate statistical test?
4. What factors related to sampling methods used help to determine which statistical test is appropriate?
5. What two characteristics of a variable also affect which statistical test should be used?
6. How does the operationalization of a variable performed before data are even collected serve to limit (or expand) our option of a statistical test that can be used? Provide original examples in your discussion.
7. What do we mean when we say that one statistical test is more "powerful" than another? What do we mean when we say that one test is more "robust" than another?
8. What factors affect the statistical power of a given test?
9. How is it possible for a test to be "too powerful"? What problems can a too powerful test create?
10. How is it possible for a test to be "not powerful enough"? What problems can a not powerful enough test create?
11. What three general assumptions must be met for a parametric test to be used?
12. Why are nonparametric tests particularly useful in many social work research projects? How can we make them more powerful?
13. Describe two ways in which a multivariate test differs from a bivariate one.
14. In what ways do multivariate analyses differ from bivariate analyses? Why are they less likely to cause a researcher to commit a Type I error?

Chapter **8**

Correlation

$\mathbf{I}$n one form or another, correlation is used in many phases of the research process—not just for analyzing data. It is discussed at this point (along with the following chapter) because it serves as a useful bridge between the topics of descriptive statistics (discussed in previous chapters) and inferential statistics (to be discussed in later chapters).

"Correlation" is a word, unlike many other terms contained in this book, that is used in statistical analyses much as it is used in everyday language. Correlation can be thought of as a generic term when used within statistical analysis. It encompasses a wide variety of statistical tests and examines the strength of a relationship between or among variables. When we wish to examine the correlation between two interval or ratio level variables, for example, we are really trying to ascertain to what degree certain values of one variable tend to be found with certain values of the other variable.

In most of the discussion in the previous chapters, we have been using the terms "independent variable" and "dependent variable." The terms "independent variable" and "dependent variable" are used to indicate the direction of influence between (or among) variables based upon logic. They generally are used in research hypotheses that suggest that one variable is believed to affect the other (more than vice versa).

In social work research we often are not seeking to demonstrate that one variable directly influences another variable; we wish only to find support for the belief that two variables that we have neither introduced nor manipulated in any way covary. If demonstration of covariance, or prediction, between variables is our study's main goal, two other terms are used to describe the relationship between variables. The variable that is used for prediction is called a *predictor variable*. The variable whose value categories (or values) we hope to predict (based upon the predictor variable) is called a *criterion variable*. As mentioned in Chapter 1, this chapter, along with the next one, will use the labels "predictor variable" and "criterion variable" in discussing the statistical concept of correlation. Correlation cannot be used to imply causality; the focus here is on covariance.

USES OF CORRELATION

Correlation is very versatile. It can be used for developing research designs and can be an integral part of developing some forms of data collection instruments, for example. It also can be used for examining the reliability of existing measuring instruments when they are used with different populations, different research situations, or at different times.

Teachers use correlation when they conduct analyses of their tests. They employ it to compare the responses to individual test questions with responses to other test questions or to student's overall performance on the test. They use correlation analyses to look for patterns in the way students answer one question compared to another or how they answer a specific question and how they perform overall on the test. Correlation can help us to conclude if a test question is a good one. As with all types of correlation analyses, however, such analyses stop at reliability.

If a correlational analysis tells us that a particular test question lacks one type of reliability, the question can also be assumed not to be valid. But if it indicates that a test question is reliable (at least in some ways), that is no guarantee that the question is valid (see Chapter 1).

Correlation is also widely used in descriptive statistics. It provides a numerical summary of the linear relationship between variables within a sample or population. It even describes the degree of correlation between two variables using simple graphs such as scattergrams.

Scattergrams

Unlike the other graphs presented in Chapter 2, which displayed how many times different values occur for a given variable (frequencies), *scattergrams* display all individual case values. Actually, they simultaneously portray all case values for two variables. They can thus begin to suggest the presence (or absence) of a correlation between variables. Each dot on a scattergram portrays the relationship between variables and represents one case (person or object).

If 23 clients, for example, completed a standardized self-administered measuring instrument that measures the variable "self-esteem," and also completed a standardized self-administered measuring instrument that measures the variable "client satisfaction with social work services," a scattergram could portray each person's score on both variables (i.e., self-esteem, satisfaction with social work services) with a single dot. The scattergram would simply have 23 dots—not 46—one to represent each of the 23 cases and their combination of measurements for the two variables.

In general, scattergrams have three general uses:

1. They are used to portray a possible relationship between variables.
2. They are used to graphically report relationships that have already been demonstrated to exist through the use of other statistical analyses.

3. They are used to identify and present patterns of possible relationships between variables that may exist within certain subsets of a larger data set but that might have tended to get "lost" when the total data set is statistically analyzed.

For example, there may be no apparent relationship between age (first variable) and job satisfaction (second variable) among blue-collar workers when we analyzed the data from a large sample of workers between the ages of 18 and 70. But when the same data were displayed using a scattergram, a relationship may have been quite evident within the age range 36–45.

Like most of the other graphs presented in Chapter 2, scattergrams use two perpendicular lines (i.e., x-axis, y-axis). Unlike the other graphs, however, scattergrams do not use the y-axis to plot and display frequencies. As can be seen in Figure 8.1, they simply plot the values of the first variable along the x-axis and the values of the second variable along the y-axis.

In a scattergram designed to detect and/or display a correlation, the x-axis is used to plot the values of the predictor variable and the y-axis is used to plot the values of the criterion variable, as shown in Figure 8.1. The terms "predictor" and "criterion" are used (rather than "independent" and "dependent") since correlation does not imply causation, a point emphasized throughout this chapter.

The values for the predictor and criterion variables for a scattergram may or may not have identical intervals. This is no problem since the values for the predictor variable can be marked off at equal intervals of five units, for example, while the values for the criterion variable can be marked off at equal intervals of ten units. Most statistical software packages that produce scattergrams automatically draw them to scale based upon the raw data that have been entered.

How might we suggest a possible relationship between variables using scattergrams? Suppose that we are interested in studying the relationship between the two variables "number of treatment sessions a client attended" (predictor variable) and his or her "self-esteem level" (criterion variable). We might hypothesize that among

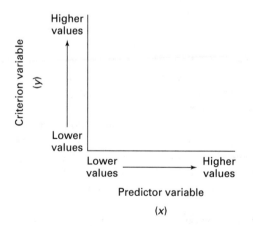

FIGURE 8.1 Basic Outline of a Graph for
Depicting Values for Two Variables

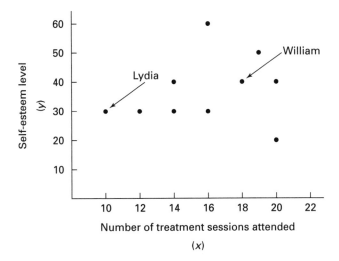

FIGURE 8.2 Scattergram: Number of Treatment Sessions
Attended and Self-Esteem Level

clients being treated for problems related to low self-esteem, there will be a positive association between current self-esteem levels and number of treatment sessions they attend; that is, the more treatment sessions they attended, the higher their self-esteem and vice versa. The number of treatment sessions attended (the predictor variable) and the client's self-esteem score (the criterion variable) could then be displayed as in Figure 8.2.

Each dot in Figure 8.2 represents an individual client's self-esteem level (y-axis) and the number of treatment sessions attended (x-axis). As can be easily seen, 10 individuals (dots on the graph) represent our small sample. Notice that Lydia, who attended 10 treatment sessions, had a self-esteem level of 30, but William, who attended 18 sessions, had a self-esteem level of 40. The fact that the dots in Figure 8.2 are scattered somewhat randomly (rather than falling in a straight line) suggests that the relationship between the two variables within our sample was by no means perfect.

Usually correlation is used to determine if a linear relationship exists between variables within a sample (or population, when all cases were studied)—descriptive types of research endeavors. But it is also sometimes used to test hypotheses about the relationship between variables (e.g., in explanatory research studies). This use of correlation (inference about relationships between variables in a population based upon their correlation within a sample) is discussed in more detail later in this chapter.

PERFECT CORRELATIONS

As noted previously, the correlation in Figure 8.2 is not perfect. An example of a perfect relationship between a predictor variable and a criterion variable can be seen in Table 8.1. The table contains two variables, "client's motivation for treatment" and

TABLE 8.1   Motivation for Treatment and Level of
Functioning ($N = 10$)

Name	Motivational Level (X)	Functioning Level (Y)
Floyd	1	2
Jane	2	3
Robert	3	4
Sue	4	5
Herb	5	6
Bill	6	7
Margareta	7	8
Ann	8	9
Dorothy	9	10
Lynne	10	11

"client's level of functioning." It simply summarizes hypothetical data for a sample of ten clients.

Each client has a pair of values. For every client value of the predictor variable (motivational level for treatment), there is a corresponding client value of the criterion variable (functioning level).

Note in Table 8.1 that if, prior to data collection, a one-tailed research hypothesis had been formulated (e.g., "Clients with higher motivational levels for treatment will have higher functioning levels than clients with lower motivational levels and vice versa"), the data would lend support to that hypothesis.

A relationship between the two variables in Table 8.1 is evident because, without exception, higher motivational levels for treatment are associated with higher levels of functioning and vice versa. Floyd, for example, scored lowest on both motivational level for treatment (1) and functioning level (2). Jane scored second lowest on both levels (scores of 2 and 3 respectively), and Lynne scored highest on both (scores of 10 and 11 respectively). This perfect relationship also can be depicted by means of a scattergram, such as the one in Figure 8.3.

In Figure 8.3, the horizontal axis (x-axis) represents the clients' individual scores (or measurements) of their motivational levels for treatment, while the vertical axis (y-axis) represents the individual scores of their functioning levels. Each dot represents a pair of scores for one person. The dots, if connected, form a straight line, indicating that the two variables are perfectly correlated. Such perfection is almost never seen in data drawn from social work research studies. It is used here to illustrate the concept of correlation in its most vivid form, prior to our discussion of the kind of correlations that we more commonly find in social work research and practice situations—nonperfect correlations.

When perfect, or even near perfect, correlations do occur in social work research, we must always wonder whether they really reflect a meaningful relationship between variables or whether what were assumed to be two variables were really just two different measurements of the same variable. In some social work agencies, for example,

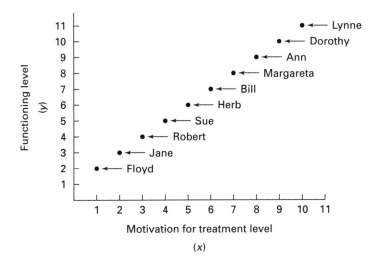

FIGURE 8.3 Scattergram of a Perfect Positive Correlation between Two Variables: Motivation for Treatment and Functioning Levels (from Table 8.1)

we probably could demonstrate a nearly perfect correlation between workers' years of employment and the total number of clients seen by them. But such a correlation would be neither meaningful nor surprising. The "two variables" may be just two different measurements of the same variable—seniority, age, or number of hours worked.

Strength and Direction

Figure 8.3 demonstrates two important characteristics of the perfect linear relationship between variables: strength and direction. With regard to strength, the overall relationship between the two variables contained in Figure 8.3 could not be stronger, as each one of the client's paired scores falls along a straight line. While Figure 8.3 is an example of a perfect positive correlation, Figure 8.4 is an example of a perfect negative correlation. In both figures, the dots fall in a straight line. In those more common situations where the relationship between variables is less than perfect, a line called a *regression line* (to be discussed in Chapter 9) can be drawn to represent "the best fit" among a scatter of dots.

In regard to the second characteristic of a correlation—direction—the relationship between the clients' motivation for treatment levels and their functioning levels, as displayed in Figure 8.3, can be described as positive. In a positive correlation, high values of x are associated with high values of y, and low values of x are associated with low values of y.

In a negative relationship, such as the one displayed in Figure 8.4, high values of one variable are associated with low values of the second and vice versa. Figure 8.4

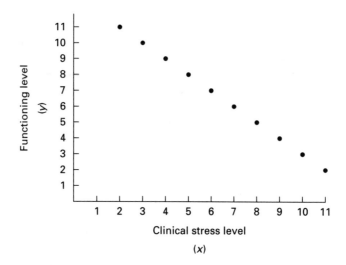

FIGURE 8.4 Scattergram of a Perfect Negative Correlation Between Two Variables: Clinical Stress and Functioning Levels

suggests that higher clinical stress levels (predictor variable) were associated with lower functioning levels (criterion variable).

NONPERFECT CORRELATIONS

In social work research, some relationships between variables may have no discernable direction as well as no strength; that is, there is no apparent relationship at all between them. Figure 8.5 displays hypothetical data in which there is no perceivable relationship between the variables, "self-esteem" and "aggression." In other words, we could not say that the more (or less) self-esteem that clients have, the more (or less) aggressive they are (at least in this sample anyway).

Virtually all relationships between variables reflect some degree of correlation, usually ranging from barely discernable to nearly perfect, that is, nonperfect correlations. Figure 8.6 is a scattergram illustrating a less than perfect positive correlation between the variables "number of treatment sessions attended" and "clients' attitudes toward their peers." The relationship is still positive, but it is not perfect, like the one reflected in Figure 8.3.

Figure 8.6 shows that three clients were seen only once by a social worker, but one client (Sue) scored a 2 on the Attitudes Toward Peers Scale, another (Robert) scored a 4, and a third client scored a 6. So, the relationship between the variables is far from perfect, even though the dots fall in an overall positive direction (bottom left to upper right). In contrast, Figure 8.7 reflects no relationship at all between the variables "depression level" and "motivation for treatment."

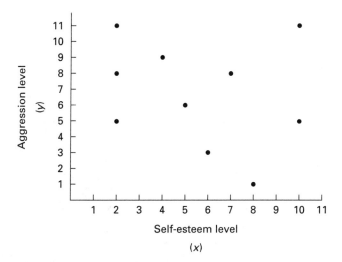

FIGURE 8.5 Scattergram of No Correlation between Two Variables: Self-Esteem and Aggression Levels

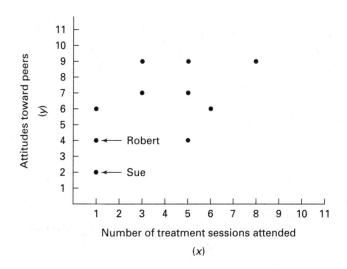

FIGURE 8.6 Scattergram of a Nonperfect Positive Correlation between Two Variables: Number of Treatment Sessions Attended and Attitudes Toward Peers

INTERPRETING LINEAR CORRELATIONS

The dots in scattergrams (each reflecting one value for the predictor variable and one value for the criterion variable for each case) can fall in a variety of patterns, such as a straight line, a "U" shape, and a "J" shape. The dots in a scattergram might look like a

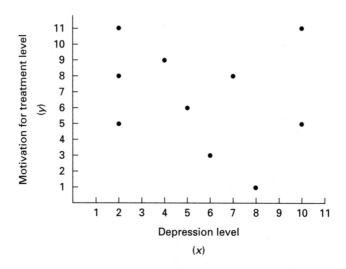

FIGURE 8.7 Scattergram of No Correlation between Two Variables: Motivation for Treatment and Depression Levels

series of waves (cyclical correlation), for example, or a line that is curved like either an arch or an upside down arch (curvilinear correlation). A clear pattern in a distribution of dots and the fact that they form a straight or curved line indicate the presence of a relationship between variables.

Observing the pattern in which the dots in a scattergram fall is useful for understanding and drawing tentative conclusions about relationships between variables. It also tells us whether it is appropriate to use certain statistical tests that examine correlation but have certain assumptions about the overall pattern of a correlation between the two variables.

The statistical tests in this chapter, for example, test for the degree to which two variables are linearly correlated. They are not used appropriately to examine relationships between variables that may be related, but not in a linear way.

Scattergrams are one way of displaying the paired values for two variables within any given data set. A more efficient way of displaying the relationship between two interval or ratio level variables is through the use of a correlation coefficient. A correlation coefficient, expressed as the lowercase italicized letter r, provides a numerical indicator of both the strength and the direction of the relationship between variables.

The Correlation Continuum

As Figure 8.8 shows, correlation coefficients range along a continuum—from -1.0 (perfect negative) at one extreme to $+1.0$ (perfect positive) at the other extreme, with 0.0 (no linear correlation) at the midpoint. A correlation coefficient cannot be greater than $+1.0$ or less than -1.0. The closer the numerical value of the correlation coefficient is to either extreme ($+1.0$ or -1.0), the stronger the linear relationship between

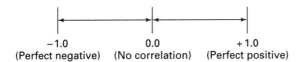

FIGURE 8.8 The Correlation Coefficient Continuum

the two variables. A coefficient of +.72, for example, is closer to a perfect correlation than coefficients of either −.60 or +.60 and therefore suggests a stronger correlation than either of the other two.

The closer the coefficient is to the middle of the continuum (0), the weaker the relationship between the two variables. A correlation coefficient that is close to 0 suggests that the linear relationship, if any, is quite weak.

The plus (+) or minus (−) sign of r indicates the direction of the relationship. The correlation coefficient (r) between a social worker's skill level and years of professional social work experience, for example, might be $r = +.45$, a positive relationship. The correlation between skill level and level of apathy regarding one's work might be $r = -.35$, indicating a negative relationship; that is, persons who are most apathetic and uninvolved in their work are likely to be less skillful and vice versa.

The sign of a correlation coefficient (+ or −) should be used only as an indicator of the direction of a relationship between variables. Thus, if a correlation coefficient is negative (that is, preceded by a minus sign), this does not mean a negative value for the correlation as it would in the usual mathematical sense. It merely indicates that, to the extent suggested by the value of the correlation coefficient, lower values of one variable tend to be found with higher values of the other variable and vice versa.

Interpreting Very Strong Correlations. As noted earlier, when a correlation coefficient approaches 1.0 (whether the sign is either positive or negative), it may have a special meaning. Very high coefficients, say .93 or .96, may indicate that the two variables that are so very highly correlated may really be just different indicators of the same variable. To use an extreme example, if we performed a correlation analysis among a group of social work students for the variables, "number of classes missed" and "number of classes attended" over the course of a semester, we would get a perfect, negative correlation coefficient (−1.0). This would not be surprising since classes missed and classes attended are indicators of the same variable, class attendance. In a less obvious way, the same interpretation might apply if the correlation coefficient between variables is very high, but not perfect. Suppose that a research study examined the relationship between assertiveness and timidness. A statistical analysis might produce a correlation coefficient of, say, −.95. Is this an important finding? Or a surprising one? Probably not. A logical interpretation might be that timidity and assertiveness are really "opposite sides" of the same concept.

Often very high correlation coefficients between variables are not of much value except, of course, to confirm that two "variables" are really one and the same. Usually, the relationship between both variables is obvious and predictable without computing a correlation coefficient. Thus, fairly strong correlation coefficients or even those that are just moderately strong may have greater potential to contribute to our body of knowledge than very strong ones.

The Coefficient of Determination

The correlation coefficient produced by a statistical test of correlation indicates the degree and the direction in reference to how the two variables co-vary. But if the coefficient (r) thus produced is squared (r^2), we can learn much more. The new number (r^2) indicates the proportion of the variation in one variable that can be "accounted for," or is "related to," the variation in values of the other variable. r^2 is called the *coefficient of determination*.

An r value of $+.80$, for example, describing the correlation between number of treatment interviews and self-esteem levels, means that 64 percent ($+.80^2 = +.64$ or 64%) of the variation in self-esteem levels is related to the variations in number of treatment interviews. The other 36 percent ($100\% - 64\% = 36\%$) of variation in self-esteem levels remains unaccounted for and is related to variation within values of other variables.

In interpreting a correlation coefficient, it is important not to treat it as if it were equivalent to ratio level data or to make statements that in any way give this impression. A correlation coefficient of $+.80$, for example, is not twice as strong as one that is $+.40$. At least in one sense—its ability to account for the amount of variation in the criterion variable from the variation in the predictor variable—a correlation of $+.80$ describes an association four times as strong ($+.80^2 = .64$; $+.40^2 = .16$; $.64/.16 = 4$).

It is also useful to remember that in those rare correlation coefficients as strong as $+.80$, there will be few exceptions to the pattern of relationships between values of one variable and values of the second variable; that is, virtually all high values of the first variable will be found in cases with high values of the second variable and vice versa. A weaker correlation coefficient (such as $+.40$) will have a much higher percentage of cases that reflect a relationship between variables opposite to the overall direction of the association.

Correlation Is Not Causation

What a correlation coefficient cannot do is tell us whether or not the value of the criterion variable has been caused by the value of the predictor variable. As suggested earlier, correlation should not be used to make any statement about causation. Why not?

Unlike a research experiment in which we introduce or manipulate the independent variable, a correlational analysis generally is used to examine the pattern of a relationship between variables for which data (on both the predictor and criterion variables) have already been randomly distributed. We do not introduce, or control, measurements of the predictor variable; rather, its natural variation is observed along with that of the criterion variable. Thus, any interpretation of correlation that implies causation goes far beyond the utility of the concept.

What is the relationship between correlation and causation? Correlation is necessary but not sufficient for proof of causation. This means that where causation exists between variables, those same two variables always will be correlated. Just because two variables may co-vary, however, there is no reason to believe that they possess a relationship that involves causation. There may be many other possible explanations for a correlation between them besides a cause-effect relationship.

Many pairs of variables tend to co-vary; they could thus be demonstrated to be correlated. Any statement suggesting causation is ludicrous. A few examples include (1) ice-cream sales as a predictor variable and drowning rates as a criterion variable, (2) bible sales as a predictor variable and whiskey sales as a criterion variable, and (3) diet drink consumption as a predictor variable and weight of individuals as a criterion variable.

More often than not, a correlation between a predictor and a criterion variable is easily explained by the effects of one or more other variables. In the previous three examples, other variables such as "temperature," "per capita income," and the "greater tendency of overweight persons to watch their caloric intake," respectively would help to explain any linear correlations between the variables that could be demonstrated using statistical analyses.

Example: Education and Financial Success. Sometimes the influence of other predictor variables on a correlation is less obvious. We all have heard media exhortations to young people to complete high school and, if possible, to go to college. The appeal usually includes correlational data about the relationship between the variables "educational level" (predictor variable) and "lifetime earnings" (criterion variable). A statement is made that the farther people go in school, the more money they will make over their lifetimes. A cause-effect interpretation of correlation data is implied. The correlation between educational level and lifetime earnings may be undeniable. Can it be interpreted to mean that continuing to stay in school will automatically increase one's earning potential? No!

The criterion variable "financial success in life" may be strongly correlated with other predictor variables such as "motivation," "intelligence," and "socioeconomic status of parents." All these variables could reflect a stronger correlation with lifetime earnings than would educational level. They may also contribute to high levels of education **and** to lifetime earnings.

The complex interaction of variables that relate to lifetime earnings argues against any statement implying causation, despite the fact that many different correlations could be demonstrated to exist. All other things being equal (and when does this ever occur?), the high school diploma or college degree might give a person an edge in being financially successful. However, this is not a conclusion drawn from only a simple correlation between the variables "educational level" and "lifetime earnings."

Using Correlation for Description

As mentioned previously, a correlation coefficient is a numerical summary of the strength and direction of the association between two interval or ratio level variables. As such, it can be used as a mathematical alternative to a scattergram for communicating to the reader of a research report how the values of one variable were correlated with the values of another variable. For example, it might be useful for the reader of a report to know that within a sample of employees studied in a social service agency, there was a high negative correlation between the variables "employee's age" and "number of claims for disability insurance." This information might be valuable, even though such a correlation may not be typical or representative of social work agencies in general. Knowing about it would help readers to better understand the unique research sample and setting of the study as well as to recognize differences between the study's setting and their own.

As suggested in Chapter 5, statistical significance does not guarantee meaningfulness. In interpreting the strength of a correlation coefficient, we must also take into consideration the way in which a correlational analysis is to be used. Even when a statistically significant correlation coefficient is obtained, the correlation may not be strong enough to represent a meaningful finding. It should also be remembered that a statistically significant, relatively low correlation coefficient may represent a meaningful finding in one study, but a relatively high correlation coefficient in another study may be relatively unimportant. Even identifying no association ($r = 0$) between variables that are believed to be related may represent the most important finding of a study.

COMPUTATION AND PRESENTATION OF PEARSON'S r

Correlations are used in different ways. Similarly, a correlation coefficient (ranging from $r = +1.00$ to $r = -1.00$) can be computed using many different statistical formulas. The most commonly used one results in a Pearson's product moment correlation coefficient, or simply Pearson's r. It is regarded as parametric and its assumptions state that both the predictor and criterion variables should be at the interval or ratio levels of measurement and normally distributed within the population.

A Pearson's r can easily be computed with the aid of a computer. Box 8.1 is provided for readers who wish to see the mathematical foundations of the r formula. It uses ratio level data on the number of spouse abuse reports (the predictor variable) and the number of child abuse reports (the criterion variable). The raw data are listed in the x- and y- columns in Table 8.2. Notice how the predictor variable and criterion variable could easily be reversed; this reversal process would mean that the number of spouse

TABLE 8.2 Number of Spouse Abuse and Child Abuse Reports in Five County Social Services Offices

Office Number	Spouse Abuse Reports (X)	Child Abuse Reports (Y)	X^2	Y^2	XY
Office 1	22	25	484	625	550
Office 2	20	13	400	169	260
Office 3	10	10	100	100	100
Office 4	15	5	225	25	75
Office 5	9	0	81	0	0
Totals . . .	76	53	1290	919	985

Box 8.1
The Correlation Coefficient

Hypothesis: There is a positive association between the the number of spouse abuse reports and the number of child abuse reports.

Null Hypothesis: There is no association ($r = 0$) between the number of spouse abuse reports and the number of child abuse reports.

Predictor Variable: Number of spouse abuse reports — ratio level.

Criterion Variable: Number of child abuse reports — ratio level.

Observed Frequencies: See Table 8.2.

Correlation Coefficient Formula:

$$r = \frac{N\Sigma XY - (\Sigma X)(\Sigma Y)}{\sqrt{[N\Sigma X^2 - (\Sigma X)^2][N\Sigma Y^2 - (\Sigma Y)^2]}}$$

where:
r = Correlation coefficient
N = Number of cases
ΣXY = Sum of xy column
ΣX = Sum of x column
ΣY = Sum of y column
ΣX^2 = Sum of x^2 column
ΣY^2 = Sum of y^2 column

Substituting values for letters:

$$r = \frac{(5)(985) - (76)(53)}{\sqrt{[(5)(1290) - (76)^2][(5)(919) - (53)^2]}}$$

$$= \frac{897}{\sqrt{(674)(1786)}}$$

$$= \frac{897}{\sqrt{1203764}}$$

$$= \frac{897}{1097.16}$$

$$= .82 \text{ (correlation coefficient)}$$

Presentation of Results:

$$r = .82, \, p < .05$$

Conclusions: The null hypothesis is rejected and the one-tailed research hypothesis is supported. In short, there is a statistically significant association between the number of spouse abuse reports and the number of child abuse reports. The coefficient of determination, r^2, is $(.82)^2$ or .67. This indicates that 67 percent of the variance in the number of child abuse reports can be explained by the number of spouse abuse reports.

abuse reports would become the criterion variable and the number of child abuse reports would become the predictor variable.

Presentation of *r*

If more than just a few bivariate correlation coefficients are reported as descriptive statistics within a research report, reporting them in tabular form may be helpful to the reader. A table designed for this purpose is called a *correlation matrix*. It lists all variables in a column on the left side and repeats them in a row along the top. The reader can find the direction and strength of a correlation between any two variables by noting the correlation coefficient that appears in the matrix where the row in which the first variable appears intersects with the column headed by the second variable.

When the results of a hypothesis testing using a correlation analysis appear in a research report, a short narrative description is usually included to elaborate on its meaning. The text might read, for example, like this:

> Among the 30 clients participating in the research study, the correlation between the number of treatment interviews they completed and their self-esteem scores was $r = +.72$, $p < .01$ (one-tailed test). This means that their self-esteem was positively correlated with the number of times they were seen by the social worker.

> Or:

> The correlation between the predictor and criterion variables for the 30 clients was $r = +.72$, $p < .01$, which indicates the presence of a statistically significant, positive correlation between the two variables.

NONPARAMETRIC ALTERNATIVES

Sometimes we cannot meet the assumptions of a parametric test like Pearson's *r*, but we still wish to compute a correlation coefficient. This is possible using various nonparametric tests that require only ordinal level data (or interval or ratio level data that are skewed). They are commonly used in situations where, if normally distributed interval or ratio level data were present, Pearson's *r* would be used. Two of the most commonly used such tests are discussed together because they are so similar that they may be considered almost interchangeable. They are Spearman's rho and Kendall's tau.

Spearman's rho and Kendall's tau

Like Pearson's *r*, Spearman's rho and Kendall's tau produce a correlation coefficient that is either positive or negative and that has a numerical value between $+1.0$ and -1.0. But while Pearson's *r* uses all the case values of two variables in its formula to see to what degree and in which direction (positive or negative) the variables are correlated, both of these nonparametric correlational procedures focus on the ranks of research participants (or objects) for each of the two variables (rather than their exact values).

Both formulas, for example, use the fact that a given person might have ranked highest in the sample (or population) on the ordinal level variable of "motivation" and third on another ordinal level variable, "socioeconomic status." Another person may have ranked fifth on both variables, another second on the first and seventh on the latter, and so on.

The actual case values for each pair of variables, while used in determining an individual's rankings on the variable, are not used in their formulas. This makes the tests about equally powerful to each other (i.e., able to detect the presence of a real correlation between variables) but slightly less powerful than Pearson's r. When both Spearman's rho and Kendall's tau are computed using case rankings for two variables within the same data set, they generally produce slightly different correlation coefficients, but very similar p-values.

Like most statistical tests, both Spearman's rho and Kendall's tau are available on many personal computer statistical software packages. They can, of course, be computed by hand as well. If this is done, however, two factors must be considered in determining which of the two slightly different formulas should be used: (1) the size of the sample and (2) the number of "ties" (more than one case sharing a ranking for a variable) present within the raw data set.

USING CORRELATION FOR INFERENCE

As noted earlier, correlation can even be used for inference—testing the likelihood that an apparent relationship between variables within a sample may be the work of chance, or sampling error. How large an r do we need when examining sample data in order to conclude that we can safely reject the null hypothesis and be able to claim statistical support for the position that two variables may be related within a population? It should come as no surprise to us that it depends on the size of the sample.

It also should come as no surprise that for a relationship between variables to be considered statistically significant, a correlation coefficient must be larger than the corresponding correlation coefficient at our predetermined rejection level. Unless previously stated and justified, the .05 rejection level is used as the reference point for determining whether we can claim statistical significance for a relationship between variables.

The table of critical values of r contained in Table 8.3 and Appendix B illustrates the strength of a correlation coefficient that is required to achieve statistical significance at various rejection levels and with various size samples. With a sample of 11 individuals, for example, a correlation coefficient of + or −.6021 is required with a two-tailed research hypothesis to reach statistical significance at the .05 rejection level (+ or −.7348 at the .01 level) and thereby to permit rejection of the null hypothesis. Of course other alternative explanations for a relationship between variables (besides chance) should have been adequately controlled too. With a sample size of 102 cases, however, rejection of the null hypothesis is possible with a much weaker correlation coefficient (+ or −.1946 at the .05 level and + or −.2540 at the .01 level). How can this be?

TABLE 8.3 Critical Values of *r*

N	Level of significance for a one-tailed test				
	.05	.025	.01	.005	.0005
	Level of significance for a two-tailed test				
	.10	.05	.02	.01	.001
5	.8054	.8783	.9343	.9587	.9912
6	.7293	.8114	.8822	.9172	.9741
7	.6694	.7545	.8329	.8745	.9507
8	.6215	.7067	.7887	.8343	.9249
9	.5822	.6664	.7498	.7977	.8982
10	.5494	.6319	.7155	.7646	.8721
11	.5214	.6021	.6851	.7348	.8471
12	.4973	.5760	.6581	.7079	.8233
13	.4762	.5529	.6339	.6835	.8010
14	.4575	.5324	.6120	.6614	.7800
15	.4409	.5139	.5923	.6411	.7603
16	.4259	.4973	.5742	.6226	.7420
17	.4124	.4821	.5577	.6055	.7246
18	.4000	.4683	.5425	.5897	.7084
19	.3887	.4555	.5285	.5751	.6932
20	.3783	.4438	.5155	.5614	.6787
21	.3687	.4329	.5034	.5487	.6652
22	.3598	.4227	.4921	.5368	.6524
27	.3233	.3809	.4451	.4869	.5974
32	.2960	.3494	.4093	.4487	.5541
37	.2746	.3246	.3810	.4182	.5189
42	.2573	.3044	.3578	.3932	.4896
47	.2428	.2875	.3384	.3721	.4648
52	.2306	.2732	.3218	.3541	.4433
62	.2108	.2500	.2948	.3248	.4078
72	.1954	.2319	.2737	.3017	.3799
82	.1829	.2172	.2565	.2830	.3568
92	.1726	.2050	.2422	.2673	.3375
102	.1638	.1946	.2301	.2540	.3211

Source: From Table VII of R.A. Fisher and F. Yates, *Statistical Tables for Biological, Agricultural, and Medical Research*, published by Longman Group, Ltd., London (previously published by Oliver and Boyd, Ltd., Edinburgh) and by permission of the authors and publishers.

The likelihood of demonstrating statistical significance with any statistical test that produces an r value (correlation coefficient) is related directly to sample size. As demonstrated in earlier chapters, it is more likely that chance, or sampling error, will cause two variables to appear to be related with a small sample than with a larger one. With larger samples, a relationship, even one that appears quite weak, is far less likely to be the work of chance, or sampling error. If there were no true relationship between variables, the law of averages (the long run) should have taken effect with the use of a large sample—any early pattern of a relationship should have disappeared as new cases were added to it.

Example: Verbal Participation Among Female Group Members

Background.   Leon is a social worker in a family service agency. He leads several treatment groups of female adolescents. He recently became aware of the wide variation in verbal participation among his group members. While virtually all the members responded when spoken to, a few never made any unsolicited comments. Over a period of several weeks, Leon made it a point to ask some of the nonverbal members why they rarely participated verbally in the group sessions.

Of the seven members he asked, five replied with essentially the same answer—each was an only child in her family and had been taught by her parents that it was not her role to initiate communication. Leon then asked three of the most verbal adolescents, who tended to dominate group discussions, how many siblings they had. Their responses were six, seven, and nine respectively.

Hypothesis.   Based on his limited inquiries, Leon began to speculate on a possible relationship between the criterion variable "number of unsolicited comments" in group treatment, and the predictor variable "number of siblings in the family." He conducted a quick literature review to learn about such phenomena as social traits of only children, communication patterns among siblings, and variations in verbal participation in adolescent groups. Most of the literature seemed to confirm his rather unscientific observation that female adolescents with more siblings are more likely to volunteer comments than those with fewer siblings. He decided that he had sufficient justification for a one-tailed research hypothesis:

One-Tailed Research Hypothesis:
Among female adolescents in treatment groups, there will be a positive correlation between the number of unsolicited comments and the number of siblings.

Methodology.   It was a policy in Leon's agency to videotape group treatment sessions for use in staff supervision. He received permission from the agency administrator and the adolescent clients to use the videotapes from all his group treatment sessions to test his hypothesis. He operationally defined a case as being a female adolescent who attended at least 75 percent of group sessions over a four-month period. Thirty-seven clients met this criterion. Leon developed an operational definition for the variable, "unsolicited comments." An unsolicited comment was judged to have been made only if both Leon and a colleague (who also viewed the tapes independently) agreed that it met that definition.

Leon totaled the number of unsolicited comments for each case and then divided by the number of sessions the client attended. This number provided the average number of unsolicited comments per session (the criterion variable) for each case. Case values for the predictor variable, "number of siblings," were acquired from agency records for each case.

Findings.   Leon used a personal computer to analyze his data. He entered a pair of measurements ("number of siblings" and "average number of unsolicited comments per session") for each case. Using Pearson's r, he achieved a correlation of $+.34$ with a corresponding $p < .025$. Leon knew that this meant that if he were to claim a relationship between the predictor and criterion variables, he would be on reasonably safe ground, assuming that something else (besides sampling error) had not produced the relationship between the two variables within his small sample. Another determination was required before support for his hypothesis could be claimed, however. Leon asked, "Was the association in the direction that he had hypothesized it would be—that is, a positive association?"

Because the correlation was positive, it meant that members who had high values for the variable "average number of unsolicited comments per session" should also tend to have high values for the variable "number of siblings," and vice versa. Yes, the data looked the way Leon had hypothesized that they would. He concluded that he had support for his one-tailed research hypothesis.

Limitations.   Leon was realistic about his findings. He had, for example, relied on a convenience sample and used only his own cases. Many potential design biases and other variables that might have affected his findings could have been present. Some bias may have been created within the sample as a result of case loss. Or, perhaps, Leon had just been a poor facilitator with certain members (those from small families) who were not used to being in group situations.

Perhaps the nature of comments that clients had made in the groups may have been misperceived when the content of the tapes was analyzed because of the poor quality of the camcorder that was used. Leon also recognized that the $+.34$ correlation coefficient between the two variables was really not that strong in an absolute sense.

Implications.   Leon's findings, even as qualified as they were, were certainly not without value. He summarized them in a weekly staff meeting for other social workers. His colleagues provided a critique of his research methods and identified several other possible design biases and rival hypotheses that if methodologically controlled would improve the design if he chose to replicate his study.

Leon and the other social workers who ran adolescent groups decided to make some adjustments to their practice methods. However, they agreed to evaluate the changes after six months. They decided to take three steps:

1. Staff would use the variable number of siblings (the data were available from the intake form) to create more homogeneous groups among new clients.

They felt that by placing what might be the most verbally assertive members (those with more siblings) in groups together, they could prohibit them from intimidating other group members who were less assertive. They also hoped that the more assertive clients would be less likely to dominate and monopolize discussion among persons most like themselves. In turn, some of those who the social workers believed to be less assertive (those with fewer siblings) might become more active and assertive in groups with persons more like themselves.

2. In other groups, new members from families with many siblings would be viewed as "at risk" to dominate discussions. Likewise, new members with no or few siblings would be viewed as at risk to be reticent to volunteer comments. This perception would affect the way in which the social worker would approach the role as facilitator with the more heterogeneous groups.

3. In all groups, leaders would facilitate discussion around such areas as attitudes toward the presence or absence of siblings, parental attitudes toward children's assertiveness, and so on.

Example: Worker Experience and Error Rates

Background.   Tanya is an administrator in a county department of social services. When she was hired, the error rate for eligibility determinations for new AFDC applications within her agency was among the highest in the state. She assumed that the problem must be related to the inadequate training of workers. She quickly took steps to increase training for all workers who had been employed by the agency for less than six months. She also required all senior workers who were not full-time supervisors to perform at least three eligibility determinations each week. To her surprise, one year after she implemented these decisions, the error rate had nearly doubled.

Tanya (and her supervisor!) were very concerned about the new error rate figures. Tanya wondered if her efforts to address a problem might possibly have made it worse. Why was increased training of newer workers, combined with greater use of more experienced personnel, associated with a dramatic increase in erroneous eligibility determinations?

In discussing this paradox with a staff member, Tanya began to speculate on what may have gone wrong. There had been a series of major changes in federal AFDC eligibility requirements over the past few years. Tanya had asked her senior workers to do more eligibility determinations because she thought that they would make fewer errors. They were not given additional training, however, to update them on the newer eligibility requirements. In fact, the use of senior workers who had not been retrained may have been a major contributor to the increased error rate.

Tanya did not wish to make another administrative decision that might not help the problem—or might make it even worse. If she were to recommend any future changes, she could not rely solely on a hunch. She intended to have data to back them up.

Hypothesis.   Tanya decided to examine the correlation between worker experience and error rate using data already available in the agency's management information system. Because she was interested in explaining differences in error rate, she labeled it her criterion variable; worker experience became her predictor variable. Based on a brief literature review and conversations with colleagues, she formulated a one-tailed research hypothesis:

One-Tailed Research Hypothesis:
There will be a positive correlation between years of worker employment and error rate.

Methodology and Findings.   Tanya used her personal computer at home to analyze the data. For each of 42 workers currently doing eligibility determinations, she entered a pair of values—number of years of experience and average number of identified errors per 100 cases (the last 100 reviewed).

The correlation coefficient reflecting the correlation between the variables "years of experience" and "error rate" was $-.21$. The corresponding p-value was greater than .05. Even if it had been less than .05, Tanya would not have been able to claim statistical support for her hypothesis. Why? The correlation within her population was negative—the correlation was in the exact opposite direction to what she predicted in her one-tailed research hypothesis.

Implications.   At first, Tanya's findings were a disappointment to her. The negative correlation suggested that the most senior workers in her sample had actually made fewer mistakes than those with less experience, not at all what she had expected. But she quickly reminded herself that the lack of support for her hypothesis did not mean that no new knowledge had been generated. In fact, her findings helped her to shift her focus away from past work experience and/or lack of recent training of senior workers as factors in the recent rise in error rates.

She then recalled that in her haste to reduce the error rate, she also had implemented another change—newer staff were given expanded training in making eligibility determinations. Perhaps the problem had been made worse by the introduction of the training for newer staff. Tanya knew that more training did not guarantee that workers would be better prepared to do their jobs. She began to question whether the training was accomplishing its goals. She decided that she would

1. design and implement an evaluative study of the current training for new eligibility workers;
2. continue to give senior workers increased responsibility for eligibility determinations and encourage them to assist newer workers in learning their jobs;
3. report her research findings to her superiors, informing them of her approaches to the problem (Steps 1 and 2) and make them aware of her concern about the high error rate and her attempts to correct it.

Example: Caregivers and the Longevity of Their Hospice Clients

Background.   Meredith is a social worker in a hospice program that provides services to caregivers of terminally ill clients. After working with hundreds of clients and their caregivers, it seemed to her that cancer clients whose caregivers were initially willing to use hospice services were more likely to live beyond their projected date of death than those who were more reluctant to use them.

Hypothesis.   Meredith decided to test the following one-tailed research hypothesis:

One-Tailed Research Hypothesis:
There is a positive correlation between caregivers' willingness to receive hospice services and the longevity of their clients.

Methodology.   Meredith tested the above one-tailed research hypothesis by conducting a small study using the nine clients who signed up for hospice services during the month of June. At the time they signed up, she and another social worker, who sat in on the initial interview, discussed each caregiver and then categorized them as "very reluctant," "somewhat reluctant," or "eager" to receive services. Then she followed each client and his or her family until the client's death, and she noted for each whether the client died "before," "at about," or "after" the time of death the client's doctor had projected when services were initiated.

Findings and Implications.   Meredith analyzed her data on the nine clients and examined the relationship between the predictor variable "caregivers' willingness to receive hospice services" and the criterion variable "longevity of the client" using Spearman's rho. She noted that her sample was small and that there were many ties in the rankings she compiled for the two variables, so she used the appropriate formula for these conditions.

It produced a correlation coefficient (r) of $+.24$ and a corresponding p-value greater than .05. By glancing at Table 8.3 or Appendix B, it can easily be seen that she needed a minimum correlation coefficient of .5822 for her analysis to produce statistical significance at the .05 level (with only nine cases).

Based upon her statistical analysis, Meredith concluded that she could not reject the null hypothesis. In short, she could not claim statistical support for her research hypothesis. She concluded that her observations may have been a bit of "wishful thinking" on her part. Just in case her hypothesis had been correct, however, she decided to test it again using a larger number of cases active in her agency over a one-year period.

CORRELATION WITH THREE OR MORE VARIABLES

Bivariate relationships frequently need further explication. Moreover, they can also be misleading. We are unlikely to explain how long a client remains in treatment, for example, based solely on data on the variables "severity of the client's presenting problem," "the client's motivation for treatment," or any other single variable. Both a systems perspective and other theories of multiple causation argue that many variables work together to affect a single variable such as a human behavior or attitude.

The accuracy of the relationship among variables can be improved by expanding the pool of available data to include more than two variables at one time in the data analysis. Decisions regarding the direction that this expansion should take as well as the additional sources and types of data needed to improve our understanding of the relationship are frequently the next critical steps along the data analysis continuum.

Partial *r*

There are some situations where we conclude that there is possibly one intervening variable that is so likely to "muddy the water" that it cannot be ignored. Often, this third variable (often called an "intervening" or "extraneous" variable) cannot be controlled by the study's research design. In order to assess a possible correlation between the variables, "age" and "amount of charitable contributions to a family service agency," for example, it may be necessary to use some method to control for a third variable, "yearly income."

A relatively simple statistical test, *partial r*, is available for this type of situation. Data on all three variables can be entered into the partial *r* formula, and a correlation coefficient can be obtained between any two of the variables while the influence of the third is mathematically "controlled" by adjusting case values.

Using partial *r*, we would be able to determine how large (and statistically significant or not) a correlation between the two variables, "age" and "amount of charitable contributions to a family service agency," would exist if the variations in the third variable, "yearly income," were not a factor in their relationship. A useful by-product of this analysis would be correlation coefficients reflecting correlations between the variables "yearly income" and "amount of charitable contributions to a family service agency" (controlling for age) and between "age" and "yearly income" (controlling for amount of charitable contributions).

A variation of the nonparametric Kendall's tau can be used when the assumptions of partial *r* cannot be met (normally distributed interval or ratio level variables). It is called *Kendall's partial rank correlation coefficient*. Like partial *r*, it is most useful in situations in which there is one potentially intervening or extraneous variable that cannot be controlled for by the research design. It thus represents an obvious other possibility for explaining the variations in values of the criterion variable, that is, it (rather than the predictor variable) may explain them.

Multiple *R*

A more sophisticated type of correlational analysis is available for situations in which we are interested in knowing the amount of variation of the criterion variable that can be explained by several predictor variables working in combination with one another. Multiple correlation (Multiple *R*) looks at a whole set of predictor variables together in order to determine the degree to which their combined variations correlate with different values of the criterion variable. It can be used to help identify the best set of predictor variables for explaining different values of the criterion variable.

It might tell us, for example, which interval or ratio level demographic variables might collectively reflect the highest correlation with a variable such as "rate of homelessness," "incidence of spouse abuse," or "degree of loneliness." An "at-risk" population consisting of people with a certain combination of characteristics might thus be identified.

Multivariate correlation analyses such as Multiple *R* often are superior to bivariate analyses, both for describing the characteristics of a sample and for testing hypotheses. They can easily examine the complexity of the interaction of three or more variables in a way that bivariate analyses cannot. They also help us avoid committing Type I errors by stumbling onto spurious (false) "relationships" that result simply from trying enough combinations of bivariate analyses until one finally reflects a statistically significant correlation.

Multiple R can extend our understanding of the relationship among variables. What if, for example, two or more predictor variables all reflect a high correlation with the same criterion variable? Would we not have an even better chance of explaining the variation within the criterion variable if we could use those two (or more) predictor variables that correlate highly with it? Yes. Logic tells us that our ability to explain the variation of a criterion variable is improved if we can determine the combined explanation capacity of a group of predictor variables.

Multiple R is designed for this task. It determines the degree to which a group of predictor variables correlate with the criterion variable. Finding the best combination of predictor variables to do this is not a simple task. We will see why.

Example: Social Work Students' Scores on a Statistics Exam.
Suppose that we want to find out how well several predictor variables might correlate with a social work student's score on a standardized statistics examination (the criterion variable). We might, for example, use four interval or ratio level predictor variables: (1) number of statistics courses taken, (2) number of hours of preparation, (3) undergraduate GPA, and (4) score on the mathematics section of the SAT. Let us assume for our purposes that they all are normally distributed.

Let us also say that the bivariate correlation between these variables and the criterion variable are, respectively, +.45, +.26, +.51, and +.74. To find out which two of these variables might be the best pair to explain the different scores that occur on the statistics examination and how well they would, in combination, explain their variation, we could not simply add the various pairs of bivariate correlations together. Why not? For one thing, adding the correlation coefficients for some of the pairs (e.g., +.51 and +.74) would produce a correlation coefficient greater than +1.00—and that is impossible. But more important, any two of the predictor variables (or three or all four of them) will share some of the same covariance with the criterion variable.

In other words, part of their bivariate correlation with the criterion variable will contribute nothing new to explaining the variation in values of the criterion variable—one predictor variable would account for some of the same variation as others. That is because the four predictor variables, in addition to having some correlation with the criterion variable, also have some degree of correlation with each other.

Continuing with our simple example, we would expect there to be a fairly high correlation between the predictor variables of "number of statistics courses taken" and "amount of preparation time," "number of statistics courses taken" and "score on the SAT mathematics section," and so on. Thus, these variables would not explain a unique amount of the variation of the criterion available. In fact, two predictor variables that are highly correlated with each other are unlikely to add much to our ability to explain variation within the criterion variable beyond what either one alone could have done. If they are perfectly correlated (+1.00 or −1.00) they are probably just two measurements of the same variable, and the use of both is redundant.

In short, Multiple R sorts out the degree to which any one predictor variable accounts for the variation in the criterion variable. It produces what is referred to as a beta weight for each predictor variable. *Beta weights* essentially are partial correlations and are based on (1) the correlation between each predictor variable and the criterion variable and (2) the correlations among the various predictor variables. By using both of these, Multiple R identifies what is unique within the correlation between a given predictor variable and a criterion variable—that is, the variation in the criterion variable associated with that predictor variable that is not already accounted for by some other predictor variable.

Even though a given predictor variable might have the highest bivariate correlation with the criterion variable (as in the case of the SAT mathematics score in our example), this is no guarantee that its beta weight will also be higher than that of the other predictor variables. If it is highly correlated with the other predictor variables, its beta weight may be relatively low.

Our example used only four predictor variables. But we probably could identify many more interval or ratio level variables that might be expected to correlate fairly highly with scores on a standardized statistics examination. Multiple R can be used with a large number of predictor variables. Unless we have a considerably larger number of cases than we have predictor variables, however, we can be led into making too much of the correlation coefficient thus produced. It might be quite high just on the basis of chance, or sampling error. To avoid this problem, Multiple R should be used only when the number of cases is substantially larger than the number of predictor variables to be included in the statistical analysis.

Variations of Multiple R.   There are variations of Multiple R, referred to as stepwise procedures, that can be very useful. One of these, referred to as the step-up procedure, involves a kind of rank ordering of the predictor variables. First, the predictor variable that is most highly correlated with the criterion variable is identified. Then, the next predictor variable that accounts for the most additional unexplained variation of the criterion variable is added to see how much the Multiple R correlation coefficient is affected.

The process can continue with other predictor variables added (in order of their contribution to the unexplained variance of the criterion variable) until we reach a "point of diminishing returns," that is, until we get down to those predictor variables that are of little value in accounting for any more variance within the criterion variable. The process allows us to narrow our list to only those predictor variables that are most important in explaining the variation of the criterion variable.

Another procedure, referred to as the step-down procedure, works in a similar way, but in the opposite direction. It begins with all the predictor variables and eliminates them one by one, starting with the one that explains the smallest amount of variation of the criterion variable. Predictor variables previously omitted can be re-added along the way to see how the multiple correlation coefficient is affected. Like the step-up procedure previously described, this procedure allows us to "winnow down" the list of predictor variables to a relatively small number that is most useful in explaining the variation of the criterion variable.

As mentioned throughout this book, there is a statistical analysis for just about any situation. There is yet another situation when still another type of correlation analysis is appropriate. Multiple R is used to obtain the correlation between one criterion variable and a group of predictor variables (sometimes called a *derived variable*). Another procedure, called *canonical correlation,* takes correlation even further. It is used to examine simultaneously the correlation between a weighted group of predictor variables (a derived predictor variable) and a weighted group of criterion variables (a derived criterion variable). The procedure is used in situations in which the criterion variable is somewhat abstract and cannot be adequately measured by using scores for any single variable.

Example: Interpersonal Skills on the Job. If we wanted to correlate a fairly abstract criterion concept, such as interpersonal skills on the job, we might have to ask coworkers to evaluate persons on several different criterion variables that are indicators of the concept, such as cooperativeness, communication ability, helpfulness, and so on. The weighted group of scores on these variables could then be correlated with another weighted group of scores on such predictor variables as education level, years of work experience, number of siblings, and so on, using canonical correlation to produce a Multiple R.

We would then be able to evaluate the Multiple R thus produced (or any other one produced by the procedures that we have described above) as to its strength and direction, using the same criteria that are used in evaluating the bivariate correlation coefficients produced by Pearson's r. All correlation coefficients, no matter what statistical procedure produced them, are interpreted in the same way, as previously described.

CONCLUDING THOUGHTS

This chapter presented just some of the many uses of correlation. It is used to design research studies, to refine data collection instruments, and to describe the relationship between and among variables within a population or sample. All correlation analyses produce a correlation coefficient that describes the strength and direction of an association (the extent of covariance) that exists between and among variables. It can be squared to gain an estimate of the amount of variation in the predictor variable attributable to the variation in the predictor variable or, when using Multiple R, to two or more predictor variables in concert.

This chapter is the first of five that describe specific statistical tests that can be used for hypothesis testing. We discussed the most commonly used test for examining the correlation between two normally distributed interval or ratio level variables (Pearson's r). We also described nonparametric and multivariate alternatives to Pearson's r that generate correlation coefficients and presented a conceptual overview of their calculations. We noted the effect that sample size has on statistical significance and the way that it mathematically explains why a correlation coefficient may be statistically significant while really quite weak.

With the statistical tests described in this chapter and with those that are described in subsequent chapters, we must take special care not to deliberately or unintentionally misrepresent our research findings. Like all statistical tests, tests of correlation do not control for possible rival hypotheses or various forms of design bias.

Chapter 9 builds upon the concepts contained within this chapter. It examines simple linear regression, another important function of statistical analyses, that we have only alluded to up to this point, prediction.

STUDY QUESTIONS

1. What can a scattergram portray that other graphs that we have examined cannot? What does each dot in a scattergram depict?
2. Construct hypothetical data on the variables "number of siblings" and "mother's highest school grade completed" for members of your class. Create a scattergram similar to Figure 8.3 to portray your data. Does the scattergram suggest that the two variables are related? If so, in which direction?
3. Why do we use the terms "predictor variable" and "criterion variable" rather than the terms "independent variable" and "dependent variable" in discussing correlation analyses?
4. In a correlation coefficient, what do the sign and the number each reflect?
5. What do we mean by linear correlation? Provide examples of variables that might be correlated in a nonlinear way.
6. What does r^2 tell us about the relationship between variables? Provide examples in your discussion.
7. Interpret each of the following hypothetical values for r: $r = -.45$; $r = +.45$; $r = +1.0$; $r = -1.0$.
8. Fill in the blanks to complete the following sentences: Correlation coefficients range from _____ to _____. A correlation coefficient suggests the _____ and the _____ of the relationship between variables. A correlation coefficient of _____ indicates a perfect positive relationship; _____ indicates a perfect negative relationship; and _____ indicates that there is no linear correlation between variables.
9. What are two nonparametric tests that can be used to examine correlation when the assumptions of Pearson's r cannot be met?
10. What do we call a type of correlation analysis that examines the correlation between two normally distributed interval or ratio level variables while controlling for the effects of a third variable?
11. What do we call the multivariate form of correlation analysis discussed in this chapter? What does it mean when we say that one predictor variable is "redundant of another" when we use this type of analysis? What do we call the procedures for adding or subtracting predictor variables based upon their ability to help explain variations in values of the criterion variable?
12. Find an article in a professional social work journal that used multiple correlation as the method of data analysis. What were the predictor variables? What conclusions did the author generate from the study? Do you feel the study was relevant to your future practice? Why or why not? What other predictor variables could the author have used?
13. When using multiple correlation, why can we not simply add together the individual bivariate correlation coefficients between two predictor variables and the criterion variable to find their combined correlation with the criterion variable? Explain.

Chapter **9**

Simple Linear Regression

As presented in Chapter 8, a correlation coefficient (expressed as an *r* value) provides us with an "overall picture" of the relationship between two variables—its strength and direction. We can use the laws of probability to determine if this relationship is sufficiently strong within a sample so that we can safely conclude that it probably was not caused by chance, or sampling error.

Another, related form of statistical analysis, *simple linear regression*, tells us even more about the relationship between two variables. By using simple linear regression, we can predict (with varying degrees of accuracy) what a value will be on the criterion variable when we know the value for a predictor variable for a person (or object).

WHAT IS PREDICTION?

In statistical analysis, prediction has a meaning similar to that of everyday usage. Specifically, it refers to determining (without measuring) what a specific value, for a variable, is most likely to be. Understanding statistical prediction involves many of the statistical concepts that we have discussed in the previous eight chapters. The mean and standard deviation (Chapter 3), the normal distribution (Chapter 4), and correlation (Chapter 8), for example, are all important to our understanding of prediction.

Let us see what statistical prediction is all about. Suppose we want to predict a new enrollee's (Joe's) score on a standardized life skills measuring instrument following a 12-week life skills training course for people with developmental disabilities. The instrument is administered in the program at 6 weeks (mid-program) and 12 weeks (termination). It produces scores that range from 0 (very poor life skills) to 100 (excellent life skills).

To make our prediction of Joe's most likely score at termination, we would have to base our estimate on some fact that we already know. If the only datum that we have is the mean life skills score at termination for all people who have completed the course, this mean (e.g., 82) would be our best estimate for predicting a final life skills score for Joe at the end of 12 weeks.

Clearly, such a prediction based on only a group's mean would provide a rather crude estimate. But we can do better. To improve our prediction, we might look to other data for help. Suppose we also know Joe's individual score from his 6-week assessment and the group's mean score after six weeks. We could use these data to make a more informed prediction about what Joe's final score is likely to be at 12 weeks.

Let us say, for example, that Joe's life skills score at six weeks was 79 and that the group's mean score at six weeks was 75. The distribution in Figure 9.1a shows that Joe scored higher than the group's mean at the 6-week assessment period. Thus, it would be reasonable to suggest that Joe would also score higher than the group's mean (i.e., 82) at the 12-week assessment period (presented in the distribution in Figure 9.1b).

Without any additional information about Joe or the program, we can statistically improve the accuracy of our prediction by considering the correlation between the scores at the 6- and 12-week assessment periods. As we know from Chapter 8, the correlation coefficient (r) between the two variables helps by telling us (roughly) how accurate our prediction will be. If the correlation is equal to zero, data from the 6-week assessment (distribution in Figure 9.1a) will not be of any help to us in predicting scores at the 12-week assessment (distribution in Figure 9.1b). In other words, we cannot compare data across the two distributions. If our correlation is $+1.0$ or -1.0, then we can make perfect predictions.

Understanding how perfect predictions are made requires knowledge about standard deviations and the normal distribution. Suppose there is a perfect positive linear correlation ($r = +1.0$) between the scores at the 6-week assessment and the scores at the 12-week assessment period. Thus, a client's position within the group at the 6-week assessment period would correspond perfectly to his or her position within the group at the 12-week assessment period. If a client's score was one standard deviation above the group's mean score at the 6-week assessment period, then his or her score at the 12-week assessment period would also be one standard deviation above the group's mean score. By using the means and the standard deviations for the two distributions of the variable at the 6- and 12-week assessment periods and the z score formula (Chapter 4), we could compute exactly what that score should be.

Let us take a closer look at Figures 9.1a and 9.1b. They show both the raw scores and the standard scores for the 6- and 12-week assessment periods. The standard deviation for the 6-week assessment period is 4, since the raw scores change by increments of 4 along the base of the 6-week distribution. This being the case, Joe would have scored one standard deviation above the mean for the 6-week assessment on the standard normal distribution (75 + 4 = 79). If the correlation between 6- and 12-week assessment scores was +1.0, we would know that Joe should have the same relative position on both normal distributions.

Thus, to predict Joe's score at the 12-week assessment period, we would find the raw score that corresponds to one standard deviation. As can be seen from the distribution in Figure 9.1b, Joe's predicted 12-week assessment score would be 87. It is one standard deviation above the mean, with $SD = 5$ (82 + 5 = 87). No matter what the

(*a*) 6-week assessment period

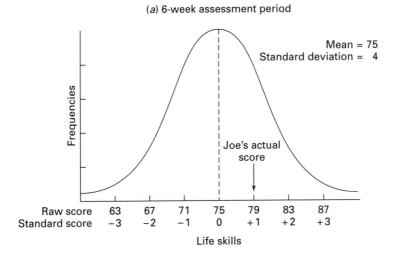

(*b*) 12-week assessment period

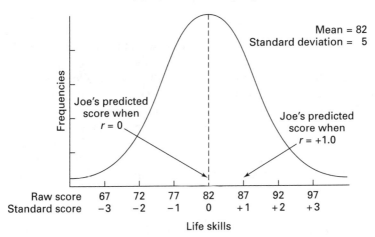

FIGURE 9.1 Standard Normal Distributions for Life Skills at 6-Week and 12-Week Assessment Periods

strength of the correlation (we are assuming it is positive), the predicted score for Joe should fall between 82 (our estimate without any information from the 6-week assessment) and 87 (our estimate when $r = +1.0$ between scores at the 6- and 12-week assessments).

As suggested earlier, however, perfect predictions are rare in the real world. Comparing the normal distributions for two variables that have a less than perfect correlation coefficient is not as straightforward as when $r = +1.0$ or -1.0. When the correlation between two variables is less than perfect, we must rely on a simple linear regression analysis to help us to make predictions.

WHAT IS SIMPLE LINEAR REGRESSION?

Simple linear regression can be used when two variables are correlated to some degree and they reflect a linear relationship when plotted on a scattergram. As stated at the beginning of this chapter, simple linear regression allows us to make predictions about the value(s) of a criterion variable by knowing the value(s) of a predictor variable.

Simple linear regression is especially useful in experimental research designs in which we are able to manipulate or introduce the value of the predictor variable. It can also be used in the types of research situations we more commonly encounter in social work. Specifically, it can be used to examine the relationship between a predictor variable and a criterion variable when we can only select for analysis—but cannot introduce or manipulate—the predictor variable.

We could use simple linear regression, for example, to examine the predictive value of a student's undergraduate grade point average (GPA), the predictor variable, on the student's GPA in graduate school, the criterion variable. Or we could use it to look at how well the number of previous felony arrests (predictor variable) for a group of offenders can predict their scores on a standardized self-report measurement instrument that measures the degree of hostility they have toward authority (criterion variable).

In either example, simple linear regression would be used to predict how well a person (or case) will "perform" on a particular variable. It would do nothing more than provide us with a technique for predicting values of one variable given our knowledge of values of another variable. Like correlation, simple linear regression does not suggest that the relationship identified between two variables is one of cause and effect.

Simple linear regression can be explained in terms of a regression equation and a regression line—two very closely related concepts. Before we discuss these important components of simple linear regression, however, we will first look at how to formulate a research question for a simple linear regression analysis and the limits of simple linear regression.

Formulating a Research Question

Simple linear regression relies heavily on the strength and statistical significance of a correlation coefficient (r) to make predictions about values of the criterion variable. It is really just an extension of correlation analyses of the relationship between interval or ratio level variables that are normally distributed. Therefore, it is not necessary to restate a research and null hypothesis when using simple linear regression. When using regression analysis, the null hypothesis—that there is no relationship between the criterion and predictor variables—would already have been tested when Pearson's r was computed.

Instead of restating the research hypothesis, we typically specify a research question when using simple linear regression. A research question for a simple linear regression analysis asks how well knowing a value of the predictor variable can improve the prediction of the value of the criterion variable for a given case. The following are possible research questions (based upon our previous examples) that can be answered using a simple linear regression analysis:

Research Question:
How much does knowing a student's GPA in undergraduate school help to predict his or her GPA in graduate school?

Or:

Research Question:
How well does knowing the number of previous felony arrests help to predict a felon's degree of hostility toward authority as measured by a standardized self-report instrument?

Limits of Simple Linear Regression

A simple linear regression analysis produces an equation, called a *regression equation*. Using the equation, we can predict (with less than total accuracy) the value of a criterion variable (*Y*) for a particular case by knowing the value for the case's predictor variable (*X*). The major benefit in doing this is that we can predict the most likely measurement for a criterion variable before we actually measure it, if we just know the measurement for the case's predictor variable.

There are limits to what we can legitimately do using simple linear regression. We cannot make predictions about measurements of the criterion variable for cases whose values for the predictor variable are either larger than the largest *X* value or smaller than the smallest *X* value used in the computation of the equation. Suppose, for example, that the predictor variable "number of hours of vigorous exercise per week" was used to predict the variable "longevity." If our sample (on which the regression equation was computed) included individuals who exercised between 2 and 15 hours per week, then we could not use the equation to predict longevity for other individuals with less than 2 or more than 15 hours of vigorous exercise per week.

Other statistical limitations of simple linear regression are the same as for Pearson's *r*. Both analyses require interval or ratio level data and both assume a normal distribution of the predictor and criterion variables (see Chapter 8).

COMPUTATION OF THE REGRESSION EQUATION

Let us use an example to show how to compute a simple linear regression equation. Suppose that we wish to find out whether among a group of adolescent female clients, there is a relationship between their educational level (predictor variable) and their assertiveness (criterion variable). Their educational level is measured by recording the last year of school completed, and their assertiveness is measured by the completion of a self-report, standardized measuring instrument that measures assertiveness.

Simple linear regression can help us predict one adolescent's assertiveness score (criterion variable) by just knowing her educational level (predictor variable), provided the two variables have been found to reflect a linear correlation. Suppose the seven clients selected for study reflect the two distributions (i.e., educational level and assertiveness level) presented in Table 9.1.

TABLE 9.1 Educational and Assertiveness
Levels ($N = 7$)

Name	Educational Level (X)	Assertiveness Level (Y)
Rochelle	9	23
Carny	12	29
Belinda	6	17
Amanda	8	21
Maria	11	27
Ky	15	35
Ruth	13	31

If we study the data in Table 9.1, we can make a number of observations. For all cases, the measurement of Y (the criterion variable, or assertiveness level) is greater than X (the predictor variable, or educational level). A close look at Table 9.1 shows that for each case, Y is more than twice the value of X. In fact, in all seven cases, Y is exactly $2(X) + 5$. We could express the relationship between the two variables as a regression equation:

$$Y' = 5 + 2(X)$$

The above equation is just a variation of the usual equation for a straight line written as $Y = a + b(X)$. In a regression equation, the notation Y' is used to denote a predicted value (not an actual one). If we plotted the data in Table 9.1 using a scattergram and connecting the dots as in Figure 9.2, we would have a straight line. Rochelle, for example, has 9 years of education (X) and has an assertiveness level of 23 (Y).

Thus, the regression equation reflects (exactly) the relationship between her education level and her assertiveness score: $Y' = 5 + 2(9) = 23$. Unlike what we would be likely to find in the real world, the equation $Y' = 5 + 2(X)$ holds true for the other six adolescents as well. The data would form a straight line when plotted on a scattergram—the variables reflect a perfect, positive correlation.

The general regression equation (when we wish to predict a value of the criterion variable) is

$$Y' = a + b(X)$$

where:

$Y' = $ the predicted Y value from a particular X value;
$a = $ the point where the regression line would intersect the y-axis, the constant;
$b = $ the slope of the line, where the amount of change in Y is directly related to the amount of change in X, the regression coefficient;
$X = $ a selected value of the predictor variable used to predict the value of the criterion variable.

Hand computations of regression equations are lengthy processes, especially for large data sets of, say, 1000 cases. Computers can do the computations, however, in very little time. Most statistical software packages are programmed to display the data

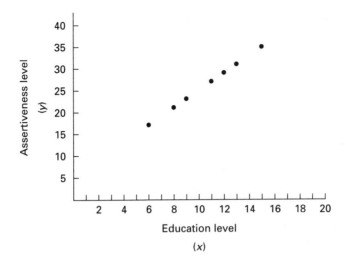

FIGURE 9.2 Scattergram of Educational and Assertiveness Levels (from Table 9.1)

within a scattergram showing dots for all cases, the correlation coefficient (r), and the regression equation. For those who may wish to see how a regression equation is calculated using formulas, Box 9.1 has been provided. It uses the data displayed in Table 8.2 in Chapter 8.

MORE ABOUT THE REGRESSION LINE

The regression line is a straight line of "best fit" for a given set of data and can be presented mathematically or graphically within a scattergram. The values in Table 9.1 as illustrated in Figure 9.2 reflect a perfect positive correlation ($r = +1.0$), but, as we repeatedly have emphasized, perfect positive correlations (and perfect negative ones as well) are very rare, especially in social work research. It is far more likely that the actual data in our example would look more like those in Table 9.2 and Figure 9.3, which reflect a less than perfect linear correlation between the two variables, "educational level" and "assertiveness level."

A straight line cannot be drawn through the seven dots in Figure 9.3, since the correlation between the two variables displayed is not a perfect one (it is neither $+1.0$ nor -1.0). We could use a computer to compute Pearson's r for the data. A computer printout would tell us that $r = +.76$ for the two variables in Figure 9.3. But to be able to predict the most likely assertiveness level for an adolescent female not among the seven cases based upon knowing her educational level we would need to do more than just compute this correlation. We would need to find or produce the line with the best possible fit—one, and only one, line—that would pass through "the center of the dots," hitting as many as possible while not missing the others by too much.

How would we find this line? What would be its slope, that is, how vertical (as opposed to horizontal) would it be? We could draw several lines through what appears

BOX 9.1
The Least-Squares Regression Equation

Problem: What is the least-squares regression equation ($Y' = a + b[X]$) for the data in Table 8.2?

Predictor Variable: Number of spouse abuse reports—ratio level.

Criterion Variable: Number of child abuse reports—ratio level.

Slope Formula:

$$b = \frac{N\Sigma XY - (\Sigma X)(\Sigma Y)}{N\Sigma X^2 - (\Sigma X)^2}$$

where: b = Slope
                N = Number of cases
            ΣXY = Sum of xy column
             ΣX = Sum of x column
             ΣY = Sum of y column
            ΣX^2 = Sum of x^2 column
            ΣY^2 = Sum of y^2 column

Substituting values for letters:

$$b = \frac{(5)(985) - (76)(53)}{(5)(1290) - (76)^2}$$

$$= \frac{897}{674}$$

$$= 1.33 \text{ (slope)}$$

y-intercept Formula:

$$a = \overline{Y} - b\overline{X}$$

where: a = y-intercept
            $\overline{Y}$ = Mean of Y column
            $b\overline{X}$ = Slope times mean of X column

Substituting values for letters:

$$a = \left(\frac{53}{5}\right) - (1.33)\left(\frac{76}{5}\right)$$

$$= 10.6 - (1.33)(15.20)$$

$$= 10.6 - 20.2$$

$$= -9.62 \text{ (y-intercept)}$$

Presentation of Results: $Y' = -9.62 + 1.33(X)$

Conclusion: A slope of 1.33 means that for every unit change in X (for every increase of 1 in the number of spouse abuse reports), there was a change of 1.33 units in Y (the number of child abuse reports increased by 1.33). Note from Box 8.1, $r = .82$.

TABLE 9.2 Educational and Assertiveness Levels ($N = 7$)

Name	Educational Level (X)	Assertiveness Level (Y)
Rochelle	9	20
Carny	12	21
Belinda	6	14
Amanda	8	25
Maria	11	21
Ky	15	28
Ruth	13	30

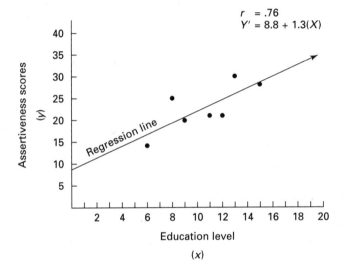

FIGURE 9.3 Scattergram of Educational and Assertiveness Levels (from Table 9.2)

to be the center of the distribution of dots, but it would be hard to determine from just visual examination which one would be the best. Some lines would hit some dots but miss others; some would be more vertical, others more horizontal.

The Least-Squares Criterion

The line that we would seek for the data in Figure 9.3, its regression line, is a line of predicted scores (Y'). As we know, the dots above and below the line represent actual scores. Notice how the actual scores above the line are predicted by the line to be lower than they actually are and the scores below the line are predicted by the line to be higher than they actually are. This is basic to an understanding of simple linear regression.

It generally (unless the correlation is perfect) does not provide perfectly accurate predictions, only "best guesses."

The way that regression analysis obtains a regression line, that is, the way that it determines its equation reflecting its slope and where it would intercept the y-axis is by using what is referred to as *the least-squares criterion*. Obviously, any straight line drawn through the center of the dots in Figure 9.3 would miss some of the dots.

The vertical distance between each of the respective dots and that line could be measured, however. Then each of these distances (referred to as deviations) could be squared and their squares added together. The sum of the squared deviations from a regression line would be different for each regression line we might draw through the dots—some would be larger; some would be smaller. The least-squares criterion asserts that the best line, the regression line that should be used, is the one that produces the smallest sum of squared deviations from that line.

Fortunately, there is a much easier and better way to arrive at a regression line for a data set than by trying an almost infinite number of lines, determining their sum of squared deviations, and then selecting the line with the "least squares." It involves the computation of the regression equation. We have already seen (Box 9.1) that a mathematical formula is available to calculate the slope and the point of the y-intercept for any pair of interval or ratio level variables.

The formula generates the linear equation for the regression line that we are seeking. Both the a value (where the line intercepts the y-axis) and the b value are likely to be fractions and not whole numbers, as in our first example, in which a perfect correlation existed. The computer-generated equation for the regression line shown in Figure 9.3 is $Y' = 8.8 + 1.3(X)$.

The Regression Coefficient (b)

In a regression equation, the regression coefficient (b) is the slope of the regression line. (Slope as used here has essentially the same meaning as it does when we refer to the slope of a hill—that is, the proportional relationship between vertical rise and horizontal distance.) For the regression line, this is stated as the amount and direction of change in Y' for each unit change in X. If b is positive, as X increases, Y' will increase at some specific constant rate. Or if b is negative, as X increases, Y' will decrease at some specific constant rate. Likewise, as X decreases, Y' will increase at some specific and constant rate. The b value suggests the rate of change in the value of Y' (the criterion variable) for each unit of change in the value of X (the predictor variable).

The slope of the regression line (b) indicates exactly where (between the vertical and horizontal axes) the line would fall. High b values reflect lines that are nearly vertical; low b values reflect lines that are nearly horizontal.

The regression coefficient (b) within a regression equation is closely related to the correlation coefficient (r) for the two variables. But, unlike the value of r, which always ranges between $+1.0$ and -1.0, the value of b may be of any size. Also, as we have suggested, r and b will always correspond in terms of positive and negative values. If r is negative, b is negative; if r is positive, b is positive.

Computer statistical software packages that give us b also give us r. We can determine the probability that any apparent relationship between the predictor and criterion variables (as expressed by the regression coefficient) may have occurred by chance. The significance level for r will be exactly the same as the significance level for b.

After the data are entered into a computer and a regression analysis is completed, the computer output will usually display both the correlation coefficient and the regression equation. The b value for Figure 9.3 is 1.3; it is seen in the upper right-hand corner of the figure. Since it is a positive number, this means that for each unit increase in X, Y' increases 1.3 points. Thus, for each one-point increase in educational level, we can predict an increase of 1.3 points in "assertiveness level" (plus the value of a).

The y-Intercept (a)

Most computer statistical software packages also display the starting point for the line. The starting point is the y-intercept, the point at which the regression line (if extended beyond the sample data if necessary, as in Figure 9.3) would cross the y-axis. This is the point that might represent the predicted value of Y when X equals zero. In our example, then, the predicted assertiveness score of an adolescent with zero years of education (theoretically) might be 8.8.

As noted above, however, we should not predict the assertiveness level of an adolescent with zero years of education since the sample data on which the regression equation was developed did not include anyone with less than six years of education. Why? Because, since we did not actually study adolescents with very little or no education, we have no way of guessing what the assertiveness of such people might be. It might be quite high. In other words, the relationship between the two variables may not be linear if female adolescents with all existing levels of education were to be studied.

Computer statistical software packages draw the correct regression line in a scattergram and also show the place where it crosses the y-axis. The value of it can be positive or negative. A positive a value tells us the regression line will meet the y-axis at a value **above zero**; a negative a value indicates the regression line (extended, if necessary) would cross the y-axis at a value **below zero**.

Predicted Y (Y′)

As we have discussed, the regression coefficient (b) and the y-intercept (a) help us to generate a regression line. Y' is the estimated score for the criterion variable, for a given value of the predictor variable. We can predict the value for a criterion variable for a single case by computing Y' for the value of X. Look at the upper right-hand corner of Figure 9.3 for the regression equation $Y' = 8.8 + 1.3(X)$. The X component of the formula is any specific value of X for which we wish to predict a Y value. The following are two calculations for the predicted Y values of two different cases when we substitute specific values for X (13 and 6 respectively):

Calculation 1:
Let us determine Y' by substituting 13 for X:

$$Y' = a + b(X)$$
$$= 8.8 + 1.3(13)$$

$$= 8.8 + 16.9$$
$$= 25.7 \text{ (predicted value of } Y \text{ when } X = 13)$$

Calculation 2:
Let us determine Y' by substituting 6 for X:

$$Y' = a + b(X)$$
$$= 8.8 + 1.3(6)$$
$$= 8.8 + 7.8$$
$$= 16.6 \text{ (predicted value of } Y \text{ when } X = 6)$$

The X values of 13 and 6 were chosen at random. They could have been any numbers within the range of the distribution of X within the sample studied. What do the X and Y' values mean? When X is 13, the predicted Y' value is 25.7 (Calculation 1); when X is 6, the predicted Y' value is 16.6 (Calculation 2). Thus, a client who has an educational level of 13 is predicted to have an assertiveness score of 25.7, and a client with an educational level of 6 is predicted to have an assertiveness score of 16.6.

An alternative approach to predicting the value of Y involves using the actual regression line as presented in a scattergram. We could find, for example, the exact value $(X = 13)$ along the x-axis of the scattergram in Figure 9.3. Next we could run a vertical line straight up until we reach the regression line. Then we could draw a straight horizontal line to the left until we touch the y-axis.

Note that we hit the same Y' as predicted in the equation above ($Y' = $ about 25.7). This method of prediction is not nearly as precise as using a regression equation. It does provide a visual understanding of the data, however, and can be used as a quick check on a result obtained mathematically. We could use the same method to check the value for Y' when $X = 6$ to verify that our math was correct.

Interchanging X and Y Variables

In our example we conceptualized years of education as the predictor variable (X) and degree of assertiveness as the criterion variable (Y). We also could have conceptualized the relationship between the two variables the other way around. Assertiveness could be thought of as the predictor variable and years of education as the criterion variable. As emphasized earlier, the labeling of variables as "predictor" and "criterion" variables needs to make theoretical and logical sense. In this instance, we could build a logical case for a relationship between the two variables in either direction.

In computing the correlation between two variables, the correlation coefficient between them would be the same regardless of which variable we label the "predictor variable" and which we label the "criterion variable." The predictor and criterion variables are not interchangeable in a regression analysis, however. If we were to tell the computer that years of education is our predictor variable and assertiveness is our criterion variable, we would get one result (the regression equation above).

On the other hand, if we programmed the computer so that assertiveness is the predictor variable and years of education is the criterion variable, we would get a different result. We must be clear which variable is intended as the predictor variable and which variable is intended as the criterion variable (as stated in the research question). We must then be careful to input our data into the computer so as to reflect this understanding if we hope to get the regression equation that we seek.

INTERPRETING RESULTS

How valuable is a prediction that can be made from a given regression line? The answer depends on the strength and significance of the correlation between the two variables. When there is a very low correlation, there is no use in even calculating the best-fitting straight line to make predictions. When there is a high correlation, however, the line can be used for predictive purposes. Thus, there is a direct relationship between the magnitude of r and the accuracy of our predictions.

If we study the formula in Box 9.1, it clearly shows how correlation is directly related to simple linear regression. As r decreases (approaches 0.0), the accuracy of prediction using simple linear regression decreases. As r increases (approaches +1.0 or −1.0), the accuracy increases.

Presentation of Y'

The presentation of Y' is straightforward. The regression equation $Y' = 3.5 + 6.8(X)$, for example, could be stated in words as "for every unit increase in X, there will be a 6.8 unit increase in Y'." Using the variables of client's educational level (X) and assertiveness level (Y), this would read, "for each one-year increase in a client's educational level, a client's assertiveness level will increase by 6.8 assertiveness points" (plus 3.5, the value of a).

The Standard Error

An indicator referred to as the *standard error* can be used to give us an estimate of how well the regression equation can predict values of the criterion variable, from known values of the predictor variable. When $r = +1.0$ or −1.0, all dots fall exactly on the regression line. In this case, the standard error equals zero. The closer the standard error is to zero, the more confident we can be that the regression equation will give us good predictions. The further r is from being perfect (+1.0 or −1.0), the more we must account for error in the equation. When $r = 0.0$, the standard error will be at its maximum.

USING REGRESSION FOR INFERENCE

While the primary function of regression is the prediction of a value of a criterion variable from knowing a value of a predictor variable, it is sometimes combined with the results of a correlation analysis to add additional information to hypothesis testing. We will examine two hypothetical examples to see how this can be done.

Example: Socializing with Family Members and Life Satisfaction

Background. Wilhelmenia is a social worker in a family service agency. Over the last year, she saw 80 clients for counseling related to depression. During this time, she formed the impression that the clients who seemed most depressed had little time to spend socializing with family members. She also noticed that clients who had a considerable amount of time to spend socializing with family members during the week did not seem as depressed as most other clients. Wilhelmenia decided to do a small-scale research study to test her hunch.

Research Question. Wilhelmenia wanted to determine how well information about the amount of client time spent socializing with family members would improve her ability to predict a client's life satisfaction level. Her predictor variable was "the amount of time the client spent socializing with family members during the previous week" (X), and her criterion variable was the "client life satisfaction level" (Y).

Methodology. Over the next several months, Wilhelmenia had each of 50 new clients who were about to be seen for counseling complete a standardized self-report measurement instrument that measures life satisfaction (interval level). She also asked each one how many hours of time he or she had spent socializing with family members during the previous week (ratio level). The life satisfaction instrument produces scores ranging from 0 (lowest level) to 200 (highest level).

Findings. Wilhelmenia entered the pairs of measurements for the two variables (one pair per case) into her personal computer and asked it to perform a simple linear regression on them. The Pearson's r and regression equation and p-level that it produced for her data were as follows:

$$r = +.70$$
$$Y' = 1.49 + 4.69(X)$$
$$p < .0005$$

Wilhelmenia studied the above findings. The relatively high Pearson's r value (and significant p-value) indicated that regression analysis was justified and might produce fairly accurate predictions for values of the criterion variable. She computed r^2 and noted that the amount of clients' time spent with family members was related to a fairly sizable amount of the variation of their life satisfaction levels ($+.70^2 = .49$, or 49%).

Based upon the regression equation generated, a slope (b) of 4.69 indicated that for each unit of increase in X, there is an increase of 4.69 units in Y'. For each additional hour of time spent socializing with family members, for example, there was an average increase of 4.69 "points" on the life satisfaction instrument (a decrease in depression).

Implications. Wilhelmenia could use her findings to predict a future client's life satisfaction just by knowing how many hours of time socializing with family members the client had spent during the week. She realized that her findings are not very generalizable to other clients with different problems (i.e., those without a presenting complaint of depression) or to other clients being treated for depression in other settings. She also knew that she could not predict life satisfaction level for clients who had spent more or less time with family members during the week than those contained in her original 50-case sample.

After completing her study, Wilhelmenia saw a 51st client, David, who came to the agency to be counseled for depression. During their first interview, David told Wilhelmenia that he had spent 15 hours socializing with family members during the previous week. Wilhelmenia computed David's predicted life satisfaction score (Y') as follows:

$$Y' = 1.49 + 4.69(15)$$
$$= 1.49 + (70.35)$$
$$= 71.84 \text{ (predicted value of } Y \text{ when } X \text{ equals 15)}$$

To test how accurate her prediction had been (using the regression equation), Wilhelmenia had David complete the life satisfaction instrument and obtained his actual score. She compared his actual score (i.e., $Y = 73$) to his predicted score ($Y' = 71.84$) and was pleased to find that they were quite close.

Example: Worker's Case Load Size and Number of Sick Days Taken

Background. Miriam is an administrator in a child protection agency. With recent cutbacks in funding, caseloads have increased for Miriam's workers. In the past, her child protection workers typically managed a caseload between 30 and 40 clients. More recently, workers were assigned to as many as 50 active cases. Miriam noticed that since caseload size had increased, there also seemed to be an increase in sick days taken by her workers.

Research Question. Miriam wondered if the size of a worker's caseload might be a good predictor of the number of sick days that the worker would take.

The predictor variable for her correlation and simple linear regression analysis was caseload size, and the criterion variable was number of sick days. Both variables, "caseload size" and "number of sick days," are at the ratio level of measurement.

To shed some light on her research question, Miriam reviewed employee records over the past year. There were 22 front-line child protection workers on staff during the year. She reviewed their employee records and randomly selected a one-month period for each worker. She noted the workers' average caseload size and the number of sick days taken during that month.

Findings. After entering the data into her personal computer, Miriam performed a simple linear regression analysis and printed the results. The printout contained the following:

$$r = +.76$$
$$Y' = -6.8 + .25(X)$$
$$p < .0005$$

Miriam noted a statistically significant ($p < .0005$) high correlation coefficient for r (+.76). Based on her findings, Miriam was quite confident that her regression equation could generate reasonably accurate predictions. The direction of the relationship between the two variables was also positive, exactly what she had expected. She noted that the regression coefficient (b) of .25 meant that for every unit change in X, there is an increase of .25 in Y. In other words, for every additional case added to a worker's caseload, it increases the number of sick days a worker is likely to take by .25.

Implications. Miriam could use her findings to predict the number of sick days that a worker might be expected to take in a month. She knew, however, that her study's findings might be useful for prediction only among those workers in her agency whose caseload was no smaller or larger than those contained in her sample of 24 cases.

Miriam used her regression equation to predict how many sick days a worker (who had a caseload of 43) would be likely to take for the month:

$$Y' = -6.8 + .25(43)$$
$$= -6.8 + (10.75)$$
$$= 3.95, \text{ rounded to 4 (predicted value of } Y \text{ when } X \text{ equals 43)}$$

Miriam's "best guess" was that a worker with a caseload of 43 would take four days of sick time during the month.

REGRESSION WITH THREE OR MORE VARIABLES

Simple linear regression has its multivariate counterpart, *multiple linear regression*. Not surprisingly, multiple correlation and multiple linear regression have many similarities. They have both theoretical and actual differences, however.

In theory, all correlation analyses (including Multiple R) are designed to analyze data where we have no control over the distribution of the variables (random variables) within the population. We simply measure the predictor and criterion variables *ex-post facto*, after they have already been distributed among the cases or objects.

Consequently, a correlation coefficient is just an indication of how these variables co-vary naturally, that is, without any of our interference. No matter how high the correlation coefficient produced, it would be presumptuous to imply that the predictor variable in any way caused the variations in the values within the criterion variable.

Linear regression analysis, however, was designed for situations for which we have experimental data—where we either introduce, or directly manipulate, the predictor variables; that is the way regression was designed to be used. In reality, regression analyses are now also used in many situations for which we have only random variables, whose distributions are beyond our control. This generally causes no major problems, so long as we are confident that the measurement of the predictor variables are accurate and other assumptions about their distributions are met.

In those relatively rare situations in which experimental research designs are employed and normally distributed interval or ratio level predictor and criterion variables exist, regression analyses (simple or multiple) are the statistical procedures of choice. If the predictor variables are really randomly distributed variables, either correlation or regression can be used, but correlation is really the more correct of the two.

Multiple linear regression is used to help us predict the value of one interval or ratio level criterion variable using the values of two or more interval or ratio level predictor variables. Multiple R produces a correlation coefficient that gives us a good idea of the degree of correlation between the group of predictor variables and the criterion variable. When squared (R^2), it can tell us what percentage of the variation within values of the criterion variable can be explained by the group of predictor variables. Multiple linear regression does even more. Through the use of a regression equation, it helps us to estimate the actual value of a criterion variable, knowing the corresponding values for two or more predictor variables.

Like simple linear regression, multiple linear regression is used along with correlation to

- decide whether an apparent relationship between the predictor variables and the criterion variable is likely to be the work of chance, or sampling error;
- present any such relationship as a mathematical equation;
- indicate how accurate the equation is as a predictor of values of the criterion variable.

What makes multiple linear regression different from simple linear regression is that it also provides an assessment of the relative value (i.e., respective contributions) of different predictor variables for predicting values of the criterion variable.

The formula for multiple linear regression is similar to that of simple linear regression, but not surprisingly, it is more complex. Like the formula for Multiple R, it takes into consideration the fact that the predictor variables are not only correlated with the criterion variable, they are also correlated to a greater or lesser degree with each other. We could not just add up their individual prediction powers, because some of the prediction power of one predictor variable duplicates the power within another predictor variable.

The regression counterpart of Multiple R's beta weights are referred to as *beta coefficients.* Like beta weights, they reflect the partial correlation of a predictor variable with the criterion variable, given the other predictor variables in the equation. There are other similarities between Multiple R and multiple linear regression as well. Stepwise procedures help us to select the smallest number of predictor variables while not sacrificing too much in our ability to predict.

Like Multiple R, this can be accomplished by using either a step-down or step-up procedure—that is, by systematically adding or dropping different predictor variables. Statistical computer software packages can quickly provide us with the best (in terms of prediction of the criterion variable) combination of two or more predictor variables that will produce the best multiple linear regression equation.

Multiple linear regression can also be used with nominal or ordinal level predictor variables. We do this by creating dummy variables (see Chapter 1) from a single nominal or ordinal level variable. The variable "marital status," for example, is at the nominal level of measurement and can contain five different value categories (e.g., currently married, separated, divorced, widowed, never married).

By creating four dummy variables, this nominal level variable could become four ratio level variables, with the value of 0 representing a state of "no measurable quantity" for each of its values. Thus, one dummy variable could be "currently married" (0 = no; 1 = yes); a second could be "separated" (0 = no; 1 = yes), a third could be "divorced" (0 = no; 1 = yes); and a fourth could be "widowed" (0 = no; 1 = yes).

In this way, a group of four dummy variables (one less than the number of value categories used for the nominal level variable, "marital status") is added to a multiple linear regression analysis as four predictor variables. Why not five? A person who has values of 0 for the first four dummy variables has never been married. To include "never marriedness" as another dummy variable is redundant and will produce misleading results when a multiple linear regression analysis is performed.

Like all statistical analyses, multiple linear regression can produce results that if we are not careful will lead us into Type I or Type II errors. It has several assumptions for its use that must be met. An advanced statistics text can help us to understand these and thus to avoid such phenomena as collinearity (two highly correlated predictor variables that can distort the results of an analysis), self-fulfilling prophecies, or regression to the mean.

CONCLUDING THOUGHTS

This chapter presented a brief overview of some of the more common uses of simple linear regression and demonstrated how it is closely related to correlation. A simple linear regression provides us with a method for predicting the value of a criterion variable if we know the value of a predictor variable. It is a group of useful techniques for those situations in which a reasonably strong linear correlation exists.

When there is little or no correlation between two variables, or the correlation is strong but not linear, creation of a simple linear regression equation is an exercise in futility. It does little to enhance our ability to predict a value(s) of the criterion variable by knowing the value(s) of one or more predictor variables.

STUDY QUESTIONS

1. What can simple linear regression do that correlation cannot do? Provide examples in your discussion.
2. What statistical insights discussed in earlier chapters in this book are critical to an understanding of simple linear regression? Describe how they relate to it.
3. Explain why it is not necessary to state a research or null hypothesis when using simple linear regression. What alternative to restating a hypothesis do researchers commonly use when performing simple linear regression analysis?
4. Discuss (using examples drawn from social work practice) why it is not a productive use of one's time to use regression when the correlation coefficient between two variables is low. Draw two scattergrams to illustrate your point (one scattergram showing a low correlation and one scattergram showing a high correlation). Discuss the two scattergrams in relation to simple linear regression.

5. What do we mean when we say that the predictor and criterion variables are not interchangeable for statistical purposes when we perform a simple linear regression? What implications does this have when we program a computer to conduct a simple linear regression analysis?

6. In your own words, explain why you think we should not predict Y' when an X value is below the minimum or above the maximum value used in generating Y'.

7. Describe two situations in which you believe it would be appropriate to perform a regression analysis in a social service agency with which you are familiar. How would the results have the potential to help the agency?

8. For each of the two major examples used in this chapter, discuss additional methodological limitations (in addition to those mentioned) that might serve to "depreciate" the statistical findings. You may wish to go to a book on social work research methods and review the section on threats to internal and external validity.

9. What type of research situations would be especially suited to the use of multiple linear regression? Give an example of how a social work practitioner might use it to predict the amount of some client behavior.

10. Describe how a social worker in your answer to the previous question might use dummy variables to include a nominal level variable such as gender as a predictor variable in the analysis.

11. Which form of multivariate analysis is designed to help us predict the value of an interval or ratio level criterion variable from the measurements of two or more interval or ratio level predictor variables that have been introduced or manipulated by the researcher?

12. Describe how dummy variables can be used to perform a multiple linear regression using a nominal level predictor variable. Provide an example.

13. How do step-up and step-down regression differ from each other? Describe how each works.

Chapter 10
Cross-Tabulation

$\mathbf{T}$he term *cross-tabulation* is a familiar one to most social workers. Actually, it is associated with two related statistical tests that analyze the relationship between nominal level variables: (1) the chi-square goodness of fit test and (2) the chi-square test of association.

THE CHI-SQUARE GOODNESS-OF-FIT TEST

Let us first examine the *chi-square goodness-of-fit test*. As with all the statistical tests presented in this book, it is a valuable test if certain conditions for its use are present. As will be seen shortly, its major limitation is that it can only be used if we have accurate information about the population from which a sample was drawn. This information is necessary because the test does nothing more than compare a value category of a nominal level variable taken from a sample with the population from which the sample was drawn.

When this test compares a specific sample with its respective population, it does not compare the sample's mean with its population's mean. Obviously, as presented in Chapter 3, it is impossible to compute a mean with nominal level data. What this test can do, however, is compare the percentage of cases for a given value category for a nominal level variable within a sample with the percentage of cases of that variable's value category within its **known** population.

Example: Left-Handed People

Let us take a simple example to make the above point a bit clearer. Let us say we know that the percentage of left-handed people within a specific population is 12 percent. We could use a chi-square goodness-of-fit test to determine if the percentage of left-handed people within a sample that was drawn from this population differs significantly from that within the population—that is, from 12 percent.

Based upon what we have learned in previous chapters about sampling distributions (Chapter 6) and about how other statistical tests work, we would probably not be surprised if the percentage of left-handed people in our sample of 30 was, say, 11 percent or 13 percent. We would not expect the difference between either of these two sample percentages and the population's 12 percent to be statistically significant. With these small percentage differences, we would not expect to be able to reject the null hypothesis in which any difference between the percentages is probably just the work of chance, or sampling error. After all, if nothing unusual were going on, we would expect our sample to contain about the same percentage of left-handed people as contained within the population from which it was drawn (12%) and either 11 percent or 13 percent are both very close 12 percent.

But what if the percentage of left-handed people in our sample was, say, 5 percent or 19 percent? Then the evidence in support of not rejecting the null hypothesis would be far less dramatic. We would need help to determine whether or not to reject the null hypothesis; that is, to determine the likelihood that chance, or sampling error, might have produced the percentage of left-handed people in the sample (a p-value). We would require satistical analysis.

The chi-square goodness-of-fit test can help us to reject (or not to reject) the null hypothesis. By applying a simple formula (contained within most statistical software packages), it can compare our sample's percentage of left-handed people with its population's known percentage of left-handed people (given our sample size), which then tells us the likelihood that the percentage of left-handed people in our sample (in relation to its population) could have been the work of chance, or sampling error.

How might we use this test? We probably would not care if a sample that we drew had a disproportionate number of left-handed people in it. But we might be most interested in (1) whether our sample differs significantly in relation to some important variable within its respective population or (2) whether our sample differs significantly from its respective population following a treatment intervention of some kind. The chi-square goodness-of-fit test can answer both of these questions.

Example: Family Support and Longevity

Kanesha wanted to examine the relationship between an independent variable, "client's level of family support at admission," and a dependent variable, "length of client survival," among the residents living in a long-term care nursing home. Using case files, she drew a simple random sample of 50 residents from the home's population of 1000. Her literature review, however, had suggested that gender may be an intervening or extraneous variable in the relationship between her independent variable and her dependent variable. She knew from the home's weekly census that its percentage of females was 72 percent. Or out of the home's population of 1000 residents, there were 720 females.

Before Kanesha conducted a statistical analysis using Pearson's r, she wanted to know if her sample (which consisted of 37 females, or 74% females) could be considered representative of the home's population of 1000 residents for the potentially intervening variable "gender." She constructed the following null hypothesis:

Null Hypothesis:
The percentage of females in my sample does not differ significantly from the percentage of females within the population from which my sample was drawn.

To test her null hypothesis, Kanesha used the chi-square goodness-of-fit test to compare her sample's percentage of females (74%) with the home's actual percentage of females (72%). The test produced $p > .05$. This is what Kanesha had hoped she would find. She was not able to reject the null hypothesis—the sample was really not "that different" from the population in relation to gender.

The percentage difference between her sample (i.e., 74%) and its population (i.e., 72%) was relatively small (i.e., 2 percentage points), and may well have been attributable to chance. In other words, her sample was sufficiently representative of the population for the variable "gender." She then went on to conduct her primary data analysis, assured that if she found a relationship between her independent variable and her dependent variable, at least it did not occur because her sample contained a disproportionately large number of males or females.

Example: Involvement in the Political Process

Max works for a community organization agency located in his precinct, a very low socioeconomic neighborhood of the inner city. One of his agency's goals is to get local residents more involved in the political process in order to demand better public services. Recent election data revealed that only 22 percent of eligible voters in the inner city voted in the last several county council elections. Max selected a random sample of 100 eligible voters in his precinct from voter registration lists and visited each one in his or her home. He stressed the importance of voting in the next month's county council election. After the election, he determined that 35 of those he had visited, or 35 percent, had voted, while the overall percentage within the precinct remained constant at 22 percent.

Max used the chi-square goodness-of-fit test to determine whether the difference between the "voting percentage" in his sample of 100 people (35%) and the percentage of those voting within the population (22%) was likely to be the work of chance, or sampling error. After all, there was a 13 point percentage difference (35% − 22% = 13% points).

The results of his analysis were that the probability (p) of a difference of that magnitude occurring with a sample of 100 just because of sampling error was $p < .05$. Max was pleased that he could reject the null hypothesis. Apparently, his sample was really different (better!) in its voting record following his intervention. He was hopeful that his home visits had made the difference (and not some alternative explanations).

THE CHI-SQUARE TEST OF ASSOCIATION

The second form of chi-square that we will examine is the *chi-square test of association*, usually referred to simply as *chi-square*. It tests the association between two nominal level variables.

No nonparametric statistical test (and probably no other statistical test) is better known than chi-square. Most of us who have been exposed to statistics as part of our professional social work education have spent some time studying it. Research articles using chi-square analyses appear frequently in our professional literature. Since we feel comfortable with the test, we are more likely to read reports that use it than studies that employ less widely known and understood statistical tests.

A major reason for the popularity of chi-square is that the value categories for each nominal level variable need only represent distinct categories and a difference of kind. This fact alone makes chi-square especially well suited for a large number of social work research situations. We often want to know, for example, if there is a relationship between two or more different methods of intervention and client success or failure. More often than not, both variables are only at the nominal level of measurement. When measuring treatment effectiveness, for example, we frequently can do little more than assign cases to value categories, such as found employment, did not find employment; abused again, did not abuse again; rehospitalized, not rehospitalized—all nominal level variables.

Other variables that may be related to treatment effectiveness also are likely to be at the nominal level of measurement. These variables could be, for example, the type of treatment provided (e.g., individual treatment, group treatment), the educational background of the social workers (e.g., B.S.W., M.S.W.), or the demographic variables of the clients (e.g., marital status, gender, religious affiliation, race).

Similarly, many other variables in social work research studies have yes-no or other dichotomous value categories that can be considered to be only at the nominal level of measurement. A small research study, for example, might measure whether a piece of social legislation passed or did not pass in different states and whether or not the local chapters of the National Association of Social Workers supported the legislation.

Another study could examine whether there is an association between whether candidates for local offices were elected (or not) and whether (or not) they had taken a pro-choice position on the issue of abortion. In all these situations, all variables are at the nominal level of measurement. Because of this fact, chi-square is an ideal statistical test to use. As we shall see, however, chi-square is not appropriate for all data analyses situations involving two nominal level variables.

As mentioned, chi-square is a statistical test of association between two nominal level variables. Thus, even if it demonstrates support for a relationship between them, it would not be appropriate to conclude that the different value categories of either variable caused the different value categories of the other. We can only state, at best, that a pattern or clustering of value categories may exist—certain value categories of one variable simply tend to be found where certain value categories of the other value are also present. Like all statistical tests of significance, chi-square can only determine whether any pattern of relationship between two nominal level variables within sample data is so strong and consistent that chance, or sampling error, is an inadequate explanation of it.

With chi-square, the specter of chance, or sampling error, plays the skeptic in a unique way; its role is central to our understanding of how it works. Let us use a simple hypothetical example to illustrate how chi-square works. Suppose that we want to find out if there is a relationship between a nominal level dependent variable, "client outcome" (i.e., success, failure), and a nominal level independent variable, "type of treatment" (i.e., group, individual), within a large alcoholism counseling program. Based on a literature review and previous experience and hunches, we feel justified in formulating the following one-tailed research hypothesis:

One-Tailed Research Hypothesis:
Clients in group treatment are more likely to abstain from alcohol for two months than clients in individual treatment.

When a one-tailed research hypothesis such as the one above is stated, and we are planning to use the chi-square statistic to test it, it is extremely helpful to depict the hypothesis in the form of a dummy table. A *dummy table* shows where we would expect to find a disproportionately large number of cases if the hypothesis is supported through testing its null hypothesis.

In our example, if we were to demonstrate support for our one-tailed research hypothesis, we would expect to find a relatively large number of cases who were in group treatment who abstained from alcohol (success) and a relatively large number of cases who were in individual treatment who did not abstain (failure). This is seen by the placement of the asterisks in the body of Table 10.1. The creation of a dummy table at the time that a one-tailed research hypothesis is formulated can later assist greatly in the interpretation of a study's findings.

As emphasized in Chapter 5, the concept of the null hypothesis always guides our decision-making process when we are testing our research hypothesis. The corresponding null hypothesis for our one-tailed research hypothesis would be as follows:

Null-Hypothesis:
There is no relationship between the type of treatment clients received and whether or not they abstained from alcohol for two months.

The null hypothesis would assert that although it may occasionally seem (within a sample) that successful treatment is more likely to occur among clients who received group treatment than among those who received individual treatment, there is not a real relationship between the variables within the population from which the sample was drawn.

To test our one-tailed research hypothesis, we could randomly select 100 cases from the program's 300 clients who are being seen for alcohol dependency problems. These 100 clients form our sample. We then ask the social workers to note for each

TABLE 10.1 Dummy Table: Type of Treatment by Client Outcome

	Results		
Type of Treatment	Success	Failure	Totals
Group	*		
Individual		*	

client they saw (1) whether the client was in individual or group treatment and (2) whether or not the client abstained from alcohol for the previous two-month period.

Type of treatment would have two possible value categories—group or individual. Client outcome also would have two possible value categories—success or failure. (Success would be operationalized as two months of alcohol abstention.) Thus, there are four possible "combinations" of value categories that could be recorded for each client, with every client falling into one, and only one, of the following four classifications.

- group treatment and client success
- group treatment and client failure
- individual treatment and client success
- individual treatment and client failure

Suppose, for example, that the 100 clients were distributed among each of the four categories as follows:

- group treatment and client success (40 clients)
- group treatment and client failure (20 clients)
- individual treatment and client success (15 clients)
- individual treatment and client failure (25 clients)

Observed Frequencies

These data (i.e., 40, 20, 15, 25) are placed into a cross-tabulation table. Thus, this table contains the actual data from the research study. The data in the four cells of Table 10.2 are the actual number of clients who possessed each combination of value categories for the two variables. Such a table (also referred to as a *chi-square table, cross-break table,* or *contingency table*) is constructed using the variable labels, value labels, and frequencies drawn from the data. A cross-tabulation table for our hypothetical data is presented as Table 10.2.

In the far right-hand column of Table 10.2, the totals for each row (adding across) are entered. Likewise, the totals for each column (adding down) are entered on the bottom line. These row and column totals are called *marginals* (marginal totals). They indicate the total number of cases that were observed to possess a given value category

TABLE 10.2 Observed Frequencies: Type of Treatment by Client Outcome (N = 100)

Type of Treatment	Results		Totals
	Success	Failure	
Group	40 (a)	20 (b)	60
Individual	15 (c)	25 (d)	40
Totals . . .	55	45	100

for each variable: group treatment (60), individual treatment (40), success (55), and failure (45). The grand total of cases (N) in the table is entered in the bottom right-hand corner (100). Note that the sum of the row totals equals the grand total, as does the sum of the column totals.

The areas where the frequencies (i.e., 40, 20, 15, 25) are placed are referred to as "cells." Table 10.2 contains two dichotomous (two-category) variables, type of treatment and client outcome; thus, it has four cells. It is, of course, possible to have variables with more than two value categories. The cross-tabulation table would then have more rows and columns and thus more cells.

By convention, small italicized letters (e.g., a, b, c, d) are used to refer to the respective cells. As can easily be seen from Table 10.2, they are lettered left to right, starting with the top row, then going to the next row, and so on.

Since the variables are at the nominal level of measurement, there is no logical sequence in which they should appear in a table. In our example, it would have been equally correct to place individual treatment above group treatment or to place failure to the left of success. By convention, however, we display the dependent variable in the columns and the independent variable in the rows, as seen in Table 10.2. If neither variable is clearly one or the other (that is, we are only interested to see if their value categories are associated), it makes no difference which variable's value categories run down the side of the table and which run across the top.

Now that our data have been placed in the cross-tabulation table (Table 10.2), we can compare the outcomes of clients who received group treatment with outcomes of those clients who received individual treatment. Such a comparison cannot be easily accomplished using only the observed frequencies as contained in Table 10.2, however.

We cannot simply compare the raw number of clients who had successful outcomes with group treatment (40) directly with the raw number of clients who had successful outcomes with individual treatment (15) and conclude that group treatment is better just because 40 is larger than 15. We would naturally expect to have more successes among those clients in group treatment than among those in individual treatment because more clients (60) were in group treatment and fewer (40) were in individual treatment.

It is possible to compensate for the difference in the number of cases in the two subsamples (individual versus group) by using percentages. Percentages "equalize" the sizes of groups. Using percentages, we can demonstrate, for example, what percentage 40 clients is of 60 clients and what percentage 15 clients is of 40 clients. Table 10.3 is a percentage table for the observed data contained in Table 10.2. It indicates that 66.7

TABLE 10.3   Percentages of Clients: Type of Treatment by Client Outcome (N = 100)

| | Results | | |
Type of Treatment	Success	Failure	Totals
Group	66.7	33.3	100.0
Individual	37.5	62.5	100.0

percent of the 60 clients who received group treatment had successful outcomes, compared with 37.5 percent of the 40 clients who received individual treatment and had
successful outcomes.

If the percentages in cells a and c and the percentages in cells b and d had been
exactly the same, we would have no reason to believe that the variables are related. The
percentages in the cells in Table 10.3 are quite different, however, and thus may not be
the work of chance, or sampling error. They seem to suggest that among clients who are
alcohol dependent, type of treatment and treatment success may be related. Yet, at this
point, it is difficult to know whether the apparent relationship is anything more than
the work of chance, or sampling error. The null hypothesis would argue that a 29.2 percentage point difference (66.7% − 37.5% = 29.2% points) is not really very large. But
is it? How much of a percentage point difference is needed to rule out chance, or sampling error, as an apparent relationship between the two variables? Percentages alone
cannot answer this question. We now need to look at expected frequencies.

Expected Frequencies

In order to answer the previous question, we need to introduce the concept of expected frequencies. *Expected frequencies* are those frequencies that we would expect to
occur most frequently in an infinite number of samples if the null hypothesis were correct—that is, if there was not a real relationship between the two nominal level variables. Unlike observed frequencies, which reflect actual data that we collected (as in
Table 10.2), expected frequencies are hypothetical numbers; they are derived using
simple math from the marginal totals in a cross-tabulation table.

To understand expected frequencies, we need to return to Table 10.2 for a
moment. Let us see how the expected frequencies for a given cell are obtained. Look
first at cell a, which contains the 40 clients who were in group treatment and who had
successful outcomes. They represent two thirds, or 66.7 percent, of the 60 clients who
were in group treatment (Table 10.3).

The expected frequency for cell a (or for any cell) is based upon the two marginal
totals that correspond to that cell; that is, the total for the row in which that cell appears
and the total for the column in which that cell appears. For cell a in Table 10.2, for
example, these two marginal totals are 60 and 55 respectively. For cell b, they are 60
and 45 respectively. For cell c, they are 40 for the row total and 55 for the column total,
and for cell d, these are 40 and 45.

The expected frequency for any given cell is computed by multiplying that cell's
row total by its column total and then dividing by the grand total for the table (N). We
can express this as a formula:

$$E = \frac{(R)(C)}{(N)}$$

where:

E = Expected frequency in a particular cell
R = Marginal total for the row in which the cell appears
C = Marginal total for the column in which the cell appears
N = Total number of cases

TABLE 10.4   Observed and Expected Frequencies:
Type of Treatment by Client Outcome ($N = 100$)

	Results				
	Success		Failure		
Type of Treatment	Observed	Expected	Observed	Expected	Totals
Group	40	(33)	20	(27)	60
Individual	15	(22)	25	(18)	40
Totals . . .	55		45		100

Using the formula, we can figure out the expected frequency for each cell:

$$\text{cell } a = \frac{60 \times 55}{100} = 3300/100 = 33$$

$$\text{cell } b = \frac{60 \times 45}{100} = 2700/100 = 27$$

$$\text{cell } c = \frac{55 \times 40}{100} = 2200/100 = 22$$

$$\text{cell } d = \frac{45 \times 40}{100} = 1800/100 = 18$$

Table 10.4 displays the expected frequency for each of the four cells in parentheses alongside the corresponding observed frequency. Note that there is only one set of marginal totals because they are constant for both the observed frequencies and the expected frequencies.

The chi-square statistic simply compares the observed frequency for each cell with its respective expected frequency. It uses a formula to produce a chi-square value, which is directly related to the size of these differences. Larger differences between the observed and expected frequencies produce larger chi-square values. Let us now turn to how a specific chi-square value is calculated using Table 10.4. Before we can do this, however, we first need to discuss degrees of freedom.

Degrees of Freedom

If we were to study the chi-square formula carefully, (Box 10.1) we could see why larger differences between observed and expected frequencies are not the only thing that generate larger chi-square values. The likelihood of obtaining a large chi-square value is also affected by the size of the cross-tabulation table on which it is computed. As used here, size refers to the number of rows and columns and, more specifically, to the number of cells in the table.

The larger the table, the more likely it is to have a large chi-square value. The more cells in a table, the more cells available to contribute to the chi-square value and the higher that value is likely to be, even if the difference between individual pairs of observed frequencies and expected frequencies is quite small.

A chi-square value must be evaluated in relation to the size of the table from which it was computed. A large chi-square value in itself may not mean a statistically significant relationship between two nominal level variables. It could have been generated by a large table with many cells, each contributing a small amount (because of small differences) to that value. Conversely, a smaller chi-square value may be statistically significant if the table from which it was produced had relatively few cells to contribute to its value. The critical values of chi-square contained in Table 10.5 and Appendix C reflect this.

The number of cells in a cross-tabulation table is expressed in terms of degrees of freedom. The *degrees of freedom* (*df*) for any chi-square analysis is equal to the number of rows minus one times the number of columns minus one (see Box 10.1). Using this formula tells us that Table 10.2 has one degree of freedom (as will all 2-by-2 tables). A 3-by-3 table would have four degrees of freedom $(3 - 1) \times (3 - 1) = 4$, a 2-by-3 table would have two degrees of freedom $(2 - 1) \times (3 - 1) = 2$, and so on.

Computation of Chi-Square

In the not too distant past, calculating a chi-square statistic (or any statistical test for that matter) was a time-consuming task. It is now a rare occasion when a chi-square analysis is undertaken with pencil and paper. When it is, there are seven steps involved:

Step 1. Place the observed frequencies into a cross-tabulation table.

Step 2. Compute the expected frequencies and add them to the table.

Step 3. Compare the observed frequencies (Step 1) with the expected frequencies (Step 2) using the chi-square formula.

Step 4. Compute degrees of freedom for the cross-tabulation table.

Step 5. Go to the appropriate line for the degrees of freedom in a critical values of chi-square table (see Table 10.5 or Appendix C) and see where the chi-square value falls.

Step 6. Go to the number to the left of where the chi-square value falls.

Step 7. Go to the top of the column in which that number appears and obtain the approximate *p*-value using the line corresponding to the type of research hypothesis used (one- or two-tailed).

The general formula that is needed to compute a chi-square statistic is contained in Box 10.1. It is used for cross-tabulation tables containing more than four cells. If there are only four cells, as is the case in our example, we would normally adjust the formula slightly by reducing the absolute difference between the observed and expected frequencies by .5 for each cell before squaring it (referred to as the *Yates Correction Factor* or the *correction for continuity*). This is a mathematical correction designed to avoid the slightly inflated chi-square value that the uncorrected general formula will produce in tables that have only four cells (referred to as 2-by-2 tables).

For the sake of simplicity (and because most cross-tabulation tables contain more than four cells), the computation illustrated in Box 10.1 does not include the use of the Yates Correction Factor. Other chi-square values displayed in the tables in this chapter, however, were derived from the corrected formula where appropriate.

TABLE 10.5 Critical Values of χ^2

	Level of significance for a one-tailed test					
	.10	.05	.025	.01	.005	.0005
	Level of significance for a two-tailed test					
df	.20	.10	.05	.02	.01	.001
1	1.64	2.71	3.84	5.41	6.64	10.83
2	3.22	4.60	5.99	7.82	9.21	13.82
3	4.64	6.25	7.82	9.84	11.34	16.27
4	5.99	7.78	9.49	11.67	13.28	18.46
5	7.29	9.24	11.07	13.39	15.09	20.52
6	8.56	10.64	12.59	15.03	16.81	22.46
7	9.80	12.02	14.07	16.62	18.48	24.32
8	11.03	13.36	15.51	18.17	20.09	26.12
9	12.24	14.68	16.92	19.68	21.67	27.88
10	13.44	15.99	18.31	21.16	23.21	29.59
11	14.63	17.28	19.68	22.62	24.72	31.26
12	15.81	18.55	21.03	24.05	26.22	32.91
13	16.98	19.81	22.36	25.47	27.69	34.53
14	18.15	21.06	23.68	26.87	29.14	36.12
15	19.31	22.31	25.00	28.26	30.58	37.70
16	20.46	23.54	26.30	29.63	32.00	39.29
17	21.62	24.77	27.59	31.00	33.41	40.75
18	22.76	25.99	28.87	32.35	34.80	42.31
19	23.90	27.20	30.14	33.69	36.19	43.82
20	25.04	28.41	31.41	35.02	37.57	45.32
21	26.17	29.62	32.67	36.34	38.93	46.80
22	27.30	30.81	33.92	37.66	40.29	48.27
23	28.43	32.01	35.17	38.97	41.64	49.73
24	29.55	33.20	36.42	40.27	42.98	51.18
25	30.68	34.38	37.65	41.57	44.31	52.62
26	31.80	35.56	38.88	42.86	45.64	54.05
27	32.91	36.74	40.11	44.14	46.94	55.48
28	34.03	37.92	41.34	45.42	48.28	56.89
29	35.14	39.09	42.69	46.69	49.59	58.30
30	36.25	40.26	43.77	47.96	50.89	59.70
32	38.47	42.59	46.19	50.49	53.49	62.49
34	40.68	44.90	48.60	53.00	56.06	65.25
36	42.88	47.21	51.00	55.49	58.62	67.99
38	45.08	49.51	53.38	57.97	61.16	70.70
40	47.27	51.81	55.76	60.44	63.69	73.40
44	51.64	56.37	60.48	65.34	68.71	78.75
48	55.99	60.91	65.17	70.20	73.68	84.04
52	60.33	65.42	69.83	75.02	78.62	89.27
56	64.66	69.92	74.47	79.82	83.51	94.46
60	68.97	74.40	79.08	84.58	88.38	99.61

Source: From Table IV of R.A. Fisher and F. Yates, *Statistical Tables for Biological, Agricultural, and Medical Research,* published by Longman Group, Ltd., London (previously published by Oliver and Boyd, Ltd., Edinburgh) and by permission of the authors and publishers.

BOX 10.1
The Chi-Square Statistic
(Without Yates Correction Factor)

Hypothesis: Clients who received group treatment are more likely to abstain from alcohol than those clients who received individual treatment.

Null Hypothesis: There is no difference between the type of treatment clients received and whether they abstained from alcohol.

Predictor Variable: Type of treatment—nominal level (group versus individual).

Criterion Variable: Client outcome—nominal level (success versus failure).

Observed Frequencies: See Table 10.2.

Expected Frequencies Formula: $E = \dfrac{(R)(C)}{(N)}$

where: E = Expected frequency in a particular cell C = Total number in that cell's column

   R = Total number in that cell's row N = Total number of cases

Substituting values for letters:

   Cell a: $E = (60)(55)/100 = 33$ Cell c: $E = (40)(55)/100 = 22$
   Cell b: $E = (60)(45)/100 = 27$ Cell d: $E = (40)(45)/100 = 18$

Chi-Square Formula: $\chi^2 = \Sigma \dfrac{(O - E)^2}{E}$

where: χ^2 = Chi-square value E = Expected frequency
   O = Observed frequency Σ = Sum of (for all cells)

Substituting values for letters:

$$
\begin{array}{ccccccc}
\text{cell } a & + & \text{cell } b & + & \text{cell } c & + & \text{cell } d \\
\chi^2 = \dfrac{(40 - 33)^2}{33} & + & \dfrac{(20 - 27)^2}{27} & + & \dfrac{(15 - 22)^2}{22} & + & \dfrac{(25 - 18)^2}{18}
\end{array}
$$

   = 8.24 (Chi-square value)

Degrees of Freedom Formula: $df = (r - 1)(c - 1)$

where: df = Degrees of freedom
   r = Number of rows
   c = Number of columns

Substituting values for letters:

   $df = (2 - 1)(2 - 1)$
   = 1 (degree of freedom)

Presentation of Results: $\chi^2 = 8.24$, $df = 1$, $p < .005$

Conclusions: The null hypothesis is rejected and the one-tailed research hypothesis is supported. In short, clients who received group treatment had statistically significant better outcomes than clients who received individual treatment.

Today, any statistical software program that has the capacity to perform a chi-square analysis will save us a lot of time. The formula for chi-square along with the formulas for expected frequencies and degrees of freedom are all pre-programmed. Using an inexpensive statistical computer software package, we could enter the data for our 100 cases in the example used in this chapter in just a few minutes.

We could then program the computer to run a cross-tabulation and to give us the chi-square and associated p-value to examine the association between type of treatment and client outcome. In just a few seconds, the output of the analysis will appear on the screen.

In our example, we would find that the chi-square value for the data contained in Table 10.2 is 8.24 without using the Yates Correction Factor and that it is reduced to 7.11 when the Yates formula is used. We would also find that there was one degree of freedom and that the p-value for the data, using either formula, was "less than .005." Almost instantly, we would be ready to interpret the results of the analysis.

Presentation of Chi-Square

The actual presentation of our findings using the chi-square statistic is straightforward. First, the cross-tabulation table (containing observed frequencies) is displayed. Second, the chi-square statistic (χ^2), the degrees of freedom (df), and the probability of chance, or sampling error (p), associated with the χ^2 value are placed at the bottom of the cross-tabulation table as they are found in Box 10.1

$\chi^2 = 8.24$
$df = 1$
$p < .005$

Interpreting the Results of a Chi-Square Analysis

Returning to our original example, which examined the relationship between type of treatment for clients who were alcohol dependent and client outcome, the corresponding p-value for our chi-square value is very small (i.e., $p < .005$), which is what we had hoped to find. Since we did not specify a different rejection level, our cutoff point for rejection of the null hypothesis would be the customary .05 rejection level, the point where we would conclude that chance would produce that large a difference between the observed and the expected frequencies less than five times out of 100.

In fact, since .005 is much (ten times) smaller than .05, we would be very safe if we were to reject the null hypothesis that there is no relationship between the variables. A $p < .005$ means that chance, or sampling error, would produce that large a difference between the observed and expected frequencies less than five times out of 1000.

Can we now say that we have statistical support for our one-tailed research hypothesis? Not yet. Chi-square is just a statistical test; it has no way of knowing what we predicted in our one-tailed research hypothesis. It simply checks to see if the difference between the observed and expected frequencies is large enough that it probably is not the work of chance, or sampling error.

In our example, a large chi-square value and a corresponding low p-value would have occurred if either those clients in group treatment had a much better record of abstinence or if the better record had been among those clients in individual treatment.

A chi-square statistical analysis only told us that the variables probably are related, but it did not (and cannot) tell us the direction of that relationship. Was it in the direction that we hypothesized or in the opposite direction?

To find out if we have statistical support for our one-tailed research hypothesis, we would compare the dummy table (Table 10.1) that we created to represent our one-tailed research hypothesis with Table 10.4. We would ask, "Where are the disproportionately large observed frequencies?" (A disproportionately large observed frequency is one that is larger than its expected frequency.) Are they in the cells where we predicted they would be (*a* and *d*) or are they in the opposite cells (*b* and *c*)?

The disproportionately large number of cases are in cells *a* and *d* in Table 10.4, just where we predicted they would be. Thus, we can reject the null hypothesis and claim support for our one-tailed research hypothesis. If the disproportionately large observed frequencies had occurred in cells *b* and *c* (where clients in individual treatment who abstained from alcohol and clients in group treatment who did not are displayed respectively), we would have reason to believe that the variables are related, but in the direction opposite to that which we predicted.

Having merely demonstrated a statistically significant association between the variables, we are still a long way from saying that clients who are alcohol dependent should be put into group treatment because they are less likely to drink again. True, the difference between the percentages of abstinence in our two subsamples was pretty substantive (66.7% for group treatment versus 35.7% for individual treatment). Before we can claim that we have uncovered a relationship that would hold for all or even any other drug dependency treatment facilities, however, we want to be very sure that the alternative explanations for a real relationship between the variables (besides chance, or sampling error) did not produce the apparent relationship between the variables.

Perhaps, for example, most of the alcohol and substance abuse workers in the agency were hired because they are especially adept at working with groups and they have less skill in individual counseling; or perhaps there was an unwritten policy that only those clients with the most severe alcohol problems are assigned to individual treatment. Either fact might explain the relatively high rate of success among clients who were in group treatment.

The most we can say about our finding of a statistically significant relationship between the variables is that most likely the variables really are associated, at least in the agency from which the sample was drawn. We can neither say with certainty, however, why this relationship occurred, nor can we predict if it will be found again in different agency settings with different staff training, agency policies, and type of group or individual treatment used, for example. Maybe we are "onto something," but only replication and other research studies—perhaps using more powerful research designs and more powerful statistical analyses—will provide further evidence that our original one-tailed research hypothesis is, indeed, correct.

Meaningfulness and Sample Size

As mentioned in Chapter 6, sample size influences whether or not a statistical significance will be achieved. When using any statistical test, the larger the sample size, the greater the chance of acquiring statistical support for the decision to reject the null hypothesis. Chi-square is no exception—large samples make it more powerful, some-times too powerful. With a very large sample, it is unlikely that statistical significance will **not** be achieved, even if the actual percentage differences between the expected and observed frequencies are small.

When we see that a chi-square test has demonstrated the presence of a statistically significant relationship between variables, it is easy to be impressed, but we need to look carefully at the sample size (N) that produced it. Like other statistical tests, a chi-square analysis can identify a statistically significant relationship between variables, but it may be a statistically significant weak relationship.

A continuation of the example that we have been using throughout this chapter will demonstrate our point. Let us suppose that we tried to replicate the results of our ear-lier research study. This time, a sample of 200 clients being treated for alcoholism was followed over a two-month period. The results of our second study are displayed in Table 10.6.

When a chi-square test is computed for the data in Table 10.6, $p > .10$ (for a one-tailed research hypothesis). Because the likelihood that chance might have produced the differences between the observed and expected frequency for these data is rela-tively large, we would lack sufficient statistical support to be able to reject the null hypothesis (i.e., $.10 > .05$).

Since the evidence in support of our one-tailed research hypothesis is now con-flicting, we might want to attempt our study for a third time, this time with a very large sample. Let us suppose that we used data on not 200 clients, as is displayed in Table 10.6, but on 10 times more—2000 clients. The data from this third study are displayed in Table 10.7.

A close look at Tables 10.5 and 10.6 reveals that the percentages of the 2000 clients in the respective cells in Table 10.7 were exactly the same as those within the compa-rable cells in our sample of 200 cases in Table 10.5. In both hypothetical studies, 60 percent of clients in group treatment abstained from drinking compared with 53.3 per-cent of clients in individual treatment. Both 2-by-2 tables have one degree of freedom. But the chi-square values are very different. The value is ten times larger in the study using the larger sample than in the one using the smaller sample.

The p-value also is very different (less than .025 with the sample of 2000, com-pared with greater than .10 with the sample of 200). The relationship between the vari-ables was not statistically significant using the data in the study with 200 cases, but it was in the study with 2000 cases. If we had used 20,000 clients, the chi-square value would be 42.9; if we had used 200,000 clients, it would be 429, and so on. Even though the percentages within the tables did not change, the strength of the association would be identical in each instance.

There is a logical reason why we should be more likely to be able to reject the null hypothesis when larger samples are used. When smaller samples are used (the "short run" mentioned in Chapter 5 when the role of probability in hypothesis testing was dis-cussed), a difference of 6.7 percentage points ($60.0\% - 53.3\% = 6.7\%$ points) may have been the work of chance, or sampling error. With the much larger samples, the "law of averages" (the "long run") should have taken over; the differences in success for the two types of treatment should have disappeared if no real relationship between them and treatment success existed.

TABLE 10.6   Observed Frequencies and Percentages:
Type of Treatment by Client Outcome ($N = 200$)

	Results					
	Success		Failure		Totals	
Type of Treatment	Frequency	Percentage	Frequency	Percentage	Frequency	Percentage
Group	30	60.0	20	40.0	50	100
Individual	80	53.3	70	46.7	150	100
Totals . . .	110		90		200	

$\chi^2 = .429$, $df = 1$, $p > .10$ (direction predicted)

TABLE 10.7   Observed Frequencies and Percentages:
Type of Treatment by Client Outcome ($N = 2000$)

	Results					
	Success		Failure		Totals	
Type of Treatment	Frequency	Percentage	Frequency	Percentage	Frequency	Percentage
Group	300	60.0	200	40.0	500	100
Individual	800	53.3	700	46.7	1500	100
Totals . . .	1100		900		2000	

$\chi^2 = 4.29$, $df = 1$, $p < .025$ (direction predicted)

The fact that a 6.7 percentage point difference still exists for the very large sample suggests that the relationship between the variables is a real one, so we probably should reject the null hypothesis. We also should remember, however, that the relationship between the variables is relatively weak, because it "shows up" only when very large samples are used.

Restrictions on the Use of Chi-Square

It is helpful to understand what an expected frequency is and where it comes from. How could we expect to understand the important concept that "the chi-square statistic compares observed frequencies with expected frequencies" if we have no idea what expected frequencies are and how they are obtained? But there is another important reason why it is useful to know how to calculate expected frequencies: They can quickly tell us if we should be using the chi-square statistic at all.

It is best to know this early in the data analysis process to avoid wasting time on a test that is inappropriate. As we noted earlier, the chi-square statistic is not appropriate for all analyses of the relationship between two nominal level variables. Its formula will not produce accurate results and it should, therefore, not be used if either of two situations exists:

1. When, in a 2-by-2 (four-cell) table, at least one cell has an expected frequency of less than 5.

2. When, in a table that is larger than 2-by-2, more than 20 percent of the cells have expected frequencies of less than 5.

A handy check on whether there is a problem with small expected frequencies in any cross-tabulation table can be performed by locating the cell with the smallest expected frequency. To do this, locate the row with the smallest marginal total and the column with the smallest marginal total. The cell with the smallest expected frequency is at the intersection of that row and column. The cell's expected frequency can be determined with the expected frequency formula. If an expected frequency in a 2-by-2 table is 5 or more, it is safe to use the chi-square statistic. If the expected frequency is under 5, chi-square should not be used.

In larger tables, additional "checks" will have to be made to see if the second "no-go" situation exists. If it does, it may still be possible to use chi-square by combining adjoining cells to form a table with fewer cells with sufficiently large expected frequencies. This process, called collapsing, should be done using common sense and logic and in a way that does not discard any more data than absolutely necessary. Value categories of a variable that are thus combined should possess a strong logical similarity to each other.

AN ALTERNATIVE TO CHI-SQUARE: FISHER'S EXACT TEST

If the expected frequency size requirements for the use of the chi-square test cannot be met, an alternative, also a nonparametric test, can be used: *Fisher's exact test*. Like chi-square, it is used with two independent subsamples. The independent subsamples may have resulted from the random sampling of cases that have been categorized as falling into two identifiable groups, such as gender (i.e., male, female) or marital status (i.e., married, not married). Or they may be the experimental and control groups to which cases were randomly assigned in a classical experimental research design.

Unlike chi-square, Fisher's exact test has one serious limitation—it can only analyze data using a 2-by-2 contingency table (four cells). If we had more than two value categories of either (or both) of the variables that we think may be associated, it would be necessary to collapse the data into a 2-by-2 table before Fisher's exact test could be used. Sometimes this would result in a loss of available measurement precision. If feasible, it might be preferable to enlarge the size of the research sample so that the requirements for the use of the chi-square test can be met.

Fisher's exact test is often used to obtain a preliminary answer to a research question. It is easily computed by hand. Subsequent to its use, more sophisticated analyses can be attempted using larger samples and/or more rigorous research designs.

USING CHI-SQUARE FOR INFERENCE

Chi-square is a test for association between nominal level variables. Let us see how we can use it within practice settings to infer whether any association between two nominal level variables within a sample might also exist within its population.

Example: Discharge Planning and Re-admission

Background.   Amelia is a social worker in a state in-patient hospital. Her main duty is to do re-admission intake interviews with previous patients. From five years of experience, she has observed that a large number of patients who are re-admitted to the hospital had been previously discharged to live with their relatives. Knowing that her social work colleagues doing discharge planning also made frequent use of boarding homes for discharged patients, she wondered why she was not seeing more re-admissions among those patients who were discharged to boarding homes. She wondered if there might not be a relationship between patients being re-admitted to the hospital and the place to which they had been discharged (boarding home versus relatives).

Hypothesis.   Amelia read all the literature on the topic that was available to her. Based on a general consensus among other social work practitioners, previous research findings, and personal observations, she designed and implemented a small-scale re-search study that would gather data to test her one-tailed research hypothesis:

> *One-Tailed Research Hypothesis:*
> Patients discharged to boarding homes will have a lower rate of re-admission to the hospital than patients discharged to live with their relatives.

Research Design.   Amelia received permission from her supervisors to select a 10 percent random sample of all files of patients discharged during the previous 18 months. Using a standardized data collection instrument that she constructed, she gathered data on a wide variety of demographic variables on the 148 patients (10% of 1480 patients = 148 patients) who were discharged to boarding homes and the 250 patients (10% of 2500 patients = 250 patients) who were discharged to relatives. Her total sample was 398 patients (148 + 250 = 398).

Findings.   Table 10.8 presents Amelia's findings.
What did Amelia learn from her data analysis (Table 10.8)? From her general knowledge of hypothesis testing, she knew that $p < .01$ meant that the differences between the observed and expected frequencies probably were not the work of chance—the likelihood that chance produced the relationship between the variables

TABLE 10.8   Readmission to Hospital by
Discharge Status ($N = 398$)

Discharge Status	Readmission?		Totals
	Yes	No	
Boarding Home	25	123	148
Relatives	71	179	250
Totals . . .	96	302	398

$\chi^2 = 6.113$, $df = 1$, $p < .01$ (direction predicted)

was less than one in 100. She was able to reject the null hypothesis and to conclude that there was a statistically significant relationship between them.

Amelia also knew that when a one-tailed research hypothesis is tested using chi-square, it is necessary to determine whether a statistically significant relationship between variables is in the predicted direction. Chi-square analysis is concerned primarily with the differences between the observed and expected frequencies within each cell. A difference is only a difference, whether it suggests numbers that are smaller or larger than predicted. Amelia knew that she must determine if the association was in the predicted direction, either by looking for the cells where disproportionately large observed frequencies occurred or by examining percentages.

Using Table 10.8, Amelia was able to determine that approximately 17 percent (25 of 148) of patients discharged to boarding homes had been re-admitted to the hospital, compared with 28 percent (71 of 250) of those discharged to relatives. These two percentages, 17 and 28, were consistent with the direction of her hypothesis; patients discharged to boarding homes were less likely to be re-admitted than patients discharged to relatives.

Conclusions.   Before Amelia drew any conclusions about the meaningfulness of the statistical significance between the variables, she knew that she must acknowledge the limitations of her research design. The validity and reliability of the data in the patient records might be a problem; in addition, there might be other factors relating to bias. There was also a long list of other variables that might have affected re-admission of the patients in her study. They included patient diagnosis, length of first hospitalization, availability of after-care services, patient's use of medication, and a myriad of other factors that she had no reason to believe were equally represented in the two groups (boarding home/relatives) of patients.

What did her findings really tell Amelia about the relationship between the setting to which patients are discharged and their re-admission? The goal of chi-square is to acquire evidence for or against the existence of an association between variables. Cause and effect knowledge was not a possibility from the beginning. This was due partly to the absence of an experimental research design and partly to the limits of the chi-square analysis itself. What Amelia learned was that, for whatever reasons, patients who were discharged to boarding homes from her particular hospital were not as likely to be re-admitted as those patients who were discharged to relatives.

Amelia also gathered data on patient diagnosis and length of first hospitalization. She could examine the relationship among these other variables and the dependent variable as well, using other appropriate statistical tests. The patient's records might have yielded insights into other variables that went into the decision to live with relatives or in a boarding home; these data could be used to enhance the results of her analysis and to shed more light on the statistical findings.

Given all the limitations that tempered the interpretation of Amelia's findings, it might seem that they were of little value. The likelihood of the existence of many other variables that might have affected whether or not a patient was re-admitted would seem to discount even further the utility of her research findings for social work practice. Yet, despite a less than perfect research design and the use of a relatively low-powered, nonparametric statistical analysis, several possible practice implications emerged.

Knowing (even without fully understanding why) that patients discharged to boarding homes in Amelia's hospital are less likely to be re-admitted than patients discharged to relatives could be valuable to her social work colleagues doing discharge planning. Patients discharged to live with relatives could be perceived as being at higher risk of re-admission.

Based on her findings in Table 10.8, Amelia began to ask certain questions:

1. Should I try to find boarding home placements for more of my clients?
2. Should I endeavor as a professional social worker to work toward the creation of more boarding home facilities?
3. Should I endeavor to provide additional sources of support for patients going to live with relatives in order to reduce the likelihood of their being re-admitted?

These applications of the research findings are still only questions. None of them indicate that Amelia or the other social workers at her hospital should make drastic modifications in their service delivery methods without careful consideration and, what is more important, without evidence of further research findings.

Any major changes in the delivery of social work services may have a negative effect on the lives of patients or clients. Changes based upon findings derived from chi-square can be especially risky. After all, the identification of a statistically significant relationship between variables using chi-square is evidence of association, not causation.

Like any type of statistical analysis, chi-square can also suggest relationships between variables that are spurious, that is, not real. They might disappear if other variables are introduced into the data analysis. Chi-square analyses are sometimes best used to tentatively identify associations between variables and to formulate critical questions that can subsequently be answered through more high-powered statistical analyses.

Example: Legislators' Voting Patterns and Tax Issues

Juan is a social worker employed by a legislative committee. He is attempting to assist in the passage of an increase in the state sales tax, which will provide additional revenues for public education. As part of his job, he recently began gathering demographic data on state legislators. He hoped to gain insight into why they might favor or oppose the proposed tax bill.

After he had examined some available data and hearsay on about 30 legislators, it seemed to him that legislators who favored the bill tended to have children who currently attended public schools; those legislators who were on record as not supporting the bill tended not to have children currently in public schools. Juan wondered whether he could find statistical support for a relationship between the nominal variables support (or nonsupport) for the bill and use (or nonuse) of public schools.

After discussion with committee members and a review of the literature available on legislators' voting patterns on various tax issues, Juan concluded that he could justify formulation of a one-tailed research hypothesis:

One-Tailed Research Hypothesis:
Legislators who currently have children attending public schools are more likely to support the bill than are legislators who do not have children currently attending public schools.

TABLE 10.9 Legislators' Support for Tax Bill by
Whether They Use Public Schools
($N = 125$)

Use Public Schools?	Support for Bill?		
	Yes	No	Totals
Yes	39	36	75
No	21	29	50
Totals . . .	60	65	125

$\chi^2 = .834$, $df = 1$, $p > .10$ (direction predicted)

Juan continued to gather data on the state's legislators, but he made a special effort to learn about and systematically record data on his two variables. He identified 160 legislators who had publicly stated support for or opposition to the tax bill. Of these, he obtained sufficient current biographical data on 125 (78 percent) to conclude with reasonable certainty whether or not they were currently sending their children to public schools. Table 10.9 presents Juan's findings.

Juan was somewhat disappointed by the findings of his chi-square analysis, yet he was grateful that he had not relied on his subjective hunches in his presentation to the legislative committee. If he had, he might have misled the committee members.

With one degree of freedom and a one-tailed research hypothesis, Juan knew his chi-square value should have been at least 2.71 (i.e., Table 10.5, Appendix C) in order to reject the null hypothesis at the customary .05 rejection level. It was not that large. He lacked sufficient evidence to reject the null hypothesis and to conclude that the legislators' use or nonuse of public schools for their children was associated with their voting preference on the tax bill (which was his original one-tailed research hypothesis).

Perhaps other variables were more closely associated with whether they favored the bill, for example, their voting record on all tax bills, their perceptions of the fairness of a sales tax versus other sources of revenue, a partner who was teaching in the public school system, and so on. Juan also knew that these other variables may have helped to obscure the presence of a relationship between the variables whose association he had tested.

The lack of statistical support for Juan's one-tailed research hypothesis in no way negated the value of his study. He avoided making an erroneous conclusion based on inadequate evidence that might have resulted in an inappropriate lobbying strategy. Portraying the motivation of legislators who opposed the bill as "self-serving" would have been a mistake. He could now spend his time more efficiently by pursuing other avenues to gain insight into the legislators' positions on the proposed tax.

CHI-SQUARE WITH THREE OR MORE VARIABLES

A variation of bivariate chi-square analyses allows us to examine the relationship between two nominal level variables while controlling for a third nominal level variable. It is particularly useful when we are concerned that a relationship between variables might be spurious. A third variable might "explain it away."

TABLE 10.10 Observed Frequencies: Type of Treatment
by Client Outcome ($N = 100$)

Type of Treatment	Results		Totals
	Success	Failure	
Group	15	35	50
Individual	25	25	50
Totals . . .	40	60	100

$\chi^2 = 3.376$, $df = 1$, $p < .05$ (direction predicted)

In the example used earlier in this chapter, we were seeking to document the existence of an association between the variables "type of treatment" and "client success." Let us return to that example. This time, suppose we repeated our research study using 100 clients and again used chi-square to analyze the data. The observed frequencies for this hypothetical study are displayed in Table 10.10.

Despite the presence of a statistically significant association between the variables, we may wonder if a third variable, for example, "gender," may explain why clients in group treatment appear to do better than those in individual treatment. We would like to control for the effects of this third variable (called a control variable) to get a better picture of the true relationship between type of treatment and client outcome.

One way to explore the effect of the third variable might be to divide our sample into its two subcategories, male and female. We could then construct two separate tables—one for female clients and one for male clients. We could use the chi-square test with each of the two subsamples to see if the relationship between type of treatment and client outcome "held up" within each of the subsamples. But there would be a better and more efficient way to accomplish the same purpose, the use of multiple cross-tabulation tables.

Use of Multiple Cross-Tabulation Tables

It is possible to examine the association between two nominal level variables while controlling for a third variable while using a single cross-tabulation table. Multiple cross-tabulation tables can be used to spread the cases in the original cross-tabulation table (e.g., Table 10.10) among a larger number of cells. (This is the opposite of the process of collapsing described earlier.) Two or more variables are displayed along one axis or even along both axes. Table 10.11 is a multiple cross-tabulation table using the same data that were used in Table 10.10, only in Table 10.11 a third variable (gender) has been added.

Notice that the results of the statistical analysis (p-value) displayed in Table 10.11 are similar to those in Table 10.10. The two methods for control of the third variable produced similar results; in both methods of analysis, we would be unable to reject the null hypothesis (using the .05 rejection level). How can we interpret this phenomenon? It probably means that the relationship between type of treatment and client outcome is not a spurious one or, if it is, at least gender is not the "culprit" that is producing the deception.

Problems with Sizes of Expected Frequencies.   It is not always possible to control for one or more variables using multiple cross-tabulation. When data are spread out within larger cross-tabulation tables, a situation may be produced in which the size requirements for expected frequencies for using chi-square cannot be met.

In Table 10.11, the 100 cases are distributed among eight cells. The expected frequencies of the eight cells in Table 10.11 would thus be smaller than the expected frequencies of the four cells in Table 10.9. They are, however, over five in a sufficiently large percentage of them to justify the use of chi-square. This happened only because the number of cases in group and individual treatment was equal, there were an equal number of males and females, and the overall number of successes and failures were similar. If the cases had not split so evenly into the various value categories, the expected frequencies may have been less than five in over 20 percent of the cells. Then we could not have used the chi-square test.

Because the use of multiple cross-tabulation tables spreads out the cases into a larger number of cells, they can be used only when relatively large samples are available and cases break fairly evenly among value categories of the variables. Even then, if at least one examined variable has been measured in a way that results in a large number of value categories, the value categories may have to be collapsed so that the cross-tabulation table has fewer cells (and sufficiently large expected frequencies) before we can use the chi-square test.

Only the expected frequency size requirement of chi-square prevents the more frequent use of multiple cross-tabulation tables for examining the effect of other variables on the relationship between variables. Theoretically, several variables could be combined along the left of the table and several more could be combined along its top. To do this, however, a very large sample would be required, larger than is found in most social work research situations.

Effects of Introducing Additional Variables.   The original association between variables will sometimes disappear when a third variable is controlled. When this happens, the relationship may have been a spurious one. Other times, the relationship between the two original variables will appear stronger when a third variable is controlled.

TABLE 10.11   Observed and Expected Frequencies: Type of Treatment and Gender of Client by Client Outcome ($N = 100$)

| | | Client Outcome | | | | |
| | | Success | | Failures | | |
Treatment	Gender	Observed	Expected	Observed	Expected	Totals
Group	Male	7	(10)	18	(15)	25
Group	Female	8	(10)	17	(15)	25
Individual	Male	13	(10)	12	(15)	25
Individual	Female	12	(10)	13	(15)	25
Totals . . .		40		60		100

$\chi^2 = 4.334$, $df = 3$, $p > .05$ (direction predicted)

In such instances, the third variable, called a *suppressor* or *obscuring variable*, may cause us to underestimate the actual strength of the association between the other variables.

When a third variable is introduced, a third result also may occur. The relationship between the first two variables may remain statistically significant. But it may be significant in one direction with one or more value categories of the third (control) variable and significant in the opposite direction within its other value categories. When this happens, it is usually not possible to summarize the findings easily; the relationship between the independent variable and dependent variable has to be described for each value category of the control variable. The third variable is said to further specify the relationship between the first two variables, and it is therefore called a *specifying variable*.

The many possible effects of the introduction of one or more additional variables to a statistical analysis remind us of the complexity of most relationships among variables. It is because of this complexity that we should exercise extreme caution in drawing conclusions about the effect of one variable on another or even about their association. A statistically significant relationship between variables can still be a spurious one. All that statistical significance tells us is that the relationship was unlikely to be the work of chance, or sampling error. Chi-square analyses are sometimes best used to tentatively identify associations between variables and to formulate critical questions that can be subsequently answered through more high-powered statistical analyses.

CONCLUDING THOUGHTS

This chapter examined two related forms of statistical analyses. It briefly addressed the chi-square goodness-of-fit test, a useful tool for comparing a sample with a population when the distribution of the value categories of a nominal level variable is known within the population. The test can be used to verify the representativeness of a sample in relation to a variable or to test whether or not a research sample differs from its population following some intervention.

Most of the chapter was devoted to the more widely used chi-square test of association. The fact that chi-square requires only nominal level data makes it ideally suited to many of the hypothesis testing needs in our profession.

Unfortunately, there are certain errors commonly made in its use. They usually entail making "too much" of a finding of statistical significance by either (1) implying that the relationship is one of more than just association, (2) overestimating the importance of findings that reflect weak relationships between variables where a finding of significance was virtually inevitable because of the use of very large samples, or (3) failing to consider that the association may be a spurious one and thus attempting to control for other variables that may be creating a false impression about the relationship that has been suggested.

Still another common error is made when chi-square is used when one or both variables are at the ordinal, interval, or ratio level of measurement. When chi-square is used, the test treats different value categories as if they are only differences in kind; it will ignore the fact that they may reflect differences in the quantity of the variable.

Unless both variables are only at the nominal level of measurement, there is very likely to be a better (often a more powerful) statistical test that can and should be used.

STUDY QUESTIONS

1. What does the chi-square goodness of fit test compare? What are two different uses for it?
2. Why is the frequent use of chi-square in social work research both good and bad? How is the test particularly well suited to social work research?
3. What do the numbers in each of the cells in a cross-tabulation table mean?
4. What is a dummy table, and what does it reflect?
5. Can chi-square tell us whether one variable causes variations in the second variable? Explain.
6. What are expected frequencies, and how are they used in chi-square testing?
7. How do degrees of freedom affect whether a chi-square value of a given size (e.g., 10.00) will be considered statistically significant?
8. What are the minimum expected frequency requirements for the use of chi-square? What other nonparametric alternative is available when the expectation for a 2-by-2 table cannot be met?
9. What is the final step in the process for determining if chi-square has demonstrated support for a one-tailed research hypothesis? Provide examples.
10. How can cross-tabulation (chi-square) be used to examine the relationship between variables while controlling for the effect of a third variable? How can this detect the presence of a spurious relationship between variables?

Chapter 11

t Tests and Analysis of Variance

$\mathbf{O}$ne of our profession's greatest needs is to execute research studies that evaluate the effectiveness of our treatment interventions. We need to know, for example, whether a particular treatment intervention is associated with positive (or negative) changes in our clients' knowledge levels, affect levels, or behavioral levels. In addition, we often need to know if one intervention is better than another to help produce the desired change within our various client systems.

In testing hypotheses related to practice effectiveness, we frequently have reasonably precise measurements of the variable we seek to influence—the dependent variable. Examples of dependent variables may be "client self-esteem," "public attitudes toward welfare recipients," "client marital satisfaction," or "incidence of spouse abuse," to name just a few.

Thanks to the work of researchers over the years, many standardized self-report measuring instruments used to measure these variables now exist. They are assumed to generate interval level data that approximate a normal distribution within the population on which they have been developed.

Other dependent variables such as "number of appointments missed," "number of stated oppositions to a proposed social service program," or "amount of illegal drugs consumed," often are at the interval or ratio levels of measurement by their very nature. Many of these variables also tend to be normally distributed within the population, making the mean an appropriate measure of their central tendency and the standard deviation an appropriate measure of their variability (see Chapter 3).

In testing research hypotheses related to practice effectiveness, the independent variable is usually at the nominal level of measurement. It may be, for example, "different types of treatment intervention," "race or gender of the social worker," or some other variable that reflects only different value categories of the nominal level independent variable. Also, the research sample available for a study is usually small; large samples are not common in social work research, particularly in clinical situations.

The three conditions briefly described above—one nominal level independent variable, one normally distributed interval or ratio level dependent variable, and a relatively small research sample(s)—are ideally suited to a statistical analysis that involves a comparison of two or more means derived from the dependent variable. This chapter presents a "family" of related statistical tests used for this purpose: (1) *t* tests and (2) simple analysis of variance, or simple *ANOVA*. Let us now turn our attention to the *t* test.

t TESTS

In many social work research situations, the dependent variable is measured within either a single sample or within two samples. In a single-sample situation, for example, we may wish to know if the sample really differs greatly from its population in relation to the dependent variable—that is, how typical is it? On the other hand, in the two-sample situation, we may wish to know if measurements of the dependent variable differ greatly between the two samples in relation to the dependent variable—that is, are the two samples really all that different from one another?

A *t* test is based on a *t* distribution (of means) referred to briefly in Chapter 6. It has many similarities to the normal distribution and resembles it ever more closely as sample sizes begin to approach 30 cases. There is actually a different *t* distribution for each sample size under 30.

We will recall that both normal distributions (Chapter 5) and sampling distributions (Chapter 6) relied heavily on a knowledge of the amount of variation (standard deviation) of a variable within the population. With this knowledge, we were able to compute a confidence interval which in turn can be used to identify just how large (or small) a mean score we would have to have to be statistically significant.

As we mentioned, the *t* distribution is especially useful in that it allows us to compute a confidence interval for interval and ratio level variables whose standard deviations within the population are unknown. This condition exists for many dependent variables we wish to examine and influence. We are unlikely to know, for example, a population's standard deviation for variables such as "number of unsafe sexual contacts per month in a given community" or "number of 'bullying incidents' within a secondary school per week."

The fact that *t* tests are parametric means that they should be used when interval or ratio level data are normally distributed. On a general level, they should not be used with a variable that is badly skewed. They are, however, quite robust; that is, if we use them with interval or ratio level variables that are only somewhat skewed, they do not produce distorted findings.

The One-Sample *t* Test

The *one-sample t test* is used when our research study contains only one sample. What does it do? It simply compares a sample's mean of an interval or ratio level variable with its population's mean. The formula for the test produces a *t*-value, which is then compared with a table like Table 11.1 or Appendix D to get a p-value. When a computer is used, however, we get both the t-value and the corresponding p-value as products of the data analysis, along with the degrees of freedom. For the one-sample t test, the degrees of freedom are the number of cases in the sample minus one.

Like the chi-square goodness-of-fit test discussed in the previous chapter, the one-sample t test can be used in two basically different situations. It can be used to (1) compare a sample's mean of an interval or ratio level variable with its population mean and (2) test hypotheses.

Comparing a Sample's Mean to Its Population's Mean.

The one-sample t test is used like the chi-square goodness-of-fit test discussed in Chapter 10. The only difference between the one-sample t test and the chi-square goodness-of-fit test is that the one-sample t test is used with interval or ratio level data and the chi-square goodness-of-fit test is used with nominal level data. The one-sample t test can be used to evaluate the representativeness of a sample in relation to some interval or ratio level variable. When used this way, to demonstrate that a sample is truly representative of the population from which it was drawn, we generally hope *not* to *reject* the null hypothesis.

In essence, we hope to generate support for the position that any difference between the two means is so small that it is probably the work of chance ($p > .05$), or sampling error—that is, our sample is indeed representative of its population.

Example: Age and Job Satisfaction.

Suppose we want to conduct a simple research study to examine the relationship between the variables "age" and "job satisfaction among AFDC social workers" (using Pearson's r). We have been told by the program's administrator that we can draw only a small random sample ($N = 30$) of workers since we need to conduct extensive interviews with them. Obviously, we would like our sample to be representative of the population of all AFDC workers in relation to what logically may be an intervening interval level variable, "size of a worker's caseload." We know from the agency's management information system that the caseload for all AFDC workers is normally distributed with a mean of 50.

We could draw our sample of 30 and then, using the one-sample t test, compare our sample's mean caseload size with the population's mean caseload size of 50. If the results of our analysis were to suggest that the difference between the two means was likely to be the work of chance ($p > .05$), we would *not reject* the null hypothesis. The sample would be "not all that different," probably close enough to be considered representative of its population in regard to the variable "size of worker's caseload."

If, however, a one-sample t test analysis compared our sample's mean with its population's mean and concluded that the difference between the two means was not likely to be the work of chance, or sampling error ($p < .05$), we would **reject** the null hypothesis. From this, we could conclude that our sample and its population really are different in regard to the variable "size of caseload." We would then conclude that our sample is not representative of its population in relation to this important variable. If we were to continue our research study using a sample that is different from its population, we would jeopardize our ability to generalize our study's findings to the population from which the sample was drawn.

TABLE 11.1   Critical Values of t

df	Level of significance for a one-tailed test					
	.10	.05	.025	.01	.005	.0005
	Level of significance for a two-tailed test					
	.20	.10	.05	.02	.01	.001
1	3.078	6.314	12.706	31.821	63.657	636.619
2	1.886	2.920	4.303	6.965	9.925	31.598
3	1.638	2.353	3.182	4.541	5.841	12.941
4	1.533	2.132	2.776	3.747	4.604	8.610
5	1.476	2.015	2.571	3.365	4.032	6.859
6	1.440	1.943	2.447	3.143	3.707	5.959
7	1.415	1.895	2.365	2.998	3.499	5.405
8	1.397	1.860	2.306	2.896	3.355	5.041
9	1.383	1.833	2.262	2.821	3.250	4.781
10	1.372	1.812	2.228	2.764	3.169	4.587
11	1.363	1.796	2.201	2.718	3.106	4.437
12	1.356	1.782	2.179	2.681	3.055	4.318
13	1.350	1.771	2.160	2.650	3.012	4.221
14	1.345	1.761	2.145	2.624	2.977	4.140
15	1.341	1.753	2.131	2.602	2.947	4.073
16	1.337	1.746	2.120	2.583	2.921	4.015
17	1.333	1.740	2.110	2.567	2.898	3.965
18	1.330	1.734	2.101	2.552	2.878	3.922
19	1.328	1.729	2.093	2.539	2.861	3.883
20	1.325	1.725	2.086	2.528	2.845	3.850
21	1.323	1.721	2.080	2.518	2.831	3.819
22	1.321	1.717	2.074	2.508	2.819	3.792
23	1.319	1.714	2.069	2.500	2.807	3.767
24	1.318	1.711	2.064	2.492	2.797	3.745
25	1.316	1.708	2.060	2.485	2.787	3.725
26	1.315	1.706	2.056	2.479	2.779	3.707
27	1.314	1.703	2.052	2.473	2.771	3.690
28	1.313	1.701	2.048	2.467	2.763	3.674
29	1.311	1.699	2.045	2.462	2.756	3.659
30	1.310	1.697	2.042	2.457	2.750	3.646
40	1.303	1.684	2.021	2.423	2.704	3.551
60	1.296	1.671	2.000	2.390	2.660	3.460
120	1.289	1.658	1.980	2.358	2.617	3.373

Source: From Table III of R.A. Fisher and F. Yates, *Statistical Tables for Biological, Agricultural, and Medical Research,* published by Longman Group, Ltd., London (previously published by Oliver and Boyd, Ltd., Edinburgh) and by permission of the authors and publishers.

Hypothesis Testing. The one-sample *t* test is also used to test hypotheses. If we attempt to gain support for a one- or two-tailed research hypothesis, we hope to demonstrate that our sample is so different from its population in regard to some interval or ratio level variable that the difference is not likely to be the work of chance, or sampling error. Thus, we seek to **reject** the null hypothesis.

Example: The State's Licensure Examination. Suppose, using AFDC caseworkers again as research participants, we hope to demonstrate statistical support for our belief that AFDC workers in our county agency do better overall on the state licensure examination than most other AFDC caseworkers. Our one-tailed research hypothesis would then be stated as follows:

One-Tailed Research Hypothesis:
Social workers at ABC county office will score higher than their peers on the state licensure examination.

We then collect the scores from all 30 of our workers who took the examination during the past five years and, using the one-sample *t* test, compare their mean score with that of all AFDC workers who took the examination during the past five years. Perhaps our sample's mean score turned out to be higher than the population's mean. That alone would not be sufficient to lend support to our one-tailed research hypothesis.

The question remains, was it that much higher? Would we be safe in concluding that our sample's higher mean score was not just the work of chance, or sampling error? The results of a one-sample *t* test analysis would answer this question. It would result in both a *t*-value and a corresponding *p*-value, which would be based on the *t*-value and degrees of freedom. If we had used .05 as our rejection level, a *p*-value less than .05 (i.e., $p < .05$) would offer support to the decision to reject the null hypothesis and would lend support for our one-tailed research hypothesis. A *p*-value greater than .05 (i.e., $p > .05$) would support a decision not to reject the null hypothesis. It would suggest that the difference between the two mean scores is probably just the work of chance, or sampling error.

When the chi-square goodness-of-fit test was introduced in Chapter 10, we described how that test can be used to see if a social work practice intervention "made a difference." Since, as we noted, the two tests are similar, it should come as no surprise that a one-sample *t* test also can determine if an intervention was effective, only it does it with interval or ratio level data.

We could, for example, select a random sample of clients with low self-esteem and offer a supplemental treatment intervention package to them for six weeks. Using a one-sample *t* test, we could then measure their self-esteem levels and compare their mean self-esteem level with the mean self-esteem level of all clients who have a similar diagnosis. This example is just a variation of the use of one-sample *t* test described in the example above.

Presentation of One-Sample t Tests. The presentation of one-sample *t* tests is straightforward. Table 11.2 provides a clear example of how this is done using the

TABLE 11.2   State Licensure Examination Scores Broken Down by Offices

Research Participants	Mean	Standard Deviation	N
Sample	90	5	30
Population	80	unknown	100

$t = 2.62$, $df = 29$, $p < .01$

previous example. As noted above, it gives the results from a hypothetical study that had the following one-tailed research hypothesis:

One-Tailed Research Hypothesis:
Social workers at ABC county office will score higher than their peers on the state licensure examination.

Using Table 11.2 as a guide for the moment, the most frequently used presentation of the one-sample *t* test entails displaying the population mean (i.e., 80), the mean of the research sample (i.e., 90), the standard deviation of the research sample (i.e., 5), the number of cases in the research sample and in the population (i.e., 30 and 100 respectively), the *t*-value (i.e., 2.62), the degrees of freedom (i.e., 29), and the corresponding *p*-value (i.e., $p < .01$).

By glancing at Table 11.2, we could conclude that the 30 workers who took the examination in ABC county had a mean score of 90 compared to the mean score of 80 for the entire population and that the workers ($N = 30$) in ABC county thus scored, on the average, 10 points higher than the population ($N = 100$) as a whole. This 10-point difference is statistically significant at the .01 level (one-tailed test). This means that a 10-point difference would happen by chance less than 1 time out of 100 with this size sample.

The Dependent *t* Test

The *dependent t test* is also called the *paired groups t test, matched groups t test, dependent groups t test,* or *correlated groups t test*. Unlike the one-sample *t* test discussed above, a dependent *t* test does not compare a sample's mean for an interval or ratio level variable with its population's mean. It does, however, compare mean scores from two samples that are related in some way. It can be used when we have two connected (or matched) samples that we measure once or when we use one sample and measure it on two separate occasions.

Use with Two Connected (or Matched) Samples Measured Once.   The dependent *t* test can easily be used when research participants are connected or matched in some way and put into two distinct samples, or groups. The two samples, for example, may consist of pairs of siblings of which one sibling is assigned to Sample A and the other is assigned to Sample B. In short, the two samples are not randomly drawn from a population and put into two separate subsamples, or groups. People (or objects) are simply connected or matched. We could, for example, administer a treatment intervention to one of the samples and use the dependent *t* test to see if there is a statistically significant difference between the two samples in relation to some interval or ratio level variable.

Use with One Sample Measured Twice.

The dependent *t* test can also be used when the same people are measured at two different times. A research design of this type is called a *one-group pretest-posttest research design*.

Using the one-group pretest-posttest research design, suppose we want to test the effectiveness of a smoking cessation program. We could draw a random sample of clients who smoke and ask them to record the average number of cigarettes they smoked one day before enrolling in a smoking cessation program (pretest). We could then record the number of cigarettes they smoked the day after they complete the program (posttest). We then could compare the mean number of cigarettes the group smoked one day **before** the program with the mean number they smoked one day **after** the program.

Like all statistical tests of inference, a dependent *t* test produces a corresponding *p*-value. It allows us either to claim a statistically significant relationship between having been in the group and mean number of cigarettes smoked (i.e., $p < .05$) or not to claim it (i.e., $p > .05$). Of course, even if the relationship was found to be statistically significant, we could not reject the null hypothesis that the intervention makes a real difference on this basis alone.

We would also have to rule out the possibility that something else may have created the apparent relationship. The time lapse between the date the data for the pretest were collected, for example, and the date the data for the posttest data were collected (and what may have occurred for our participants in the interim) may be a more plausible explanation than the intervention for any reduction in cigarette smoking.

The presentation of the dependent *t* test using a one-group pretest-posttest research design is simple. Table 11.3 provides the results of a hypothetical research study with the following one-tailed research hypothesis:

One-Tailed Research Hypothesis:
Pregnant teenagers will have increased child-rearing skills after they undergo a child-rearing skills training workshop.

A five-day child-rearing skills training workshop was offered to 22 pregnant high school students. The group's mean child-rearing skills score was calculated before the skills training workshop (pretest) and after it (posttest).

TABLE 11.3 Child Rearing Skill Scores for Pregnant Teenagers Before and After the Child Rearing Skills Training Workshop ($N = 22$)

Pretest	Posttest	Difference
4.8	5.8	1

$t = 2.53$, $df = 21$, $p < .01$

Table 11.3 displays the results of the study using a dependent *t* test analysis. Notice that the students had a pretest mean score of 4.8 and a posttest mean score of 5.8. The difference between the two means was 1 point (5.8 − 4.8 = 1). This 1-point difference is statistically significant at the .01 level with 21 degrees of freedom ($N − 1$ for this *t* test). This means that a 1-point difference would happen by chance less than 1 time out of 100 with this size sample even if the workshop had no real effect on child-rearing skills. Thus, we can reject the null hypothesis and, if all other competing explanations for the apparent relationship can be ruled out, we can claim support for the one-tailed research hypothesis.

The Independent *t* Test

Another variation of the *t* test, the *independent t test*, is especially useful for research studies using a relatively small number of cases. Like the dependent *t* test, it also compares the means of two samples. But to use the independent *t* test correctly, the two samples must be independently drawn from a population. That is, no case in one sample is connected to any case in the other sample, as they are when the dependent *t* test is used.

The two groups do not have to contain an equal number of cases, which often is the situation in social work evaluations of treatment effectiveness. Often two subsamples (e.g., clients in group treatment, clients in individual treatment) naturally tend to be unequal in size. Even in the most carefully designed research studies that randomly assign an equal number of cases to two subsamples, clients are likely to drop out of treatment before the study is completed. Any resulting discrepancy between the sizes of the two subsamples presents no problem for the independent *t* test. The formula for the test automatically controls for it.

When using the independent *t* test, cases selected for study are divided into two samples for the dichotomous independent variable (e.g., Intervention A, Intervention B; female therapist, male therapist). In experimental research designs, the two samples usually are the experimental group (Sample 1) and the control or comparison group (Sample 2).

Mean scores of the two samples are compared using the formula for the independent *t* test, producing a *t*-value and a corresponding *p*-value. On the basis of chance, or sampling error, the means of the two samples are likely to be somewhat different; the results produced by the test are an analysis of the amount of that difference.

If the difference turns out to be so small that chance, or sampling error, is the likely explanation for this difference, the null hypothesis cannot be rejected. We can conclude that the difference between the means of the two groups is too likely to be a function of chance and does not reflect a real relationship between the independent and dependent variables.

On the other hand, if the results indicate that the difference is large enough that it is unlikely to be the work of chance, or sampling error, we may be able to reject the null hypothesis and conclude that the difference observed in the sample indeed reflects a real relationship between the two variables. Chance, or sampling error, will have been effectively discounted as a possible explanation for the apparent relationship between them.

With small samples such as those often used in social work practice research, even a fairly large difference between two means may be due to chance, or sampling error.

But there comes a point where a difference between two means is sufficiently large that chance alone is unlikely to have produced it. When is this point reached? The independent t test tells us. It determines the statistical likelihood of making a Type I error if we were to reject the null hypothesis.

Example: Study Guide for the State Merit Exam.   As illustrated in Chapter 2, a hypothetical study guide could be developed to help social workers prepare for the state merit exam. To evaluate the effectiveness of such a study guide, we might randomly select 15 of the 30 social workers who plan to take the exam and provide them with a copy of it. We could give them specific directions to spend part of their study time each night using the guide as instructed.

The 15 social workers who used the guide could be regarded somewhat loosely as the experimental group; the remaining 15, who did not use it, could be regarded as the control group. After all 30 social workers took the state merit exam, their results could then be compared. We would not directly compare the individual score of each person who used the guide (experimental group) with the score of each person who did not use the guide (control group). Instead, we would compare the mean exam score of the 15 social workers in the experimental group with the mean exam score of the 15 social workers in the control group.

In comparing the means for the two groups using the independent t test, we would be able to determine the answer to certain questions. Is the mean difference between the two groups large enough to allow us to reject the null hypothesis (that any apparent relationship between using/not using the guide and the social workers' scores on the exam is the work of chance)? How confident can we be that the difference was not due to chance, or sampling error? Is the difference in the direction that we predicted? Does the data analysis suggest that the use of the study guide might help other social workers taking the state merit examination, not just those in the experimental group?

Of course, as with all statistical testing, even if it can be demonstrated that a statistically significant relationship between the two variables exists, there are still other possible explanations for it. Perhaps, for example, the guide served to remind the social workers to prepare for the exam. Consequently, they may have put more time and energy into studying than did those in the control group.

Maybe the guide itself was of no direct help at all. Even if other possible alternative explanations could be ruled out (in addition to chance), another question still would have to be addressed: Is the relationship between the variables a meaningful one? Does the size of the mean difference in scores on the exam, for example, justify the purchase price of the guide? The answer to this question, like others related to the practical value of the research findings, might be a difficult one.

MISUSE OF *t* TESTS

As with the chi-square test, the popularity of t tests sometimes can lead to their misuse. The tests are familiar to us, easily understood, and relatively nonthreatening. Consequently, there may be a tendency to want to use them, even in situations in which they are inappropriate and in which other, more appropriate tests should be used. Two common misuses are (1) ignoring the shape of the distribution of the interval or ratio level dependent variable within the population and (2) using the "shotgun" approach to data analyses.

Ignoring the Distribution of the Dependent Variable

As noted earlier, *t* tests are designed for use in those situations when the interval or ratio level dependent variable is considered to be normally distributed within the population. If a variable within the population is badly skewed, other tests (such as those nonparametric alternatives to be discussed), should be used in their place. The value of research findings can be seriously jeopardized if *t* tests are used with interval or ratio level data that are badly skewed within the population from which the samples were drawn.

The Shotgun Approach to Data Analyses

A second common misuse of the independent and dependent *t* tests (two sample tests) involves calculating the tests using a single dependent variable and a long list of dichotomous independent variables. In some particularly glaring examples of this "shotgun" approach to data analyses, researchers have run hundreds of tests with little basis in the literature for believing that the independent and dependent variables might be related. To their delight, they have found a statistically significant relationship between a few independent and dependent variables.

Findings of a few statistically significant relationships between variables that are derived through using large numbers of two sample tests are not surprising. In fact, we would probably be more surprised if none of the relationships between the variables proved to be statistically significant! Probability theory alone suggests that a spurious relationship thus found may not be a real one. The "finding" is probably due to a process sometimes referred to as "data dredging." It likely was produced by a variation on the old principle that "with an infinite number of monkeys, an infinite number of typewriters, and an infinite amount of time, some monkey, some time, somewhere, will write a Pulitzer Prize winning novel!"

Expressed another way, by trying enough combinations, one is almost certain to stumble onto one of those very rare ($p < .05$) phenomena that occurred simply because of chance, or sampling error. Making too much of this can result in a Type I error, since the results are unlikely to be replicated within a second pair of samples. In situations in which there is reason to believe that many different independent variables may be related to the dependent variable, other multivariate statistical tests should be used that are specifically designed for such situations.

USING *t* TESTS FOR INFERENCE

t tests can be used in a variety of ways when it comes to inference. Two examples will demonstrate how they can be used for inferential purposes.

Example: Treatment of Marital Problems

Background.   Rose is a social worker in a large family service agency. In her agency's orientation procedure, she was taught that the best format for marital counseling is to see both partners (husband and wife) together. Five years ago, she treated 20 couples, all of whom could only be seen individually (husband *or* wife) because of their work schedules. She was surprised to observe that although they were never seen as a couple after their initial interviews, all 20 couples seemed to make excellent progress in solving their marital problems.

Over the years, Rose saw more and more couples on an individual basis. Since she believed she was having good client outcomes, she encouraged six of her colleagues to also counsel couples with marital difficulties by seeing them separately rather than together. The other social workers were also pleased with their clients' excellent progress.

However, Rose was not ready to conclude that the individual counseling format was really preferable to couple counseling. She decided to conduct a small-scale research study to see if she could find statistical support for her hunch that couples seen individually make better progress toward solving their marital problems than couples seen together.

As Rose began to search the social work literature, she found considerable support for the position that marital satisfaction is best enhanced when couples are treated in counseling together, not individually. But as she ventured into the literature from other fields such as psychology and pastoral counseling, Rose found a fair amount of support for the belief that success in marital counseling may be more likely to result from individual counseling. A reason sometimes given is that clients tend to discuss areas of dissatisfaction more readily and candidly when the spouse is not present.

Hypothesis.   Rose concluded that the professional literature was conflicting. She felt that her own observations, however, and those of her colleagues were sufficient to tilt the balance enough to justify a one-tailed research hypothesis:

One-Tailed Research Hypothesis:
Among couples receiving marital counseling, those seen individually will reflect a statistically significant higher level of marital satisfaction after ten weeks than those seen together.

Methodology.   Rose designed a small-scale research study to test her one-tailed research hypothesis. She received permission from the agency director and her clients to randomly assign new clients who requested marital counseling during a three-month period to either individual counseling or couple counseling. In a research sense, the clients were randomly assigned to one of two groups. All six social workers who had previously used and were experienced with both the couples counseling and the individual counseling formats participated as counselors in Rose's study.

Beginning the next month every other couple seen at intake was assigned to one of the six social workers to be seen together for counseling 50 minutes per week; the remaining couples were assigned to be seen individually for 25 minutes each per week.

Those who could not agree to this arrangement were also seen but were not included as research participants in the study.

The counseling method (i.e., individual, couple) was the independent variable. The dependent variable, "marital satisfaction" (to be measured after ten consecutive weeks of counseling), was measured using a widely used, standardized measuring instrument that measures marital satisfaction. The measuring instrument produces interval level data.

Fourteen couples were assigned to individual counseling sessions, and 14 were assigned to be seen as couples. Twelve couples in individual counseling completed ten weeks of treatment, and 13 couples in couples counseling completed ten weeks of treatment. After all 25 couples completed the marital satisfaction measuring instrument, Rose took the score for each partner and averaged it with that of his or her spouse to get a "couple score."

Then she computed the mean couple score of those who were seen individually (experimental group) and compared it with the mean couple score of those who were seen together (control group). The variable "marital satisfaction" has been found to be normally distributed, so Rose felt justified in using the independent *t* test for her statistical analysis. She was attempting to determine whether the difference between the mean scores for the two groups was sufficiently large to allow her to reject the null hypothesis. She hoped to be able to conclude that a real relationship between the two variables was the likely explanation for the differences observed in her research sample.

Findings.   The *t*-value for Rose's data was 1.312. From a table of critical values of *t* (Table 11.1 or Appendix D), she learned that she needed a minimum *t*-value of 1.714 to be able to reject the null hypothesis (using a rejection level of .05, a sample of 25 [23 degrees of freedom], and a one-tailed research hypothesis).

Rose noted that if she were to reject the null hypothesis based on the analysis of her data, she would have slightly more than a 1 in 10 (10%) chance of committing a Type I error (1.312 is slightly smaller than 1.319). Thus, she lacked statistical support for her one-tailed research hypothesis. Her initial disappointment was made even worse when she looked at the mean score for both groups.

The clients who had participated in individual counseling scored somewhat worse, on the average, than did those clients seen together. Rose studied her findings some more. She then realized that her lack of demonstrated support for a relationship between counseling method and marital satisfaction might reflect a useful finding in and of itself. Her inability to reject the null hypothesis could be interpreted to mean that it makes little difference which counseling method is used.

Conclusions.   Rose also wondered how she could have been mistaken. The findings from her study were inconsistent with her previous impressions. She wondered whether she and the other social workers had perhaps merely perceived their individual counseling clients as doing better because of their surprise that these clients did about as well as those seen in couple counseling. Of course, she also wondered whether her initial one-tailed research hypothesis might still be correct.

Perhaps the true relationship between the independent variable and the dependent variable had been hidden by biased measurements or the influence of rival hypotheses (e.g., the social workers' greater experience with couple counseling). As she thought about it, Rose concluded that additional studies employing more rigorous research designs were indicated.

In the interim, before further research studies could be conducted, Rose wondered what practical use she could make of her findings. During the next agency staff meeting she presented the results of her study. She was able to draw implications for social work practice within the agency. As frequently happens in social work research, her research study generated more questions than answers. These questions, however, served to focus the staff's attention on potentially productive areas of inquiry. Based on her findings, Rose and other staff members began to ask the following questions.

1. Since type of counseling (individual or couple) may have little or no effect in enhancing marital satisfaction, should continued attempts be made to encourage clients to enter couple counseling if they resist or if it represents a scheduling difficulty for them?
2. Should involvement of both partners in counseling continue to be a requirement for counseling, or should this policy be changed?
3. Should funds be allocated for a staff development program to enhance the social workers' use of individual counseling in treatment of marital problems?
4. Should the staff develop a single treatment model that combines individual and couple counseling, or should the professional staff be allowed freedom to select the counseling format that they prefer to use?

The above four questions, along with others, ranged from issues that affected the individual social work practitioner to those that related to agency policies. The principal value of Rose's study was to call into question certain unchallenged practices within the agency and to encourage the staff either to justify or to discard them based upon further examination. Even if no changes resulted, the social workers would be practicing on a sounder theoretical base until subsequent research findings provided a more definitive answer to the questions.

Example: Staff Turnover

Background. Antonia is the director of social services for a large state health agency. In her professional role, she oversees social work services offered in the 50 district offices throughout the state. It was recently brought to her attention that her agency was having a serious problem with social work staff turnover. A preliminary examination of agency data revealed that the problem was statewide and appeared to be normally distributed among the 50 district offices.

Antonia spoke with the personnel officer who was responsible for conducting exit interviews with employees leaving the agency. At first he preferred not to suggest possible reasons why so many social workers were resigning. But after Antonia assured him that she did not plan to ask him to identify workers who made complaints to him, he volunteered that the reasons given by many of the social workers for leaving appeared to be amazingly similar. He recalled that "many" of them seemed totally frustrated with their lack of autonomy in decision making.

While the social workers recognized that in some professional and administrative matters the final decision had to be made by their supervisors, they saw no reason why many other decisions could not be made by them and their fellow professionals through a more democratic process.

Antonia thought about what she had been told. While her first inclination had been to be annoyed with the district supervisors for their apparent autocratic approach to decision making, she quickly realized that she had to take much of the responsibility for their supervisory style. She had come to rely on the use of staff authority when it seemed so effective with workers in her secretarial pool. She had hired trainers from outside the agency and required that all district supervisors attend training in the use of staff authority.

She had also commented regularly at supervisors' meetings how effective she thought the approach was. Apparently the supervisors were only responding to Antonia's message that extensive use of staff authority is a sign of good supervision. By allowing their social workers only to advise them but not to make or implement decisions, the supervisors were really complying with Antonia's implicit directive.

Hypothesis.   Antonia knew that she needed an objective way to determine whether social workers' level of autonomy in decision making was related to staff turnover. She did not want to trust the impressions of the personnel officer without further data. She would not attempt to help all her supervisors to become more democratic in delegating decision making until she could be reasonably certain that some relationship existed between the two variables. She decided to conduct a small-scale research study to test the following one-tailed research hypothesis:

One-Tailed Research Hypothesis:
There will be a lower mean rate of staff turnover in democratic decision-making environments than in autocratic ones.

Methodology.   Antonia knew that recent management literature stressed the use of quality circles as a promising way to solve some administrative problems by arriving at decisions via the group process. (The approach is characteristic of Theory Z management methods that have been viewed as successful in Japan for many years.) Antonia had been considering the use of quality circles anyway and saw this as a good time to try them. Quality circles seemed to her to be a good way to create a more democratic approach to decision making in the district offices.

Antonia randomly selected ten districts to serve as her experimental group. She then provided release time to the ten district supervisors to attend an out-of-state workshop on the use of quality circles. She told the supervisors that she expected them to implement quality circles in their supervision, and she requested a report on their methods of implementation to ensure that this had been done. They were asked not to share their experiences with other district supervisors.

At the same time, Antonia randomly selected ten other districts as her control group. These district supervisors were given no additional training and no new instructions on how they should handle decision making in their district offices.

After one year, Antonia computed a mean rate of turnover for districts in the experimental group and for those in the control group. She had two categories of the dichotomous nominal level independent variable "decision-making environment" (i.e., democratic, autocratic). Her dependent variable (turnover rate) was at the ratio level of measurement. The situation seemed to be well suited to use the independent t test to test whether there might be statistical support for her one-tailed research hypothesis.

Findings.   Antonia compared the mean turnover rate for the two groups using the independent t test. The mean turnover rate of the experimental group was lower than the mean turnover rate of the control group. The t-value for Antonia's data was 1.992. She concluded that there were 18 degrees of freedom (10 + 10 = 20; 20 − 2 = 18). Using a table like Table 11.1 or Appendix D, she noted that, for the row corresponding to 18 degrees of freedom, the t-value from her statistical analysis fell between 1.734 and 2.101. She moved to the left (1.734) and observed that it was in the column headed by .05 for one-tailed tests and .10 for two-tailed tests. The p-value corresponding to her data under the one-tailed research hypothesis was therefore less than .05.

From her knowledge of statistics, Antonia knew that she had found support for a statistically significant relationship between the independent variable and the dependent variable. She knew that if she were to reject the null hypothesis, she would have less than a 5 percent chance of committing a Type I error on the basis of statistical probability alone. She also was pleased to see that the relationship was in the direction she had predicted; the mean turnover rate for district offices in the experimental group was lower than the mean turnover rate for district offices in the control group.

Implications.   Because her study had been very limited in scope, Antonia was reluctant to view her findings as an unequivocal endorsement of the expanded use of quality circles (or other more democratic methods of decision making) as a way to reduce staff turnover. She recognized that it would be precipitous on her part to proceed to implement her findings as though she had uncovered a simple cause-effect relationship. Her study's research design had certainly not eliminated the two alternative explanations (i.e., rival hypotheses, design bias) as possible explanations for the difference between the two staff turnover rates.

Certain methodological questions remained. How much did the opportunity to go out of state for training, for example, positively affect the morale of the supervisors in the experimental group? Perhaps they came back in a better mood and thus were more inclined to be more considerate of their workers. If so, this may have been a better explanation than the implementation of quality circles for their lower mean staff turnover rate. Or did the workers view the supervisors in the experimental group as more considerate simply because they made an effort to try something new? If so, this might have been a major factor in the lower mean turnover rate.

Despite the fact that Antonia's findings would have to be viewed as tentative, she was still able to use them both to understand the problem of staff turnover and to begin to address it through her actions. In light of her findings, she asked herself the following six questions:

1. How can I adjust my supervisory style with district supervisors so that I do not unintentionally communicate to them that I expect extensive use of staff authority relationships in the supervision of their workers?
2. How can I help district supervisors to identify decisions that are more appropriately made using the democratic process? How can I make them feel more comfortable using this process?
3. How can I help district supervisors to identify decisions that are inappropriate for the democratic process (e.g., personnel matters) and to continue to use staff authority (and other less democratic approaches) for these decisions without harming the morale of their workers?
4. What use of the democratic process, besides quality circles, would help social workers feel that they have more input into decisions if they possess the necessary expertise?
5. Would it be advisable to send all district supervisors to quality circle training out of state?
6. What further research studies can be designed to provide additional support for the finding that democratic decision making is associated with low staff turnover?

After thinking about the above six questions and others that emerged from her study, Antonia discussed her ideas for implementing her findings with friends who are social work administrators in other large social service agencies. She then settled on a plan of action.

At the next meeting of all district supervisors, Antonia shared the findings of her research study. She reiterated her support for the use of staff authority in certain situations but also stated her belief that social workers at all levels are professionals and need to be involved in decision making. She emphasized that she believed over reliance on autocratic supervisory approaches can hurt morale and, even more important, does not take advantage of the expertise of other staff in addressing problems.

She supported these contentions by asking a former district supervisor of the experimental group to use part of the next supervisors' meeting to teach all the supervisors (including herself) the basic principles of quality circles. In the meeting, the other nine district supervisors who had used them were asked to share their experiences as well.

Antonia was convinced that sharing decision making in certain situations by district supervisors with their respective workers was indicated. In another meeting she emphasized this belief to the supervisors. Consistent with it, she allowed them to decide individually whether they preferred to receive training in quality circles so as to implement that technique in their district offices or to develop their own plans (with her approval) for introducing ways to increase democratic decision making among their supervisees.

Finally, Antonia set aside time to develop a more comprehensive and larger-scale study of staff turnover. This study would examine other factors, in addition to approaches to decision making, that the literature suggests are related in some way to staff morale and turnover. She hoped that ultimately the findings from this larger-scale study could be generalized to other social work settings and that a report of the findings would have the potential for publication in a professional social work journal.

SIMPLE ANALYSIS OF VARIANCE (ONE-WAY *ANOVA*)

The second major group of statistical tests that form the generic term "analysis of variance" is called *simple analysis of variance*, hereafter called *simple ANOVA*. It is sometimes called *one-way analysis of variance*. These tests are appropriate for use in hypothesis-testing situations when the nominal level independent variable has three or more value categories. Like an independent *t* test, a simple *ANOVA* is used when the dependent variable is at the interval or ratio level of measurement. It should be obvious by now that the independent *t* test mentioned above compares means between only two subsamples. The key words here are "only two." The key words with a simple *ANOVA* are "three or more."

While *t* tests produce a *t*-value that can be compared with a table (i.e., Table 11.1) to determine whether or not it is justifiable to reject the null hypothesis, the variations of a simple *ANOVA* produce an *F*-ratio with its own table, (not included in this book) that allows us to make this same determination. When using computer software for data analyses, however, both a *t* and a simple *ANOVA* will automatically generate *p*-values along with their respective *t*-values or *F*-ratios.

Let us use an example to illustrate how a simple *ANOVA* works. Suppose for a moment, that within a large psychiatric outpatient clinic, all professional staff perform case management functions. Each staff member works on a team whose members share the same professional discipline as the worker. Since there are only three professional disciplines among the workers, there are three teams. (If there had been four disciplines among the workers, there would have been four teams, and so on.) We want to know if clients are more satisfied with one team (that is, with one professional discipline) than with the other two. To attempt to find out, we formulate the following two-tailed research hypothesis:

Two-Tailed Research Hypothesis:
Among clients seen by case managers, the professional discipline of the case managers is related to client satisfaction.

We could use a standardized measuring instrument that yields interval or ratio level data to measure the dependent variable, "client satisfaction." There are three categories of the independent variable "professional discipline of case manager"—(1) psychologist, (2) social worker, and (3) psychiatric nurse. We could compare the three possible combinations of pairs of means (client satisfaction) using three independent *t* tests—that is, (1) psychologist and social worker, (2) psychologist and nurse, and (3) social worker and nurse.

As noted in the previous discussion, however, we would be using the same means repeatedly and thus increasing the likelihood of chance, or sampling error, producing a spurious but statistically significant relationship. Besides, why conduct three separate statistical analyses when one will do nicely?

In our example, a simple *ANOVA* tells us if the differences among the three mean client satisfaction levels are related to the discipline of the professional. Specifically, a simple *ANOVA* would tell us the probability (*p*), considering degrees of freedom (based on the size of the samples), that any differences in mean client satisfaction levels among the three disciplines might have been produced by chance, or sampling error.

Computation

A simple *ANOVA* is not easy to compute by hand. Nevertheless, it is a very useful test to know. In our example, it would compare the mean client satisfaction level for each of the three subsamples (i.e., one for each professional discipline) with the grand mean— the mean client satisfaction level for all three professional disciplines (ignoring discipline). Thus, a simple *ANOVA* examines how much the mean of each subsample (each individual value category of the independent variable) differs from the means of the other subsamples as well as from the grand mean (all the subsamples). A simple *ANOVA* examines these differences (referred to as the "between groups variance") as well as the amount of variability of client satisfaction within each subsample (referred to as the "within groups variance").

The fact that our clinic may employ more social workers as case managers than the other two professional disciplines, for example, presents no problem. Like an independent *t* test, the subsamples used in a simple *ANOVA* need not be of equal size.

It should be pointed out that a simple *ANOVA* does not tell us which subsample mean is statistically different from the other subsamples' means. It only tells us if there is (or is not) a statistically significant relationship among the subsamples' means. If there is a statistically significant relationship among them, then we still need to identify which subsample mean is statistically different from the other subsamples' means. There are many ad hoc statistical methods that can help us with this. One commonly used one is called the *Duncan test*.

As we have mentioned, the complexity of the formula for a simple *ANOVA* precludes calculating it by hand. Nevertheless it is a powerful parametric test. It can easily identify relationships between variables that other, less powerful statistical tests might miss. As a general rule, however, more powerful tests also are more restrictive than less powerful ones—that is, more conditions for their use must be met. A simple *ANOVA* is no exception.

In addition to the requirements of the other parametric statistical tests, a simple *ANOVA* should be used only when the amount of variance for a dependent variable within each subsample is approximately equal. In our hypothetical study we could not use a simple *ANOVA* if, for example, the amount of variation in satisfaction among clients seen by social workers tended to be much greater than among clients seen by one or more of the other two professional disciplines.

A NONPARAMETRIC ALTERNATIVE: THE MANN-WHITNEY *U* TEST

There are several nonparametric options that are available if the conditions for *t* tests or a simple *ANOVA* cannot be met. Some of these are briefly discussed in Chapter 12. We will mention only one—the one that is probably used most frequently in social work research, the *Mann-Whitney U test*, hereafter called *U* test.

The *U* test is simply a nonparametric option to the independent *t* test. It is used with a dichotomous nominal level independent variable and an ordinal, interval, or ratio level dependent variable that need not be normally distributed (as required for use of the independent *t* test). Like the independent *t* test, the *U* test also attempts to reject the null hypothesis. The *U* test determines if the differences between two independent subsamples, with respect to the dependent variable, are the work of chance, or sampling error.

The *U* test is ideally suited for research studies involving two small independent subsamples (i.e., dichotomous independent variable). Thus, it is frequently used in quasi-experimental research situations to determine whether a "treatment" given to an experimental group, but not to the control group, appears to result in a difference within a dependent variable.

Like the independent *t* test, the *U* test does not need two groups of identical size (or subsamples). The same formula is used with very small samples (under eight) or larger ones, but we must be careful in interpreting results to use the table of critical values (not included in this book) that is designed to adjust for sample size.

Unlike a simple *ANOVA*, a *U* test is easily computed with a pocket calculator. It is based on the assumption that a good indicator of the difference between the two groups is the number of cases in one group that fall below each respective score of the other group when all scores are rank ordered.

The logical premise underlying it is that the presence of a disproportionate number of higher scores drawn from one group and of lower scores drawn from the other group probably suggests that on the whole, the two groups really are different in regard to the dependent variable. The *U* test is a mathematical way of determining whether this pattern is sufficiently strong to support a rejection of the null hypothesis.

Like other nonparametric options, the *U* test often is used as a "preliminary method" of examining relationships between variables without investing great amounts of effort into data analyses. Because it requires only ordinal level data, it is appropriate for situations in which the development of a new data collection instrument precludes any claim that there is adequate measurement precision to generate normally distributed interval or ratio level data. Because it requires only a small sample size, it also lends itself well to a preliminary analysis of possible relationships.

Example: Employees with "Attitude Problems"

Shanti is a social worker employed by a large corporation. During July he had 17 referrals of workers identified as having "attitude problems" on the job. He asked each of their supervisors to name another worker at the same level whom they would describe as having a "very good attitude" who might participate with him when the problem worker was being counseled. Seven of the supervisors complied with his request; the other ten did not.

Shanti saw all 17 workers (seven with their coworkers and the other ten alone) for five sessions. After the fifth interview, he asked their respective supervisors to complete a standardized measuring instrument that measures an employee's "attitude toward work." He then rank ordered the scores of all 17 workers and used the *U* test to test his one-tailed research hypothesis:

One-Tailed Research Hypothesis:
The experimental group (counseling involving the coworker approach) will have higher job attitude scores than the control group (counseling involving the supervisor-supervisee approach).

He quickly noted that three of the top four attitude scores were achieved by members within the experimental group.

In fact, the *U* test did not allow Shanti to reject the null hypothesis. Two of the lowest scores also came from experimental group members. Even if the *U* test had achieved statistical significance, alternative explanations for a true relationship (e.g., lack of random assignment to groups, the effect of other variables), could not have been ruled out because of the lack of rigor of Shanti's simple research design. Shanti decided to tighten up the design and to pursue his inquiry further by using larger, randomly selected samples and by including a pretest of worker attitudes.

As suggested earlier, the *U* test is useful for comparing the rankings of a variable within two subsamples. However, if there are more than two subsamples (value categories of the nominal level independent variable), there is another, related nonparametric test that can be used—the *Kruskal-Wallis test*. It works very much like the *U* test, ranking all scores, sorting the rankings into subsamples, and then examining how many cases in other subsamples are ranked below each case in a given subsample. Generally speaking, a Kruskal-Wallis test is the nonparametric analog of a parametric simple *ANOVA*. We could state this as an analogy: A Kruskal-Wallis test is to a *U* test what a simple *ANOVA* is to an independent *t* test.

Still another nonparametric test that is used for a variety of purposes, the median test, is sometimes used in situations in which we wish to examine the relationship between a nominal level independent variable (with more than two value categories) and an interval or ratio level dependent variable that is skewed. It is discussed in Chapter 12.

MULTIVARIATE ALTERNATIVES

Multiple Analysis of Variance

A *multiple analysis of variance* (*MANOVA*) is designed for situations where we wish to test for a relationship that involves two or more dependent variables. Like a simple *ANOVA*, a *MANOVA* entails a comparison of means, but it compares the means of the two or more interval or ratio level dependent variables across the value categories of the independent variable. Thus, it compares groups (sets) of means compiled from several dependent variables.

In situations where *MANOVA* is used, a series of simple *ANOVAs* could have been inappropriately used instead. But to do so would fail to address the importance of intercorrelation among the two or more dependent variables. The formula for *MANOVA* takes this into consideration.

Factorial Designs

Other variations of analysis of variance, called *factorial designs*, are available for situations in which we wish to examine the relationship among two or more nominal or ordinal level independent variables and one interval or ratio level dependent variable. We could, for example, examine the relationship among the discipline of the worker and the gender of the worker and the dependent variable "client satisfaction." The relationship would be a complex one, and the formula is correspondingly complex since we are now venturing once again into the area of multivariate analyses—statistical testing that has the potential to examine the interaction among three or more variables.

Three-way analysis of variance is used as we might guess it is used. It examines the relationship among three nominal or ordinal level independent variables and one interval or ratio level dependent variable. Still another type of test altogether, *Hottelling's* T^2, is appropriate when there are two or more independent variables as well as two or more dependent variables. A discussion of the complexities of this test and of the special uses and requirements of factorial designs is beyond the scope of this book. An advanced statistics text is recommended for those readers who wish to go beyond our brief mention of multivariate alternatives to *t* tests and simple *ANOVA*.

CONCLUDING THOUGHTS

The family of related tests that involve a comparison of two (*t* tests) or more (simple *ANOVA*) means are well suited to social work research. They are both versatile and powerful. *t* tests (for use with two means) and simple *ANOVA* (for use with three or more means) are being used increasingly for social work hypothesis testing.

The simple examples contained in this chapter illustrated how we can use *t* tests and simple *ANOVAs*. While these tests often are used in major research projects that have extensive funding and use sophisticated research designs, they also are valuable for preliminary, limited efforts.

In addition, while those statistical findings that support research hypotheses are of practical value at many different levels for the social work practitioner, nonsupport for research hypotheses can be of equal value. If a research study is designed and implemented well and statistical testing is conducted correctly, we can advance the body of knowledge available to social work practitioners, whether statistical support for a research hypothesis is found or not.

STUDY QUESTIONS

1. What is the appropriate combination of levels of measurement of two variables for using either an independent *t* test or a dependent *t* test?
2. Why do the sample size and subsample size comparability requirements of the independent *t* test frequently make it ideally suited for social work research?
3. If using the independent *t* test, the null hypothesis were correct, would the mean value of a variable in one sample be very similar to, or very different from, the mean value for that variable in the other sample?
4. What do *t* requirements say about using *t* tests with interval or ratio level variables that reflect a skewed distribution within the population?
5. What are the formulas for degrees of freedom for the three *t* tests described in this chapter?
6. What additional step is required in determining whether a *t*-value that is statistically significant reflects support for a one-tailed research hypothesis?
7. Explain why a *t* test that does not result in a finding of statistical significance may still produce a finding that is useful for the social work practitioner. Provide an example.

8. Provide an original example of how one could use a one-sample *t* test to evaluate practice effectiveness within a social agency with which you are familiar.

9. Find an article in a professional social work journal that reports on the use of the dependent *t* test. What was the study's hypothesis? How did the author interpret the study's results? Do you feel the test was used appropriately? If so, why? If not, why not? What contribution did the article make to the profession's knowledge base?

10. What conditions for use of the Mann-Whitney *U* test make it particularly well suited for the individual practitioner who wishes to evaluate the effectiveness of a new treatment method? Provide a social work example in your discussion.

Chapter 12

Additional Nonparametric and Multivariate Tests

The preceding four chapters presented some of the most widely used statistical procedures—correlation (r), regression, cross-tabulation (χ^2), and analysis of variance (t tests and *ANOVA*). Although these tests are used to analyze data in a large number of statistical situations, there are many other situations in which they cannot be used. This chapter presents other useful parametric and multivariate tests that were not included in the preceding three chapters.

NONPARAMETRIC TESTS

Four additional nonparametric statistical procedures that are especially useful to social workers are (1) McNemar's test, (2) the median test, (3) the Kolmogorov-Smirnov two-sample test, and (4) the Wilcoxon sign test.

McNemar's Test

The *McNemar's test*, also referred to as the *test for the significance of changes*, is popular in research situations that employ a one-group pretest-posttest research design. It entails the measurement (twice) of a two-category nominal level variable using a single research sample. Thus, the McNemar's test is frequently used in determining if a type of social work intervention may have had an impact and, if so, whether the intervention's impact was the desired direction. The test could be used, for example, to determine if an educational program on the life experiences of Southeast Asian refugees seemed to produce a desired change in attitudes about them among community members who attended an educational program (the intervention).

In social work practice and research we often wonder whether an intervention (the independent variable) had any effect at all on the dependent variable. Because of the existence of so many intervening variables that can influence the dependent variable, it may be hard to know just how influential our intervention may have been in any changes that have occurred. The McNemar's test offers the opportunity for at least a preliminary insight into these issues. It can tell us to what extent an intervention is associated with change, in addition to determining if the changes that occurred were in the desired direction.

Example: Hiring Additional School Social Workers.   Chester is a school social worker. He requested time to address a meeting of a parents' group to present his arguments for hiring four additional school social workers for the district, a proposal currently being considered by the school board. He wondered whether the parents really would be influenced by his arguments one way or the other (or would just listen politely). Before Chester even considered giving up more of his evenings to speak to other parents' groups, he wanted to know if his remarks had an effect. He needed to know if his presentation, or intervention, was associated with a change in parents' thinking and, if so, whether the change would be in a desired direction.

Chester predicted that his presentation would influence parents' thinking on the issue. But he was not sure in which direction they would be influenced. Thus, he concluded that he had a two-tailed research hypothesis:

Two-Tailed Research Hypothesis:
Parents who attend his presentation will reflect changes in their attitudes about hiring additional social workers following his presentation.

Just prior to his presentation to the parents' group, Chester gave a sheet of paper and a pencil to each parent. On the paper, he asked each parent to include an identifying number (for anonymity) and to indicate if he or she was in favor of hiring the four additional social workers. These data would form his pretest data. Immediately after his presentation, he once again gave all parents a sheet of paper and a pencil and asked them to supply the same identifying number and to again indicate if they were in favor of hiring the additional social workers. These data would form his posttest data. Based on pretest and posttest data supplied by the parents, Chester classified each parent into one of four mutually exclusive categories:

1. Favored before, favored after—cell *a*
2. Favored before, did not favor after—cell *b*
3. Did not favor before, favored after—cell *c*
4. Did not favor before, did not favor after—cell *d*

Chester placed his raw data into a 2-by-2 cross-tabulation table (Table 12.1) like the ones described in Chapter 10. He then used the chi-square formula (with the Yates Correction Factor) to compute a chi-square value. He checked the table of critical values (e.g., Table 10.5 or Appendix C) to see whether he had statistical support to reject the null hypothesis.

TABLE 12.1 Significance of Change Analysis (McNemar's Test): Positions on Proposal Before and After Chester's Presentation

Before Presentation	After Presentation		Total
	For	Against	
For	6 (a)	26 (b)	32
Against	10 (c)	8 (d)	18
Totals . . .	16	34	50

$\chi^2 = 5.58$, $df = 1$, $p < .02$

In Table 12.1, the totals on the right side represent the numbers of parents for and against the proposal before (pretest) Chester's presentation (32 and 18 respectively). The totals along the bottom of the table represent the numbers for and against it after (posttest) the presentation (16 and 34 respectively). The numbers within the body of the table (its four cells) represent individual cases, as they do in a cross-tabulation table. The 50 cases (parents) were distributed among the table's four cells based on a pair of measurements—whether or not a parent favored the proposal before the presentation and whether or not he or she favored the proposal after it.

Thus, if Ms. Aguilar favored the proposal before Chester's presentation, for example, but opposed the proposal after his presentation, she would be one of the 26 cases in cell b. Or if Mr. Owens was against the proposal before his presentation and was still against it after the presentation, he would be one of the 8 cases in cell d.

The McNemar's test simply looks at change. Cells b and c include parents who changed their position; cells a and d contain parents who had no change in their position. Since the McNemar's test is really not very interested in cases where no change occurred (cells a and d), the focus of its analysis is on cells b and c.

The null hypothesis suggests that some change would likely have occurred with some cases, but whatever change occurred probably would be the work of chance, or sampling error, not Chester's presentation. Without Chester's presentation, logic states that about half of any changes that occur would be in one direction and half in the other direction. These changes would theoretically "cancel each other out," and the number of parents favoring or opposing the proposal to hire more social workers would remain about the same after the presentation as they were before it.

Statistically, the McNemar's test seeks to determine whether the null hypothesis can be rejected by demonstrating that the preponderance of change that occurred was in only one direction. From the data in Table 12.1, Chester was able to reject the null hypothesis ($p < .02$). Unfortunately, the direction of most of the changes that occurred indicated that his presentation may have been associated with negative results (parents' turning against the proposal) rather than positive ones (parents' deciding to support the proposal).

Only 14 parents failed to change their positions (cells a and d). But of the 36 who changed them (cells b and c), only 10 moved from negative to positive (cell c), while 26 (cell b) who had previously favored the proposal opposed it after the presentation. The demonstration of a statistically significant change was an endorsement of Chester's ability to influence parents' attitudes. The results of his presentation, however, were not what he had sought.

Chester speculated on the meaning of his study's findings. Had he said something to "turn off" the parents? Why had so many of them been negatively affected by his presentation? Before he gave any more presentations to parents' groups, he planned to review carefully what he had said and how he had said it.

As can be seen, the McNemar's test is quite limited. It is used in research situations that involve a two-category nominal level dependent variable that is measured twice for the same sample of cases. Because it is ideal for many one-group pretest-posttest research designs that evaluate the effect of a method of practice intervention, it can be a useful test for the social work researcher or practitioner. It often is used as a preliminary to more high-powered statistical analyses.

The McNemar's test and another simple test that requires only a nominal level dependent variable, *Yule's Q*, often is used to obtain a preliminary answer to a research question. It is easily computed by hand. Subsequent to its use, more sophisticated data analyses can be attempted using larger samples and/or more rigorous research methods.

Median Test

Another easily calculated nonparametric test for situations in which we lack a normally distributed interval or ratio level dependent variable is the *median test*. Like the independent *t* test, it employs the use of a measurement of central tendency. But unlike the independent *t* test, which compares a mean of one sample with a mean of another sample, the median test examines those cases that fall above and below the median for a skewed interval or ratio level dependent variable. Like other statistical tests, it is designed to assess the likelihood that two independent subsamples (e.g., experimental group, control group) are sufficiently different from each other in regard to the dependent variable to warrant the rejection of the null hypothesis.

The median test is relatively simple. Scores are rank ordered for the dependent variable, and the median for all scores is computed. Then the number of scores above and below the median (those at the median are simply dropped or added to one group or the other) are tabulated for both categories of the dichotomous nominal level independent variable, and the frequencies are placed into a cross-tabulation table.

Because it uses the median as the cutoff point for the dependent variable, the median test divides the sample into two equal-sized groups (half above the median and half below the median). With larger samples (30 or 40 or more total cases) that also reflect a reasonably even split in the number of cases in a dichotomous nominal level variable (two subsamples), the expected frequencies may be large enough to justify the use of the chi-square test to complete the data analysis. When the total number of cases (both groups) is small, Fisher's exact test is substituted to see if the relationship between the two variables is statistically significant.

The median test is based on the assumption that if the two groups are not really different or reflect differences that can be attributable to chance, each will have approximately the same percentage (subsample sizes need not be equal) of cases above and below the median of the dependent variable. A clustering above the median by one group and below the median by the other group may indicate a real relationship between the two variables, depending on the strength of the pattern and the degree to which other alternative explanations have been ruled out.

Example: Client Referral Beulah is a social worker employed in a genetic counseling center. She observed that only about half of pregnant women over 40 years of age who were referred for amniocentesis (a medical procedure that determines if a fetus has any genetic problems) followed through with the referral. In her observation, she noticed what she thought might be a factor related to this phenomenon. It seemed to her that women who did not follow through on the referral tended to have several children already; those who did follow through seemed to have fewer children. Thus, she formulated a one-tailed research hypothesis:

One-Tailed Research Hypothesis:
Women with more children are less likely to complete a referral than those with fewer children.

The variable "number of children," is at the ratio level of measurement. Beulah knew, however, that the variable is not normally distributed—it is skewed. Thus, she decided to use the median test. She grouped the data into four cells of a contingency table based on where each case fell in regard to the two-category nominal level dependent variable (i.e., completed referral, did not complete referral) and the ratio level independent variable, "number of children" (i.e., above the median, below the median). In this situation, the variable "number of children," is the independent variable, and whether or not the women completed the referral is the dependent variable.

The criteria for size of expected frequencies for chi-square were met, so she completed her statistical analysis using the formula for chi-square (using the Yates Correction Factor). Her initial one-tailed research hypothesis was confirmed by the median test—women with more children were less likely to complete a referral than those with fewer children. She speculated on her findings, wondering whether the possible birth of a child with, for instance, Down's syndrome was of less concern in larger families because additional child-care help was available from older siblings. She decided to pursue the possible explanation in subsequent research studies.

The example we are using is a little unusual for use of the median test in that the independent variable was at the ratio level of measurement, but badly skewed. More typically, it is the dependent variable that is at the interval or ratio level of measurement, but skewed, while the independent variable (e.g., type of treatment) is at the nominal level of measurement. The median test is a good one when either combination of measurement precision is present.

All too frequently, for example, we observe that the criteria for the independent *t* test cannot be met and immediately turn to chi-square. If we had used the median test first, however, it would have sorted the values of the interval or ratio level variable so as to take better advantage of the level of measurement precision that was available. The median test would at least treat the skewed interval or ratio level variable as being more than nominal. As we know from Chapter 10, chi-square treats all variables as if they were at the nominal level of measurement. To use chi-square in such situations, however, increases the risk of an error in drawing conclusions about a relationship between variables.

Like the McNemar's test, the median test has no formula of its own. It really would be more accurate to describe both not as tests, but as procedures for assigning cases into the cells of a contingency table. Then the formula for chi-square, or Fisher's exact test, is applied to produce a p-value.

Kolmogorov-Smirnov Two-Sample Test

The *Kolmogorov-Smirnov two-sample test* (hereafter referred to as the K-S test) has some similarities with the median test. It compares more than just central tendency data, however. It compares (between two samples) the dispersion, skewness, and other characteristics of the distribution of values of an ordinal level variable (or skewed interval or ratio level variable); that is, it compares the entire shape of the two samples' distributions. (A variation, the K-S one-sample test, works similarly, except that it compares the distribution of a variable within a sample with another, theoretical distribution of the variable.)

The K-S test is based on the assumption that if the two subsamples' value categories of a dichotomous nominal level variable are randomly drawn from the same population and the null hypothesis is correct, the overall distribution of the ordinal level variable (or skewed interval or ratio level variable) should be very similar for each of the two subsamples.

If differences between the two subsamples are considerable, they are probably not just random deviations that exist because of chance, or sampling error. They indicate a real relationship between the two variables. In short, the K-S test is a way of determining if the differences in the distribution of the values of the ordinal level variable (or skewed interval or ratio level variable) are large enough to rule out chance, or sampling error, and to reject the null hypothesis.

If ordinal data are used, the K-S test compares the cumulative frequencies for intervals in the variable (e.g., how many cases were rated "not improved" or "slightly improved" for the control group versus the experimental group). More specifically, the test focuses on the point (interval) at which the cumulative frequency difference between the two subsamples was the largest.

Example: Punitive Attitudes Toward AFDC Clients.   Roosevelt is a county director in a public assistance agency. Several of his African-American workers had complained that Caucasian workers seemed to have excessively suspicious and punitive attitudes toward their AFDC clients. They told him that they believed that the African-American clients who were being seen by Caucasian workers were not trusted and were assumed to be "cheaters."

No valid and reliable measuring instrument for the variable "suspicious and punitive attitudes," was immediately available. Roosevelt concluded, however, that the variable "number of referrals for fraud investigation" was an acceptable way to operationalize the variable. Although an exact count of referrals was possible, when used as a measurement of attitudes (the real dependent variable), ordinal measurement of the variable was all that could be claimed.

Roosevelt compiled a count of fraud referrals for each worker during the previous three months. He then assembled a cumulative frequency distribution for African-American workers and for Caucasian workers (the independent variable), using eight intervals of number of referrals for each. The decision to use eight intervals (referrals ranged from 9 to 32) was made in an effort to "conserve" the precision of measurement available (using three intervals would throw away too much data) while not "cutting too thin" by claiming that, for example, a difference of only one referral was a valid indicator of a real difference in attitude.

Having identified the interval at which the cumulative frequency distributions were most different from each other, Roosevelt applied the K-S test. He learned that, in fact, there was little real difference between African-American and Caucasian workers for the measurement of the variable, at least not enough to rule out chance, or sampling error, and to be able to reject the null hypothesis.

While Roosevelt did not totally discount the complaints of his African-American workers (a better measurement might have revealed an attitudinal difference), he did feel that he lacked sufficient evidence to confront his Caucasian workers about what some of his fellow African-American workers perceived as a potential problem. He chose instead to reinforce what he believed to be appropriate attitudes toward AFDC clients in future staff meetings.

The K-S test is useful in looking at the relationship between an ordinal level dependent variable (or skewed interval or ratio level variable) and a nominal level dichotomous independent variable when just a comparison of central tendency may be insufficient. By examining the whole distribution of values of the dependent variable, we get a more complete picture of the similarity of two subsamples contained within the independent variable. Still another test, the *Wald-Wolfowitz runs test*, goes even further in that it identifies some of the more subtle differences in distributions of variables that the K-S test does not detect.

Wilcoxon Sign Test

Sometimes we find ourselves with ordinal level measurements that are "very close" to interval level measurements. This is frequently the case with newly developed measuring instruments that measure attitudes, perceptions, or beliefs. Often, just the amorphous nature of the concept being measured prevents us from claiming that the values we assign reflect precise intervals—that is, equal difference in quantity of the variable.

The *Wilcoxon sign test* is useful in those situations in which, for example, we know that a score of 65 on an anxiety scale reflects more anxiety than a lower score of 60 and where we also believe that this difference is greater than the difference in anxiety reflected in two other lower scores, say 62 and 60. If this latter determination can be made, we would be throwing away available measurement precision if we were to look at only the direction (more, less, or the same) of difference between pairs of matched cases that constitute two subsamples.

In using the Wilcoxon sign test to evaluate the relative effectiveness of two forms of social work intervention, an assumption is made. If the form of intervention used makes no difference, there will be essentially no difference in regard to the dependent variable among the cases in one group and their counterparts in the other group (the null hypothesis).

The ideal situation for using the Wilcoxon sign test involves the use of perfectly matched pairs of cases (identical twins?). Since this is rarely possible, however, cases are usually matched based on a pretest measurement of one or more of the most likely intervening variables.

Once matched pairs are identified, one member is randomly assigned to one group; the second goes to the other group. After the intervention, the Wilcoxon sign test examines the amount of difference between each pair as well as the direction of the difference. In the process, the differences between pairs are themselves rank ordered. If the preponderance of differences suggests higher scores for one group and the greatest differences are also among those cases, the Wilcoxon sign test is likely to suggest a statistically significant difference between the two groups. The null hypothesis can be rejected. The stronger the pattern in this direction, the more likely the null hypothesis can be rejected and vice versa.

As should be evident by now, the Wilcoxon sign test is used as a nonparametric alternative to the dependent *t* test. Both tests are used when we measure a dependent variable for the same sample at two different times. The Wilcoxon sign test is used with "ordinal plus" level data whereas the dependent *t* test is used with interval or ratio level data.

Example: Social Adjustment of College Students.

Linnette is a social work counselor in a student health center. Over the years, she has wondered whether college students having social adjustment problems benefited more from counseling by untrained student volunteers or by professional social work staff. Using standard intake screening measurements over a one-month period, she identified a group of prospective clients who were all diagnosed as having "moderate social adjustment problems." Before assignment for counseling, she identified 15 matched pairs (matched on such key variables as gender, grade point average, and the like) and randomly assigned one member of each pair to be seen by a student volunteer and the other member to be seen by a social worker. After six one-hour counseling sessions, all clients were administered a standard measuring instrument that measured the dependent variable "social adjustment."

The measuring instrument, which Linnette considered an indicator of college students' social adjustment, was deemed to be capable of generating the "ordinal plus" level data required for use of the Wilcoxon sign test. Data were compared for each pair, and the direction and amount of the differences were noted. The differences were then rank ordered.

Linnette was pleased to learn that the students who were seen by the social workers scored much better on the measuring instrument than did those seen by student volunteers ($p < .05$). The Wilcoxon sign test allowed her to reject the null hypothesis. She was, of course, not ready to discount student volunteers as effective counselors based on this single small-scale research study. She wondered, however, whether student volunteers might be used more effectively in working with students having other problems. She also decided to replicate her study, using another standardized measurement of social adjustment to see if consistent findings would be obtained.

As should be evident by now, there are many statistical tests that can be used to analyze data. Which specific test to use is determined by several factors (the shape of the distribution of the variable within the population from which the sample was drawn, sample size, level of measurement, and so on). A quick look back at Figure 7.1 underlines a point that we have made repeatedly—parametric tests have their non-parametric analogues. For example, Figure 7.1 indicates that the independent t test is similar to the Mann-Whitney U test; the dependent t test is similar to the Wilcoxon sign test; Pearson's r is similar to Spearman's rho; and so on.

MULTIVARIATE TESTS

We now turn to three multivariate techniques that are frequently being used since computer analysis of data has become available within most academic and practice settings. They are (1) discriminant analysis, (2) factor analysis, and (3) cluster analysis.

Discriminant Analysis

In social work research we often find ourselves with several interval or ratio level independent variables and a single nominal (or ordinal) level dependent variable. We want to increase our ability to predict the value categories of the nominal level dependent variable such as recidivism (e.g., abused again, did not abuse again), rehospitalization (e.g., rehospitalized, not rehospitalized), or electoral involvement (e.g., voted, did not vote) by identifying a group of interval or ratio level independent variables that will do the best job of predicting the variation within the value categories of the dependent variable.

The dependent variable can be dichotomous, as in the previous examples, or it can contain three or more value categories such as "religious affiliation" (e.g., Christian, Muslim, Jewish, Buddhist, Hindu). We may want to know what "kind" of people select the various denominations, that is, what group of interval or ratio level independent variables might be most helpful in predicting a person's religious affiliation. In either situation, discriminant analysis may be the procedure that is indicated.

A multivariate discriminant analysis creates a derived variable (in this case called the *discriminant function*) from the weighted values of several independent variables. Stepwise variations of the procedure likewise are available. Statistical computer software programs also can produce a useful table (often called a *confusion matrix*). It displays the type and number of errors that a given group of independent variables produce. It includes the number of cases that actually were in a given value category of the nominal (or ordinal) level dependent variable and the number that the independent variables would have predicted to be there. It thus allows us to know the likely number of prediction errors in any direction if a certain group of independent variables were to be used and to assess whether that number would be acceptably low.

Discriminant analysis is closely related to multiple regression. In a statistical sense, however, it is less powerful than multiple regression because it requires only nominal (or ordinal) level measurement of the dependent variable. It should not be used with an interval or ratio level dependent variable. Why throw away measurement precision and statistical power unnecessarily? To use a discriminant analysis rather than a multiple regression analysis with an interval or ratio level dependent variable would be the equivalent of using Mann-Whitney U when the requirements for an independent t test can be met.

Factor Analysis

Along with its other uses, *factor analysis* provides a way of reducing many items, or questions, contained in a measuring instrument to a smaller number that are believed to measure essentially the same variable. In designing multi-item measuring instruments to measure a variable, for example, a factor analysis can be used to reduce the number of items in the instrument without losing the instrument's measurement capacity.

When we first design a measuring instrument, we may have many more items than we ultimately hope to use. We may have included virtually any item that we think might measure the variable that we are trying to measure. We would like to know, for example, which items are redundant, that is, two or more items that measure the same thing, so that we can eliminate some of them. Factor analysis can help us with this task.

A factor analysis relies heavily on the concept of correlation. It examines to what degree peoples' responses to one item correlate with their responses to other items. Two or more items that produce the same response, or nearly the same response, are assumed to be measuring the same variable. Those items that produce dissimilar responses are assumed to be measuring something else. In a measuring instrument that measures the variable "attentiveness in class," for example, one item might ask how frequently a student has fallen asleep in class. Another item might ask how often the student yawns in class.

If, in a large sample of students, there is a strong pattern (positive correlation) of responses wherein individual students tend to respond either "frequently" to both items or "never" to both items, it may be assumed that the two items measure the same dimension of attentiveness. If, however, individual students tended to give very different responses to the two items we might conclude that the two items measure two different dimensions of attentiveness.

Using a variation of correlation analyses, a factor analysis groups items into factors (which can be thought of loosely as variables) based on the responses to them within a large data set. Returning to our example, it might list four different items in one factor because responses to them were similar among individuals. This would indicate that all four items probably are measurements of the same factor (the same abstract underlying dimension that we are attempting to measure). We could then look at the four items themselves to determine what they have in common.

If two of the four items ask about head nodding and resting one's head on one's hand, we may decide to label this factor something like "physical manifestations of attentiveness." We may decide that any one of the items may be sufficient and the other three can be deleted, or we may wish to leave two, three, or all four of them in the next version of the scale as a now-identified subscale.

The factors derived from a factor analysis are dimensions that are independent of other factors. This does not mean, however, that an item will show up in only one group of items (a factor) formed by a factor analysis. An item may be a part of two (or even more) factors.

Questions of how many items or how many factors to retain are complicated ones. Among other considerations, we may ask how long a measuring instrument can be before respondents refuse to complete it. One product of a factor analysis is helpful in this regard. It is an *eigenvalue*, which is a number that corresponds to the number of items that a given factor represents. If we had a factor with an eigenvalue of 4.3, for example, the factor would be the equivalent of 4.3 items. A factor with an eigenvalue of only .8 would be the equivalent of less than one item in terms of its contribution to measurement of a variable. In the interest of efficiency, a measuring instrument usually retains only those factors that have relatively high eigenvalues. A value such as .8 would suggest that retaining its corresponding factor would only make the instrument unnecessarily long and cumbersome. It would add little to the measurement of the variable.

There are a number of other features of factor analyses that allow us to construct just about any form of measuring instrument that we require. Factors can be refined using a process called *factor rotation*. While the process is complicated and has many different variations, all of them are designed to help us develop more precise meanings of the factors within any given data set.

A second practical use of a factor analysis, in addition to instrument construction, is for the preliminary screening of large groups of variables prior to multiple regression or discriminant analyses. Redundant independent variables, which appear as part of the same factors, can be identified, and we may be able to eliminate all but one, thus making the job of either type of analysis much easier.

Factor analyses have many practical uses in fields such as business and marketing. A restaurant owner may do a factor analysis of customers' food preferences to try to identify menu items that are redundant (i.e., may appeal to the same customers). Once identified, some of these items can be eliminated and replaced with others that have the potential to broaden the restaurant's clientele base while not having to offer more menu alternatives.

Marketing managers sometimes perform factor analyses to determine what factors lead people to buy a certain product. Then they develop magazine advertisements based upon the results of their analyses. The advertisements are written carefully to avoid redundancy (the same factors) while covering all identified factors.

A social work manager might use a factor analysis for making similar everyday, practical decisions. Discharge summary records data, for example, could be used to determine which factors constitute the variable "client satisfaction." Then staff development sessions could be used to build in all the factors while not engaging in unnecessary and inefficient redundancy ("overkill").

Factor analyses can be helpful in improving many forms of evaluation in social work. They can be used, for example, to refine measuring instruments used by students to evaluate their instructors, by eliminating redundancy and not placing disproportionate weight on what may be a single indicator of teaching effectiveness such as, "does the instructor know students' names?" or "how nice is the instructor?"

Cluster Analysis

While a factor analysis performs the task of clustering items into factors, a *cluster analysis* is used primarily to cluster cases. Put simply, it is used to form subsamples of cases based on the fact that they have similar measurements (values) in relation to a certain variable. Consequently, a cluster analysis makes hypothesis testing possible (by creating value categories of a variable) rather than by actually testing a hypothesis.

While a cluster analysis has some similarities to a discriminant analysis, there is one important difference. A discriminant analysis begins with one nominal or ordinal level variable that is already "sorted" into value categories and attempts to learn how the categories differ. In a cluster analysis, however, there are no clearly defined value categories. Thus, the goal of a cluster analysis is to form groups (or subsamples of cases) that are similar to each other (but different from cases in other subsamples).

We might conduct a discriminant analysis using people's religious affiliations as our nominal level variable and proceed to try to identify those variables (e.g., income, education level, age) that might **distinguish** one religious affiliation from another. But we might use a cluster analysis, for example, to attempt to **create** groups based upon similar beliefs about a divine being or other religious beliefs.

After the cluster analysis, each group formed would probably contain persons who represent a variety of religious affiliations but who hold similar beliefs. The beliefs of individuals in any one group would be different from those of persons in the other groups. Yet, a member of a group may have the same religious affiliation as a member of another group.

The example above suggests an important use of cluster analyses. Sometimes the similarity of people's attitudes, beliefs, values, or behaviors is of more utility to us than their label or diagnostic category. It might be useful, for example, to employ a cluster analysis to a group of clients with psychological disabilities based upon their frequency of several self-defeating behaviors, rather than upon their DSM-IV diagnosis. We could then use the clusters, or groups, thus formed to constitute different treatment groups that would have quite different therapeutic goals.

CONCLUDING THOUGHTS

This chapter presented only a few of the more commonly used nonparametric and multivariate methods that, along with those discussed in more detail in earlier chapters, are seen fairly frequently in the social work literature. While an in-depth examination of them is beyond the scope of this introductory book, we think that a conceptual introduction to a few of these useful techniques is appropriate for any student of statistics. While mathematics plays a part in understanding a statistical analysis, logic is equally important. It is the latter that we have chosen to emphasize. We have chosen to sacrifice comprehensiveness for simplicity to accomplish our goal of providing a "reader-friendly" introduction to statistics.

STUDY QUESTIONS

1. Why would the McNemar's test be especially well suited for social workers who wish to evaluate the impact of a group experience on a stereotype about minorities? Specifically, how could it be used?
2. When would the median test be preferable to the chi-square test if interval or ratio level data do not meet the necessary criteria for the use of the independent groups *t* test? Provide an original example of how it could be used.

3. Why is the Kolmogorov-Smirnov two-sample test a more comprehensive comparison of ordinal or skewed interval level data drawn from two samples than the median test?

4. What specialized type of sampling is best for the Wilcoxon sign test? For what parametric test that we have studied is it a logical nonparametric alternative?

5. What do all the tests in this chapter and those described elsewhere in this book have in common? How do they work in a similar manner?

6. Discuss the possible disadvantages of using statistical tests that are less well known.

7. Using other statistics books, find additional nonparametric tests that this chapter did not discuss and add them to Figure 7.1 under the appropriate headings. How are the other tests similar to the ones discussed in this chapter? How are they different?

8. Which multivariate statistic could be used to create treatment groups of clients that are homogeneous in relation to such variables as attitudes toward abortion, attitudes toward corporal punishment, and so on? Provide an example of its use.

9. Which multivariate statistic examines the relationship between more than one independent variable and a nominal or ordinal level dependent variable? Provide an example of its use.

10. Explain how factor analyses use the concept of reliability to reduce a large number of variables to a small number of factors. What is an eigenvalue, and what does it represent in a factor analysis?

11. Which forms of statistical analyses described in this book are used primarily for research design tasks rather than for prediction or inference?

References and Further Reading

Anderson, D.R., Sweeney, D.J., & Williams, T.A. (1986). *Statistics: Concepts and applications.* St. Paul, MN: West.

Andrews, F.M., Klem, L., Davidson, T.N., O'Malley, P.M., & Rodgers, W.L. (1994). *A guide for selecting statistical techniques for analyzing social science data* (3rd ed.). Ann Arbor, MI: Institute for Social Research, University of Michigan.

Blalock, H.M., Jr. (1979). *Social statistics* (2nd ed.). New York: McGraw-Hill.

Bohrnstedt, G.W., & Knoke, D. (1988). *Statistics for social data analysis* (2nd ed.). Itasca, IL: F.E. Peacock.

Brown, R.W. (1992). *Graph it! How to make, read, and interpret graphs.* Englewood Cliffs, NJ: Prentice-Hall.

Coleman, H., & Unrau, Y.A. (1996). Phase three: Analyzing your data. In L.M. Tutty, M.A. Rothery, & R.M. Grinnell, Jr. (Eds.). *Qualitative research for social workers: Phases, steps, and tasks.* (pp. 88–119). Needham Heights, MA: Allyn & Bacon.

Craft, J.L. (1990). *Statistics and data analysis for social workers* (2nd ed.). Itasca, IL: F.E. Peacock.

Darlington, R.B., & Carlson, P.M. (1987). *Behavioral statistics: Logic and methods.* New York: Free Press.

Davidson, F. (1996). *Principles of statistical data handling.* Thousand Oaks, CA: Sage.

Foddy, W.H. (1988). *Elementary applied statistics for the social sciences.* New York: Harper & Row.

Freund, J.E. (1988). *Modern elementary statistics* (7th ed.). Englewood Cliffs, NJ: Prentice-Hall.

Gabor, P.A., Unrau, Y.A., & Grinnell, R.M., Jr. (1998). *Program evaluation for social workers: A quality improvement approach for the social services* (2nd ed.). Needham Heights, MA: Allyn & Bacon.

Grinnell, R.M., Jr. (Ed.). (1997). *Social work research and evaluation: Quantitative and qualitative approaches* (5th ed.). Itasca, IL: F.E. Peacock.

Guilford, J.P. (1950). *Fundamental statistics in psychology and education* (2nd ed.). New York: McGraw-Hill.

Heyes, S. (1986). *Starting statistics in psychology and education.* London: Weidenfeld & Nicolson.

Howell, D.C. (1987). *Statistical methods for psychology* (2nd ed.). Boston, MA: Duxbury Press.

Kachigan, S.K. (1991). *Multivariate statistical analysis* (2nd ed.). New York: Radius Press.

Khazanie, R. (1986). *Elementary statistics: In a world of applications* (2nd ed.). Glenview, IL: Scott, Foresman.

Kiess, H.O. (1989). *Statistical concepts for the behavioral sciences.* Needham Heights, MA: Allyn & Bacon.

Krishef, C.H. (1987). *Fundamental statistics for human services and social work.* Boston, MA: Duxbury Press.

Lewis-Beck, M.S. (1995). *Data analysis: An introduction.* Thousand Oaks, CA: Sage.

Loether, H.J., & McTavish, D.G. (1988). *Descriptive and inferential statistics: An introduction* (3rd ed.). Needham Heights, MA: Allyn & Bacon.

Miller, E.L. (1986). *Basic statistics: A conceptual approach for beginners.* Muncie, IL: Accelerated Development.

Reid, S. (1987). *Working with statistics.* Cambridge, MA: Polity Press.

Shavelson, R.J. (1988). *Statistical reasoning for the behavioral sciences* (2nd ed.). Needham Heights, MA: Allyn & Bacon.

Stahl, S.M., & Hennes, J.D. (1980). *Reading and understanding applied statistics* (2nd ed.). St. Louis: Mosby.

Tutty, L.M., Grinnell, R.M., Jr., & Williams, M. (1997). Quantitative data analysis. In R.M. Grinnell, Jr. (Ed.), *Social work research and evaluation: Quantitative and qualitative approaches* (5th ed., pp. 475–500). Itasca, IL: F.E. Peacock.

Tutty, L.M., Rothery, M.A., & Grinnell, R.M., Jr., (Eds.). (1996). *Qualitative research for social workers: Phases, steps, and tasks.* Needham Heights, MA: Allyn & Bacon.

Unrau, Y.A., Krysik, J.L., & Grinnell, R.M., Jr., (1997). *Student study guide to accompany the fifth edition of Social Work Research and Evaluation: Quantitative and qualitative approaches.* Itasca, IL: F.E. Peacock.

Weinbach, R.W., & Grinnell, R.M., Jr. (1996). *Applying research knowledge: A workbook for social work students* (2nd ed.). Needham Heights, MA: Allyn & Bacon.

Wilcox, R.R. (1987). *New statistical procedures for the social sciences: Modern solutions to basic problems.* Hillsdale, NJ: Lawrence Erlbaum.

Williams, M., Tutty, L.M., & Grinnell, R.M., Jr. (1995). *Research in social work: An introduction* (2nd ed.). Itasca, IL: F.E. Peacock.

Wright, S.E. (1986). *Social science statistics.* Needham Heights, MA: Allyn & Bacon.

Yegidis, B., Weinbach, R.W., & Morrison-Rodriguez, B. (1998). *Research methods for social workers* (3rd ed.). Needham Heights, MA: Allyn & Bacon.

Glossary

This glossary is designed as a general reference for the student of statistics. Many of the terms are discussed in detail in the text. Others, which sometimes appear elsewhere in the statistical literature, also have been included.

Absolute frequency distribution. A table that displays the frequencies for various measurements of a variable.

Acceptance region. The outcome of a statistical test that leads to the acceptance of the null hypothesis.

Allowance factor. Used in constructing confidence intervals, it is the distance (on the measurement scale) between the sample statistic and the limits of the interval. We both add and subtract the allowance factor to find, respectively, the upper and lower limits of the confidence interval.

Alpha error. See Type I error.

Alternative hypothesis. See research hypothesis.

Analysis of variance. A statistical technique by which it is possible to partition the variance in a distribution of scores according to separate sources or factors; a statistical measure to test the differences among the means of three or more groups; sometimes referred to as *ANOVA*.

ANOVA. The abbreviation for the statistical procedure known as analysis of variance.

Antecedent variable. A variable that precedes the introduction of the independent variable.

A priori probability. The probability of a future event calculated from prior knowledge of the number of possible outcomes and their relative frequencies.

Arithmetic mean. See mean.

Axes. Reference lines that delineate the two (or sometimes three) dimensions of a graph; the horizontal and vertical lines in a graph upon which values of a measurement or the corresponding frequencies are plotted.

Bar graph. A graphical technique of descriptive statistics that uses the heights of separated bars to show how often each score occurs; graphical representation of a frequency distribution table in which each measurement category is represented by a bar that extends to the appropriate distance in the frequency dimension; usually has spaces between bars to represent nominal level data.

Beta coefficient. When using multiple regression, a mathematically derived indicator of the amount of prediction of the criterion variable that is attributable to any one predictor variable.

Beta error. See Type II error.

Beta weight. When using Multiple R, a mathematically derived indicator of the amount of variation in the criterion variable that is attributable to any one predictor variable.

Biased sample. A sample unintentionally selected in such a way that some members of the population are more likely than others to be picked for sample membership; if we wish to make generalizations about the population based on sample observations, it is desirable to avoid biased samples.

Bimodal distribution. A frequency distribution with two modes reflecting equal or nearly equal frequencies.

Binary variable. A dichotomous variable whose values are 0 (reflecting absence of any quantity of the variable) and 1 (reflecting presence of the variable).

Bivariate analysis. A statistical analysis of the relationship between two variables.

Box plot. A graph that reflects both the central tendency and variability of the distribution of a variable. In one of its most common variations, lines are used to indicate the "five-number summary," that is, the minimum value, the 25th percentile, the median, the 75th percentile, and the maximum value.

Canonical correlation. A statistical procedure that examines simultaneously the correlation between a weighted group of criterion variables (a derived predictor variable) and a weighted group of criterion variables (a weighted criterion variable).

Causal relationship. A relationship between two variables for which we can say that the presence or absence of one

variable determines the presence or absence of the other or that values of one variable result in specific values of the other variable.

Causality. A relationship of cause and effect; the effect will invariably occur when the cause is present; causality is usually statistical; changes in the causal variable (independent variable) will on the average, alter values of the affected variable (dependent variable).

Cell. A compartment in a matrix or table, such as in a cross-tabulation table.

Central limit theorem. The assumption underlying mathematically derived sampling distributions. It states that for a skewed distribution of a variable within a population, the distribution of means from samples of fixed sizes drawn from the population will approach a normal distribution if the sample sizes are large (generally defined as "over 30"). The sampling distribution will have the same mean as the population mean and its variance will be the population variance divided by the sample size.

Central tendency. A typical value for a variable within a data set; one of several descriptive statistics used to reflect a middle value within an array of case values.

Chance. The probability of an event occurring because of some random variation. Sometimes referred to as sampling error.

Chi-square, or goodness-of-fit, test. A technique of inferential statistics used to decide whether a sample with a given frequency distribution could have occurred by chance from a population with a known frequency distribution (or known percentage composition); a nonparametric statistic that allows us to decide whether observed frequencies are essentially equal to or significantly different from expected frequencies.

Chi-square table. See Cross-tabulation table.

Chi-square test of association. A common statistical procedure used to analyze the association between two nominal level variables. It is usually referred to simply as *chi-square*.

Class frequency. Number of observations falling in a class (referring to a frequency histogram).

Cluster analysis. A multivariate statistical procedure that, among its other uses, groups together those cases that have similar measurements (values) in relation to certain variables.

Coding. The act of categorizing raw data into groups or giving the data numerical values.

Coefficient of determination. The proportion of variation in a scattergram that is explained—that is, the proportion of variation of the criterion variable accounted for by the predictor variables; the coefficient of determination is equal to r^2, where r is the Pearson's r for the two variables.

Coefficient of nondetermination. Equal to $1 - r^2$; the proportion of the variation of the criterion variable that is not accounted for by the predictor variable.

Conceptualization. The first step in the measurement process, in which the researcher selects which variables need to be measured; delineating the exact meaning of the independent and dependent variables.

Concomitant variation. The case in which two variables vary together; individuals who differ with respect to variable x will also differ with respect to variable y.

Confidence interval. A range of values within which we are willing to assert with a specified level of confidence that an unknown parameter value lies; computed from sample statistics, the width of the confidence interval depends on the rejection level stated, the sample size, and the variability within the sample.

Confidence level. The probability that a population parameter lies within a given confidence interval.

Confidence limits. Upper and lower boundaries of confidence intervals.

Confounding variables. Variables operating in a specific situation in such a way that their effects cannot be separated; they occur when the effects of an extraneous variable cannot be separated from the effects of the dependent variable; the effects of the extraneous variable thus confound the interpretation of research results.

Confusion matrix. A table that displays the type and number of errors that a given group of predictor variables have produced; a product of discriminant analysis.

Constant. A characteristic that has the same value for all individuals in a research study.

Contingency table. See cross-tabulation table.

Continuous random variable. A random variable that may theoretically assume any value between two points on the measurement scale; it can thus have an infinite number of possible values between those points.

Control group. A group of people who do not receive the experimental treatment; a group used for comparison purposes; those people to whom no experimental stimulus is administered but who resemble members of the experimental group in all other respects; in an experimental research design, a group in which the independent variable is left unchanged; serves as a reference to compare the effect of manipulating the independent variable in the experimental group(s).

Control variable. A variable, other than the independent variable(s) of primary interest, whose effects we can determine; an intervening variable that has been controlled for in the research design; a variable that is included in designs as an independent variable for the purpose of explaining (controlling) variation.

Correction for continuity. An additional step added to the formula for chi-square if there are only four cells (a 2-by-2 table) entailing the subtraction of .5 from the absolute difference between the expected and observed frequencies for each cell prior to squaring it. It is also known as the *Yates Correction Factor.*

Correlated *t* test. See Dependent *t* test. See also *t* test.

Correlated variables. Variables whose values are associated; values of one variable tend to be associated in a systematic way with values in the others.

Correlation coefficient. A single statistic that indicates both the strength and direction of the relationship between two ordinal, interval, or ratio level variables; correlation coefficients have values between $+1$ and -1, with positive values indicating positive relationships and negative values indicating negative relationships; two commonly used correlation coefficients are the Pearson's product-moment correlation coefficient (Pearson's *r*) and the Spearman's rho.

Correlation matrix. A table used to display the correlations among three or more pairs of variables.

Correlational analyses. Statistical methods that allow us to discover, describe, and measure the strength and direction of associations between and among variables; include the various techniques of computing correlation coefficients and regression analyses.

Covariate. The measure used in an analysis of covariance for adjusting the scores of the dependent variable.

Criterion variable. The variable whose values are predicted from measurements of the predictor variable.

Critical region. A set of outcomes of a statistical test that leads to the rejection of the null hypothesis.

Critical value. A value of a test statistic that demarcates the region of rejection and that is thus used as a criterion for statistical significance in hypothesis testing; the value of the statistic that marks the significance level.

Cross-break table. See cross-tabulation table.

Cross-tabulation table. A table showing the joint frequency distribution of two or more nominal level variables; presents how often each combination of values of

each variable occurs; the entries in the table show the number of observations falling into the cells.

Cumulative frequency distribution. A frequency distribution that gives the number of scores that occur at or below each value of a variable.

Cumulative frequency polygon. A frequency polygon that shows how often scores occur at or below each value of a variable.

Cumulative percentage distribution. A table that shows what percentage of scores occur at or below each value of a variable.

Cumulative proportion graph. A graph in which one axis represents values of a variable and the other represents the proportion of the distribution that falls below those values (i.e., their cumulative proportions); when the data have been grouped, each point on the graph is plotted over the upper true limit of the interval it represents; each point thus represents the proportion of the observations falling at or below that interval.

Cumulative proportion table. A summary table of a group of observations that has one column listing values of a variable and another column indicating the proportion of the distribution that falls at or below each value; when the data have been grouped, the table lists intervals on the measurement scale rather than individual values.

Curvilinear correlation. A relationship between variables that if displayed using a scattergram, would form one or more curves; a relationship between two variables that is not linear.

Data. The numbers, or scores, generated by a research study; the word "data" is plural.

Datum. Singular of data.

Degrees of freedom. A characteristic of the sample statistic that determines the appropriate sampling distribution; the number of ways in which the data are free to vary; the number of observations minus the number of restrictions placed on the data; a number related to the sample size in a way that depends on the particular statistical technique employed; in many statistical tests, degree of freedom, or *df*, is needed in order to look up critical values.

Dependent events. Events that influence the probability of occurrence of each other.

Dependent *t* test. A hypothesis-testing procedure used to decide whether two given dependent samples could have occurred by chance, or sampling error; sometimes referred to as a dependent groups *t* test, correlated groups *t* test, paired groups *t* test, or matched groups *t* test.

Dependent variable. The variable that we do not directly introduce or manipulate; after the different levels of the independent variable have been administered, all research participants are measured, in the same way, on the same dependent variable; a variable in which the changes are results of the level or amount of the independent variable(s); also, the variable whose variations are of most interest to the researcher; when used with correlation or regression, it is referred to as the criterion variable.

Derived variable. The correlation between one criterion variable and a group of predictor variables.

Descriptive statistics. Methods used for summarizing and describing data in a clear and precise manner; strictly speaking, descriptive statistics apply only to the people (or objects) actually observed; methods for data reduction.

Design bias. Any effect that systematically distorts the outcome of a research study so that the results are not representative of the phenomenon under investigation. Includes measurement bias and sampling bias.

Deviation from the mean. The distance of a single score from the mean of the distribution from which the scores come.

Deviation score. The difference between the mean of a distribution and an individual score of that distribution; deviation scores are always found by subtracting the mean from the score; a positive value indicates a score above the mean; a negative value indicates a score below the mean.

Dichotomous variable. A variable that can take on only one of two values.

Direct relationship. A relationship between two variables in which high values of one variable are found with high values of the second variable and vice versa; the status of the relationship between two correlated variables is either positive or negative.

Directional hypothesis. A hypothesis stated in such a manner that the direction of the relationship between variables is hypothesized for the results; it uses a statistical test with only one region of rejection, that is, a one-tailed test; a directional test is called for only when certain assumptions can be made; because the region of rejection is located entirely at one end of the distribution in a directional test, fewer deviant values of the observed statistic will lead to rejection of the null hypothesis than in the nondirectional test with the same rejection level.

Directional test. See directional hypothesis.

Discrete measurement. Measurement that can generate only certain values that are separated by discrete intervals.

Discrete variable. A variable that can assume only a finite number of values.

Discriminant analysis. A form of multivariate statistical analysis that is used to classify cases into two or more values of a nominal or ordinal criterion variable based upon measurements of a group of interval or ratio predictor variables.

Discriminant function. A derived variable created in multivariate discriminant analysis that represents the weighted values of several independent variables.

Dispersion. The amount that values of a variable tend to cluster around a measure of central tendency within a data set. It is alternately referred to as "spread" or "variability."

Distribution. The pattern of frequency of occurrence of scores; the total observations or a set of data for a variable; when observations are tabulated according to frequency for each possible score, we have a frequency distribution.

Distribution-free method. A method for testing a hypothesis or setting up a confidence interval, for example, that does not depend on the form of the underlying distribution.

Distribution-free tests. A term referring to a large family of statistical tests that, in general, do not require assumptions about the precise shape of the population distribution; the population distribution of a variable need not be normal in shape and data need not be at least interval level; also called nonparametric tests.

Dummy table. A cross-tabulation table that contains asterisks to reflect where disproportionately large frequencies will be found if a directional hypothesis is supported.

Dummy variable. A variable that is created by converting a qualitative variable into a binary variable.

Duncan test. A statistical procedure for identifying which subsample mean reflects a statistically significant difference from the other subsample means using analysis of variance (*ANOVA*).

Eigenvalue. In factor analysis, a quantity that corresponds to the equivalent number of variables that a derived factor represents.

Empirical frequency distribution. A frequency distribution tabulated from data that have actually been collected (as opposed to a theoretical frequency distribution, which is constructed from theoretical or mathematical considerations).

Empirical sampling distribution. A sampling distribution generated by actually taking random samples and measuring each sample's characteristics.

Error of estimation. Distance between an estimate and the true value of the parameter estimated.

Error of measurement. In measurement, the extent of its inaccuracy.

Estimate. Number computed from sample data used to approximate a population parameter.

Estimator. Rule that tells us how to compute an estimate based on data contained in a sample; an estimator is usually given as a mathematical formula, as in regression analysis.

Expected frequencies. In the chi-square test, the frequencies of observations in different categories (cells) that would be most likely to appear if the null hypothesis were true.

Expected value. The long-run average of a random variable over an indefinite number of samplings.

Expected value of a statistic. The mean of a statistic's sampling distribution.

Experiment. A research study in which we have control over the levels of the independent variable and over the assignment of people (objects) to different conditions.

Experimental group. In an experimental research design, the group in which the independent variable is manipulated or introduced.

Extraneous variable. See intervening variable.

***F*-ratio.** The between-group estimates of the variance of the sampling distribution of the mean divided by the within-group's estimate; the *F*-ratio can be viewed as a measure of the strength of a treatment effect.

***F* statistic.** A test statistic that is used to compare variances from two normal populations; used in analysis of variance.

Factor analysis. A statistical method for identifying certain factors or dimensions that exist within a data set.

Factor rotation. A group of statistical procedures designed to develop more precise meanings of the factors created through a factor analysis.

Factorial designs. Variations of analysis of variance (*ANOVA*) that are used to examine the relationship among two or more nominal or ordinal independent variables and one interval or ratio dependent variable.

Factorial experiments. Experimental research designs that look at the separate effects and interactions of two or more independent variables at the same time.

Fisher's Exact test. A nonparametric statistical test that can be used to examine the association between two dichotomous nominal level variables when the size requirement for expected frequencies for using chi-square cannot be met.

Five-number summary. A concise description of the distribution of the values of a variable within a sample or population. It consists of the minimum value, the 25th percentile, the median, the 75th percentile, and the maximum value. It can be portrayed graphically in a box plot.

Frequency. Number of observations falling in a cell or value category of a specific variable.

Frequency distribution. A table or graph that presents the number of times (frequency) with which different values of the variable occur in a group of observations; a technique of descriptive statistics that shows how often each score occurs.

Frequency polygon. A graphic technique of descriptive statistics that uses the height of connected dots to display the shape of the distribution of a variable; graph of a frequency distribution in which the horizontal axis represents different values of a variable and the vertical axis represents frequencies with which those values occur; in constructing a frequency polygon, a dot is placed over each value of the variable at a height corresponding to the appropriate frequency; the dots are then connected with lines to form a polygon.

Frequency table. In its simplest form, a two-column table with one column listing values of a variable and the other column listing the frequency with which the different values occur within a group of observations. Columns for percentages, cumulative percentages, and cumulative frequencies may also be included.

Grouped cumulative frequency distribution. An extension of a grouped frequency distribution that shows how often scores occur at or below each interval.

Grouped frequency distribution. Table or graph in which frequencies are not listed for each possible value of the variable; rather, a frequency is listed for each of a number of intervals on the measurement scale; each interval is a range of values; all observations falling within the limits of the interval add to the frequency count for that interval; grouped frequency distributions are used most often when data represent observations on a continuous variable.

Grouped frequency histogram. A histogram that shows how often scores occur at given intervals.

Grouped frequency polygon. A frequency polygon that shows how often scores occur at given intervals.

Histogram. A graphic representation of a frequency distribution in which the horizontal line represents values of a variable and the vertical line represents frequencies with which those values occur; a bar is constructed over each value of the variable (or the midpoint of each interval, if the data are grouped) and extended to the appropriate frequency; the term histogram usually refers to such a graph for interval or ratio data, whereas the term bar graph usually refers to such a graph for nominal or ordinal data; a graphic technique of descriptive statistics that uses the heights of adjoining bars to show how often each score occurs.

Horizontal axis. The horizontal dimension of a two-dimensional graph; it usually represents values of the independent variable in frequency distributions; sometimes called the x-axis.

Hottelling's T^2. A statistical test used to examine the relationship among two or more independent variables and two or more dependent variables.

Hypothesis. See research hypothesis.

Hypothesis testing. A technique in inferential statistics in which we make a decision about the state of reality in the population;

the decision consists of either accepting the state of reality proposed by the null hypothesis or rejecting the null hypothesis in favor of the research hypothesis; usually postulates a very specific set of conditions; a technique of inferential statistics that helps us decide whether research results are attributable to chance.

Hypothetical population. A statistical population that has no real existence but is imagined to be generated by repetitions of events of a certain type.

Independent samples design. An experiment in which people are assigned to different groups on a completely random basis; samples are drawn in such a way that the particular subjects chosen for one sample have no influence on which subjects are chosen for the other sample.

Independent *t* test. A statistical test used to decide whether two given independent samples could have occurred by chance, or sampling error. See also *t* test.

Independent variable. The variable we believe to be associated with the different values of the dependent variable; the variable that is manipulated or introduced in a research study in order to see what effect differences in it will have on those variables proposed as being dependent on it.

Inferential statistics. Statistical methods that make it possible to draw tentative conclusions about the population based on observations of a sample selected from that population and, furthermore, to make a probability statement about those conclusions to aid in their evaluation.

Interaction. When the effect of one factor on a response depends on the level(s) of one (or more) other factor(s); the effect of one independent variable upon another; the failure of one independent variable to remain constant over the levels of another; two treatments are said to "interact" if scores obtained under levels of one treatment behave differently under different levels of the other treatment.

Interquartile range. A statistic used as a measure of variability; the distance between the 75th and 25th percentiles;

the interquartile range is more stable than the simple range and can be used with ordinal level data; it does not, however, reflect the value of every observation in the group (as does the standard deviation); the median and interquartile range are often used together to describe a group, since both are based on percentiles.

Interval measurement. A measurement that, in addition to ordering scores, also establishes an equal unit so that distances between any two scores are of a known magnitude; a measurement in which objects, events, or processes are assigned to ordered categories that are separated by equal intervals; any measuring device that is capable not only of placing people (or objects) in their rank order on a characteristic but can also measure the differences between them in regard to that characteristic.

Intervening variable. A variable whose existence is inferred, but it cannot be manipulated; a variable that may affect just what influence (if any) an independent variable has upon a dependent variable; also referred to as a confounding variable or an extraneous variable; when controlled for in a research design, it is known as a control variable. In its most specific usage, a variable that may have come between (in time) the introduction of the independent variable and the dependent variable and may thus have affected the latter.

Inverse relationship. A relationship between two variables in which high values of one variable are found with low values of the other variable and vice versa; sometimes referred to as a negative relationship or negative correlation.

Kendall's partial rank correlation coefficient. A nonparametric test designed to examine the correlation between two variables of at least ordinal level while controlling for a third variable of at least ordinal level.

Kendall's tau. A correlation coefficient showing the strength and direction of a relationship between ranks of two variables in a number of paired observations; it can thus be used when one or both variables produce data at the ordinal level or when interval or ratio data are badly skewed; it is sometimes used as a quickly computed substitute for Pearson's r.

Kolmogorov-Smirnov one-sample test. A nonparametric test that compares the overall distribution of a sample with another theoretical distribution in relation to an ordinal or skewed interval or ratio dependent variable.

Kolmogorov-Smirnov two-sample test. A nonparametric test that compares the overall distribution of two samples in relation to an ordinal or skewed interval or ratio level dependent variable. It identifies the point at which the two samples reflect the greatest difference.

Kruskal-Wallis test. A nonparametric statistical test that can be used to examine the relationship between a nominal variable with more than two values and an ordinal or skewed interval or ratio level variable. It is a common nonparametric alternative to simple, one-way *ANOVA*.

Kurtosis. A quality of the distribution of a set of data dealing with whether or how much the data "pile up" around some central point; the quality of "peakedness" or "flatness" of the graphic representation of a statistical distribution.

Least-squares criterion. The principle that the best regression line is one that would result in the smallest sum of squared deviations from the line.

Leptokurtic distribution. A relatively peaked frequency distribution; a frequency distribution that is more concentrated around the mean than the corresponding normal distribution.

Level of confidence. A term used in constructing confidence interval estimates of parameter values to specify our confidence that the interval includes the parameter value; using procedures for constructing a 95 percent confidence interval, for instance, we would enclose the true parameter value within its limits

on 95 percent of such attempts; the higher the level of confidence, the wider the interval.

Level of measurement. Refers to the degree to which characteristics of the data may be modeled mathematically; the higher the level of measurement, the more statistical methods are applicable.

Level of significance. See rejection level.

Limits of confidence intervals. The upper and lower values at the two ends of a confidence interval; in a symmetrical confidence interval, the limits are located one allowance factor above and below the sample statistic.

Linear correlation. A correlation between variables that if displayed using a scattergram would approximate a straight line.

Linear relationship. A relationship between two variables in which a straight line can be fitted satisfactorily to the points on the scattergram; the scatter of points will cluster elliptically around a straight line rather than around some type of curve.

Line of best fit. See regression line.

Lower confidence limit. Smaller of the two numbers that form a confidence interval; in frequency distributions where data have been grouped, it is the lower boundary of an interval on the measurement scale.

Mann-Whitney *U* test. A nonparametric test that is used to examine the relationship between a dichotomous nominal level variable and an ordinal or skewed interval or ratio level variable. It is a common alternative to the parametric independent t test.

***MANOVA* (multiple analysis of variance).** A form of multivariate statistical analysis used to compare the means of two or more interval or ratio level dependent variables across the value categories of a nominal level independent variable.

Marginals. The count of frequencies with which certain responses occur; in a cross-tabulation table, the row and column totals.

Matched pairs test. A statistical test for the comparison of two population means; the test is based on paired observations, one from each of the two populations; in the two-sample experiment, a procedure in which the entire subject pool is arranged in matched pairs, where pair members are similar (matched) on important characteristics; one member of each pair is then assigned to each group.

Matrix. A two-dimensional organization; each dimension is composed of several positions or alternatives; any particular "score" is a combination of the two dimensions as, for example, in a correlation matrix.

McNemar's test. A nonparametric test used to examine both the direction and amount of change in a group of cases in a pretest-posttest situation where the criterion variable is at the nominal level. It is sometimes called the *test for significance of changes*.

Mean. A term shared by several measures of central tendency (arithmetic mean, harmonic mean, geometric mean, and quadratic mean), all of which are computed using the value of every observation in the data set; in a general sense, the mean is equivalent to the average of all of the values within a data set.

Mean deviation. Measure of variability, that is, literally the mean (absolute value) of the deviations about the mean.

Measure of central tendency. A single number that describes the location, or relative magnitude, of a typical score within a sample or population; synonymous with the term "average;" the mode, median, and mean are examples of central tendency.

Measure of variability. A single number that describes how spread out a group of scores is within a sample or population; the range, variance, and standard deviation are examples of variability.

Measurement. In the most general sense, the assignment of labels to observations according to a rule or system; in statistics, measurement systems are classified according to level of measurement and may produce data that can be represented in numerical form or in words; the assignment of numerals to objects or events according to specific rules.

Measurement bias. A systematic source of measurement distortion that can occur because of any of a wide variety of phenomena.

Median. A measure of central tendency defined as the point on the measurement scale where 50 percent of the observations fall above it and 50 percent of the observations fall below it; it thus coincides with the 50th percentile; it is useful in skewed distributions because it is not as sensitive as the mean to the presence of a few outliers (extremely high or low values); it requires at least ordinal level data.

Mesokurtic distribution. A frequency distribution that is neither excessively peaked nor excessively flat; the normal distribution is a mesokurtic distribution.

Midpoint of an interval. The value located halfway between upper and lower limits of an interval, found by adding upper and lower limits and dividing by 2; when graphing or computing statistics from grouped data, the midpoint of each interval is sometimes used to represent all observations appearing in that interval.

Mode. A measure of central tendency; the most frequently occurring value in a distribution of scores (in grouped distributions, the midpoint of the interval with the highest frequency).

Most powerful test. The statistical test that has the smallest probability of producing a Type II error.

Multiple-group design. An experimental research design with one control group and several experimental groups.

Multiple linear regression. A multivariate statistical procedure that is used to predict the value of an interval or ratio level criterion variable using the values of two or more interval or ratio level predictor variables.

Multiple R. A form of multivariate statistical analysis that determines the amount of variation in a criterion variable that can be explained by the combined variation of a group of predictor variables.

Multivariate analysis. A statistical analysis of the simultaneous relationship among three or more variables.

Mutually exclusive events. In applications of probability theory, two or more events that cannot both happen on a single trial; on a single flip of a coin, for example, the events "heads" and "tails" are mutually exclusive.

Negative relationship. The situation in correlational analysis in which high values of one variable tend to be associated with low values of another and vice versa; negative relationships are indicated by negative correlation coefficients.

Negative skew. A descriptive term applied to frequency distributions with many high values and few extremely low values; on a frequency polygon, negative skew produces a "tail" in the direction of low values—to the left; skewness in which the mean is less than the mode.

Negatively skewed distribution. See negative skew.

Nominal measurement. A measurement that simply classifies elements into two or more mutually exclusive categories, indicating that elements are qualitatively different but not giving order or magnitude; a measurement in which objects, events, or processes are assigned to categories having no inherent order; the level of measurement whose only requirement is that each observation falls in one, and only one, measurement category; also referred to as categorical measurement; it is the lowest level of measurement.

Nondirectional test. A statistical test with two regions of rejection, that is, a two-tailed test; the area under the sampling distribution curve equal to the rejection level is divided into two equal parts at each end of the distribution, creating two regions of rejection; an observed statistic in either region leads to rejection of the null hypothesis; a test used when we have not predicted the direction of a relationship between two variables.

Nonparametric tests. Usually refers to statistical tests of hypotheses about population probability distributions, but not about specific parameters of the distributions; a test that does not require a normal population distribution; a method for testing a hypothesis that does not involve an explicit assertion concerning a parameter; hypothesis-testing procedures that do not make stringent assumptions about population parameters.

Normal distribution. A symmetrical, bell-shaped curve that often arises when a trait is composed of a large number of random, independent factors; the curve possesses a specific mathematical formula.

Null hypothesis. A statement concerning one or more parameters that is subjected to a statistical test; a statement that there is no relationship between the two variables of interest; the belief that any apparent relationship between or among variables within one or more research samples has been caused by chance, or sampling error; the hypothesis that is tested when seeking to gain statistical support for a research hypothesis.

Null research hypothesis. A relatively rare form of research hypothesis in which the researcher predicts that no statistically significant relationship between variables will be found. It is the third form that a research hypothesis can take (along with one-tailed or two-tailed research hypothesis).

Obscuring variable. A third variable that may cause a researcher to underestimate the true strength of the relationship between the independent and the dependent variables. Also called a *suppressor variable*.

Observation. An objectively recorded fact or item of datum; statistics are usually applied to collections of observations. Also referred to as a case.

One-sample *t* test. A hypothesis-testing procedure used to decide whether a given sample could have occurred by chance, or sampling error.

One-tailed research hypothesis. A form of research hypothesis in which the researcher predicts that a statistically significant relationship between variables will be found and also predicts the direction of that relationship.

One-tailed test. See directional hypothesis.

One-way analysis of variance. See simple *ANOVA*.

Ordinal measurement. A measurement that classifies and ranks elements or scores; a procedure that is capable of rank ordering individuals (or objects) on a particular characteristic but that cannot distinguish how different each is from the others; a measurement in which objects, events, or processes are assigned to ordered categories; the level of measurement above nominal but below interval; the data represent at least ordinal scale measurement if each observation falls into one, and only one, category and if observation categories can be rank ordered.

Origin. The point of a graph at which the *x*-axis and *y*-axis intersect.

Outcome. A possible result of an experiment or observation; in probability applications, the result of an experimental trial; see also probability.

Outlier. An extreme value of a variable within a data set that is either larger or smaller than most other values within the variable's distribution.

Paired observations. An observation on two variables, where the intent is to examine the relationship between them; paired observations form the raw material of correlational analyses; recording both a person's height and weight and keeping both of those measurements associated with the same person constitute collection of a paired observation.

Parameter. A characteristic of a population determined from observations on every member of the population; population parameters of interest to us include the mean, range, median, standard deviation, and many others; also a characteristic of a mathematical relation whose value must be specified before the expression can be evaluated; a measure computed from all observations in a population.

Parameter estimates. Attempts to estimate the values of population parameters (e.g., the mean) from statistics computed on a sample selected from the population; estimates may consist of a single value (a point estimate) or a range of values (confidence interval).

Parametric tests. Statistical methods for estimating parameters or testing hypotheses about population parameters; a statistical test in which the null and research hypotheses are stated in terms of population parameter values; an example is the test for the significance of the difference between two means; procedures that make relatively stringent assumptions about population parameters.

Pareto chart. A graph portraying the cumulative frequencies and cumulative percentages for a frequency distribution of a variable.

Partial *r*. A test of correlation in which the relationship between two variables is examined while holding a third, potentially intervening or extraneous variable constant.

Pearson's product-moment correlation coefficient. A correlation coefficient that specifies the strength and direction of a relation between two interval or ratio level variables; it is the most commonly used statistic in correlational analyses; also called Pearson's *r*.

Percent. Synonymous with "in 100" or the number of cases out of 100.

Percentage distribution. A table that displays the percentage of cases that were found to have each of the respective measurements of a variable.

Percentile. A point on the measurement scale below which a specified percentage of the group's observations fall; the 20th percentile, for instance, is the value that has 20 percent of the observations below it.

Percentile rank. A transformed score that tells us the percentage of scores falling at or below a given score.

Perfect relationship. A relationship between two variables in which the value of one variable is known if the value of the other variable is specified; a relationship, either direct or inverse, in which there is a perfect predictability between the two variables; when all points in the scattergram lie exactly on the regression line.

Pie chart. A graph that displays the frequency distribution of a variable as portions of a circle reflecting percentages of the whole.

Platykurtic distribution. A frequency distribution that has a relatively flat shape; a distribution that is less concentrated around the mean than the corresponding normal distribution.

Point estimate. A single value, produced by application of inferential methods to observations on sample members, that is our best guess of a parameter value.

Population distribution. A distribution of all the scores in a population; a collection of all observations identifiable by a set of rules; a designated part of a universe from which a sample is drawn; the complete group of potential observations.

Positive relationship. The situation in correlational analyses that exists when high values of the first variable tend to be associated with high values of the second variable, and low values of the first variable tend to appear with low values of the second.

Positive skew. A descriptive term applied to frequency distributions with many low values and a few extremely high values; on a frequency polygon graph, positive skew produces a "tail" in the direction of the positive values; skewness in which the mode is less than the mean.

Positively skewed distribution. See positive skew.

Power of test. See statistical power.

Prediction. The estimation of scores on one variable from data about one or more other variables.

Predictor variable. The variable that, it is believed, allows us to improve our ability to predict values of the criterion variable.

Probability. A measure of likelihood; the number of outcomes in which an event can occur divided by the total number of possible outcomes; reported as a p-value.

Probability distribution. For discrete random variables, the probability distribution is a relative frequency distribution; the relative frequencies associated with values indicate the probabilities of their occurences.

Proportion. A fraction of one.

Quartile. A percentile that is an even multiple of 25; the 25th percentile is the first quartile, the 50th percentile is the second quartile (it is also the median), and so forth.

Random variable. A variable that can assume different values; there is a probability associated with occurrence of different values of the variable, and these probabilities constitute a probability distribution.

Range. Difference between the largest and smallest numbers of an array plus one; the distance between the highest and lowest values in a distribution (more accurately, the distance between the upper true limit of the highest value and the lower true limit of the lowest value); it is used as a measure of variability.

Ratio measurement. A measurement that, in addition to containing equal units, also establishes an absolute zero point within the scale; a measurement in which objects, events, or processes are assigned to ordered categories that are separated with equal intervals, and where the zero point is not arbitrary; the highest level of measurement; it is reached when each observation falls in one, and only one, category; when observation categories can be ordered; when there are equal intervals between adjacent categories on the measurement scale; and when a value of zero represents a zero quantity of the variable being measured.

Raw score. A numerical value assigned to an observation that is expressed in the original units of measurement; a score obtained directly by measuring some characteristic of a person, event, or process in a research study.

Regression analysis. A variation of a correlational analysis that makes possible prediction of the value of one variable from observations on another variable; these predictions are based on a collection of previously made paired observations on both variables; regression analyses require that the two variables be fairly strongly correlated and that the relation between them approximate a linear one.

Regression equation. A derived equation in the form of $Y' = a + b(X)$ that makes it possible to predict the value of a criterion value from a value of a predictor variable.

Regression line. A hypothetical line that goes through data points and that uses the method of least squares; one of two least-squares lines through a scatter plot of paired observations; each regression line constitutes the collection of predicted values for one of the variables; the straight line of best fit (usually according to the least-squares criterion) for a set of bivariate data; the line of best fit in a scattergram; mostly used to predict values of the y variable from values of the x variable.

Rejection level. Set of values of a statistical test that indicates rejection of the null hypothesis; a probability associated with the test of a hypothesis using statistical techniques that determine whether or not the null hypothesis is rejected; the commonly used rejection level is .05; probability of rejecting the null hypothesis when it is true; also called the alpha level.

Rejection region. A specific region of a normal curve that, when it contains a

measurement from a sample, suggests that it is safe to reject the null hypothesis.

Relative frequency distribution. A table or graph that shows observation categories and the proportion of the group that falls within each value category—that is, the relative frequency of each category; the proportion of observations that falls in one category or interval; in probability applications, the relative frequency of an event is the proportion of trials on which the event occurs.

Reliability. The consistency of a measurement instrument.

Reliability coefficient. A measure of the consistency of a statistical test; there are several methods of computing a reliability coefficient, depending upon the test and the specific situation.

Replication. Repetition of the same research procedures (usually by a second researcher) for the purpose of determining if earlier results can be duplicated; the collection of two or more observations under a set of identical experimental conditions.

Research hypothesis. A prediction that two or more variables will be found to be related; the hypothesis to be supported if the null hypothesis is rejected; also called the alternative hypothesis.

Rival hypothesis. Theoretical alternatives for explaining the apparent relationship between the independent (or predictor) variable(s) and the dependent (or criterion) variable(s); other variables that might explain variations within the dependent (or criterion) variable(s).

Robustness. Refers to the property that certain hypothesis-testing procedures have of yielding accurate results regardless of whether all assumptions for the test are strictly satisfied.

Sample. A subset of the population under study; a subset of a population often used synonymously with "group" and "condition" when discussing research designs; sometimes referred to as a research sample.

Sample distribution. The frequency distribution of all observations in a sample; when a number of different samples are selected from one population, each sample will probably have a sample distribution slightly different from other samples.

Sample statistic. Characteristics of samples; statistics computed from observations on sample members; the mean of a sample is a sample statistic because only members of the sample contribute to its value; the mean of a population is a parameter (rather than a statistic) because all members of the population contributed to its value.

Sampling. A method of selecting members of the population for inclusion in a research study; strictly speaking, proper sampling procedures must be used if inferences about the population are to be made from sample statistics; two broad categories of sampling procedures are random (probability) sampling and non-random (nonprobability) sampling.

Sampling bias. Refers to the systematic distortion of a research sample. It can occur for any of a variety of reasons and produces a sample that is not representative of its population. Not to be confused with sampling error.

Sampling distribution. A theoretical distribution that can be specified for any statistic that can be computed for samples from a population; it is the frequency distribution of that statistic's values that would appear if all possible samples of a specified size N were drawn from the population; it is the foundation of inferential statistics because it allows one to specify the probability with which different values of the statistic appear; it is assumed that a statistic computed from sample observations is one value from such a distribution.

Sampling error. Refers to the natural phenomenon whereby sample statistics tend to differ from population parameters; the degree to which the sample can be predicted to vary from the population in relation to some variable based on this phenomenon. Sometimes referred to as chance. Not to be confused with sampling bias.

Scattergram. A graphic representation of the relationship between two interval or ratio level variables; a two-dimensional graph in which each axis represents values of a different variable; paired observations on both variables are represented as dots on the graph; it may be used as a preliminary step in a correlational analysis or to portray in graphic fashion the strength and direction of a relationship between two variables; sometimes referred to as a scatter plot.

Score. A numerical value assigned to an observation; also called data.

Score interval. In a grouped frequency distribution, the range of observed values is divided into a number of score intervals; the frequency distribution table lists the number of observations that fall into each score interval.

Semi-interquartile range. Half the interquartile range, sometimes used as a measure of variability.

Sign test. Nonparametric statistical test used to compare the same sample at two different times.

Simple ANOVA. A statistical test used to decide whether two or more samples could have occurred by chance from populations with equal means.

Simple linear regression. A statistical procedure that produces an equation that makes it possible to predict the value of the criterion variable for a given value of the predictor variable.

Skewed distribution. A distribution in which more observations fall on one side of the mean than on the other side.

Skewness. A quality of the distribution of a set of data dealing with whether the data are (or are not) symmetrically distributed around a central point.

Spearman's correlation coefficient. A correlation coefficient showing the strength and direction of a relationship between ranks of two variables in a number of paired observations; it can thus be used when one or both variables produce data at the ordinal level or when interval or ratio data are badly skewed; it is sometimes used as a quickly computed substitute for Pearson's r; also referred to as Spearman's rho.

Specifying variable. A third variable that can further explain a relationship between the independent and dependent variables that is statistically significant but that seems to exist in two different directions.

Spurious relationship. Occurring because of chance, or sampling error; not a "real" relationship that exists beyond the sample or samples in which it was identified.

Stability. The degree to which a statistic's value remains constant when it is computed for a number of different groups that are essentially alike but that differ in a few values; in inferential statistics, a stable statistic is one whose value remains stable from sample to sample when all samples are taken from the same population.

Standard deviation. A common measure of variability; it requires at least interval level data and reflects the value of every observation in the distribution; like other measures of variability, it is a single number whose size indicates the spread, or dispersion, of the distribution; a measure of variability that is the square root of the variance; it represents a specified distance along the baseline of a distribution curve.

Standard error. An estimate of how well a regression equation can predict values of the criterion variable from known values of the predictor variable.

Standard error of a statistic. The standard deviation of the underlying (sampling) distribution of the statistic.

Standard error of estimate. In the regression situation, the standard deviation of observed values around the regression line; the smaller the standard error of estimate, the more precisely we can predict scores of the criterion variable.

Standard error of the difference. Refers to the standard deviation of the sampling distribution of the difference for independent samples.

Standard error of the mean. The standard deviation of the underlying (sampling) distribution of the mean. It is the square root of the variance of the mean.

Standard normal distribution. The normal distribution with a mean of zero and a standard deviation of one.

Standard score. A score stated in units of standard deviation from the mean of the distribution; a negative score indicates a score below the mean and a positive score indicates a score above the mean; an individual observation that belongs to a distribution with a mean of 0 and a standard deviation of 1; any distribution of raw scores can be transformed into a distribution of standard scores without changing the shape of the distribution or the relative order or distances between members because the transformation to standard scores is linear; also referred to as a z score.

Statistical decision. Choosing between states of possible reality on the basis of probability considerations; hypothesis testing involves a statistical decision in which we either accept or reject the null hypothesis.

Statistical power. The ability of a statistical test to reject correctly the null hypothesis; a test's ability to detect a true relationship between or among variables.

Statistically significant. Judged too unlikely to have occurred by chance. A statistically significant relationship between variables within a sample or samples is probably not the work of sampling error. However, other variables or conditions may have produced it.

Statistics. In comparison to the term parameters, statistics refers to the characteristics of a sample rather than to the characteristics of a population; in the context of descriptive statistics, measures taken on a distribution; in the context of inferential statistics, measures or characteristics of a sample; in a more general sense, the theory, procedures, and methods by which data are analyzed; the area of study that includes methods for producing and interpreting statistics; generally speaking, statistical methods are applied in an attempt to understand large masses of data, to discover and describe characteristics of the data that are not apparent from casual observation, and to describe characteristics of a group of observations rather than single observations.

Stem-and-leaf plot. A graph consisting of numbers which reflect the actual case values of all cases in a frequency distribution.

Structural variables. In data analyses, those characteristics formed by combining units from lower levels of analysis.

Suppressor variable. A third variable that may cause a researcher to underestimate the true strength of the relationship between the independent and dependent variables. Also called an *obscuring variable*.

Symmetrical distribution. A distribution in which, for every observation on one side of the mean, there is another observation at an equal distance on the other side of the mean; in a symmetrical distribution, the left half of the polygon (or histogram) is a mirror image of the right half; a distribution with a frequency polygon whose left and right sides will coincide if it is folded in the middle along a vertical line.

Transformed standardized score. A score that allows us to tell at a glance where it falls in a distribution of scores; a standard score that has been transformed so that it now belongs to a distribution with any mean and standard deviation we wish; transformed scores are used most often in evaluating test scores.

Trimmed mean. A measure of central tendency calculated by first trimming a small percentage (usually 5%) of values off the upper and lower limits of an array of case values and then averaging the remaining values.

True limits of a number. The upper and lower points on the measurement scale that enclose all values of the variable actually represented by a number.

***t* test.** A group of parametric tests that use the *t* distribution to examine the issue of inference; determines if there is a statistically significant difference between the means of two samples or between a sample's mean and its population's mean.

Two-tailed research hypothesis. A form of research hypothesis in which the researcher predicts that a statistically significant relationship between variables will be found but does not predict the direction of that relationship.

Two-tailed test. See nondirectional test.

Type I error. Error that occurs when the null hypothesis is rejected when a true relationship between variables does not exist; also called *alpha error*.

Type II error. Error that occurs when the null hypothesis is not rejected when a true relationship between variables exists; also called *beta error*.

Unbiased estimator. Estimator that has a probability distribution with the mean equal to the estimated parameter; an estimate of a parameter is said to be unbiased if its expected value is equal to the parameter.

Unbiased statistic. A statistic computed in a manner such that the mean of its underlying distribution is the parameter that the statistic estimates.

Underlying sampling distribution of a statistic. The distribution (usually theoretical) of all possible values of the statistic from all possible samples of a given size selected from the population.

Unimodal. Refers to a distribution with only one mode.

Univariate analysis. Statistical analysis of the distribution of values of a single variable.

Upper confidence limit. Larger of the two numbers that form a confidence interval.

Upper limit of an interval. In frequency distributions where data have been grouped, the upper boundary of an interval on the measurement scale.

Validity. The degree to which a measurement instrument accurately measures what it is claimed to measure.

Variability. Dispersion of a distribution; the extent to which values differ among themselves; variability is not the name of a specific statistic; rather, it is the term applied to the characteristic of dispersion.

Variable. A characteristic that takes on different values; any attribute whose value, or level, can change; any characteristic (of a person, object, or situation) that can change value or kind from observation to observation.

Variance. Measure of variability that is the average value of the squares of the deviations from the mean of the scores in a distribution; measure of data variation; the mean squared deviation from the mean; the squared standard deviation, sometimes called the mean square.

Variation. Sum of the squared deviations about the mean; in some applications, variation is useful in its own right as a measure of variability; also called sum of squares.

Vertical axis. The vertical dimension of a two-dimensional graph; it usually represents frequency in frequency distributions, relative frequency in relative frequency distributions, and cumulative proportion in cumulative proportion graphs; when experimental results are graphed, it usually represents values of the dependent variable.

Weighted mean. The average of a group of scores that are weighted to reflect their different levels of importance. The weighted mean is widely used to compute student final grades when different graded exercises or examinations have been assigned different percentages of the course grade.

Wilcoxon Sign. A nonparametric statistical test that examines the relationship between two "ordinal plus" variables within two matched case samples.

x variable. The variable plotted on the x-axis of a scattergram and the "predictor" variable (used to predict the y variable) in regression; usually the independent variable in a research study.

Yates' Correction Factor. In computing the obtained chi-square statistic, a mathematical correction that should be applied when $df = 1$.

Yule's Q. One of several easily computed statistical tests that often is used for exploratory data analysis, that is, to determine if relationships between variables are sufficiently "promising" to examine, using more powerful forms of analysis.

y variable. The variable plotted on the x-axis in a scattergram and the "predicted" variable (predicted from the x variable) in regression; usually the dependent variable in a research study.

z score. A transformed score that tells us how many standard deviations a score lies away from the mean in a distribution.

Z test. A hypothesis-testing procedure used to decide whether a given sample could have occurred by chance from a population with a given mean and known standard deviation.

Zero relationship. The situation that exists when values of one variable are not related in any way to values of another variable; with a zero relationship, knowing the value of one variable gives us no indication of the value of the other; perfect zero relationships are represented by correlation coefficients of 0.

Appendices

APPENDIX A Areas of the Normal Curve

Area under the normal curve between mean and z score

z	.00	.01	.02	.03	.04	.05	.06	.07	.08	.09
0.0	00.00	00.40	00.80	01.20	01.60	01.99	02.39	02.79	03.19	03.59
0.1	03.98	04.38	04.78	05.17	05.57	05.96	06.36	06.75	07.14	07.53
0.2	07.93	08.32	08.71	09.10	09.48	09.87	10.26	10.64	11.03	11.41
0.3	11.79	12.17	12.55	12.93	13.31	13.68	14.06	14.43	14.80	15.17
0.4	15.54	15.91	16.28	16.64	17.00	17.36	17.72	18.08	18.44	18.79
0.5	19.15	19.50	19.85	20.19	20.54	20.88	21.23	21.57	21.90	22.24
0.6	22.57	22.91	23.24	23.57	23.89	24.22	24.54	24.86	25.17	25.49
0.7	25.80	26.11	26.42	26.73	27.04	27.34	27.64	27.94	28.23	28.52
0.8	28.81	29.10	29.39	29.67	29.95	30.23	30.51	30.78	31.06	31.33
0.9	31.59	31.86	32.12	32.38	32.64	32.90	33.15	33.40	33.65	33.89
1.0	34.13	34.38	34.61	34.85	35.08	35.31	35.54	35.77	35.99	36.21
1.1	36.43	36.65	36.86	37.08	37.29	37.49	37.70	37.90	38.10	38.30
1.2	38.49	38.69	38.88	39.07	39.25	39.44	39.62	39.80	39.97	40.15
1.3	40.32	40.49	40.66	40.82	40.99	41.15	41.31	41.47	41.62	41.77
1.4	41.92	42.07	42.22	42.36	42.51	42.65	42.79	42.92	43.06	43.19
1.5	43.32	43.45	43.57	43.70	43.83	43.94	44.06	44.18	44.29	44.41
1.6	44.52	44.63	44.74	44.84	44.95	45.05	45.15	45.25	45.35	45.45
1.7	45.54	45.64	45.73	45.82	45.91	45.99	46.08	46.16	46.25	46.33
1.8	46.41	46.49	46.56	46.64	46.71	46.78	46.86	46.93	46.99	47.06
1.9	47.13	47.19	47.26	47.32	47.38	47.44	47.50	47.56	47.61	47.67
2.0	47.72	47.78	47.83	47.88	47.93	47.98	48.03	48.08	48.12	48.17
2.1	48.21	48.26	48.30	48.34	48.38	48.42	48.46	48.50	48.54	48.57
2.2	48.61	48.64	48.68	48.71	48.75	48.78	48.81	48.84	48.87	48.90
2.3	48.93	48.96	48.98	49.01	49.04	49.06	49.09	49.11	49.13	49.16
2.4	49.18	49.20	49.22	49.25	49.27	49.29	49.31	49.32	49.34	49.36
2.5	49.38	49.40	49.41	49.43	49.45	49.46	49.48	49.49	49.51	49.52
2.6	49.53	49.55	49.56	49.57	49.59	49.60	49.61	49.62	49.63	49.64
2.7	49.65	49.66	49.67	49.68	49.69	49.70	49.71	49.72	49.73	49.74
2.8	49.74	49.75	49.76	49.77	49.77	49.78	49.79	49.79	49.80	49.81
2.9	49.81	49.82	49.82	49.83	49.84	49.84	49.85	49.85	49.86	49.86
3.0	49.87									
3.5	49.98									
4.0	49.997									
5.0	49.99997									

Source: The original data for Table 4.3 came from *Tables for Statisticians and Biometricians*, edited by K. Pearson, published by the Imperial College of Science and Technology, and are used here by permission of the Biometrika trustees. The adaptation of these data is taken from E.L. Lindquist, *A First Course in Statistics* (revised edition), with permission of the publisher, Houghton Mifflin Company.

APPENDIX B Critical Values of *r*

N	Level of significance for a one-tailed test				
	.05	.025	.01	.005	.0005
	Level of significance for a two-tailed test				
	.10	.05	.02	.01	.001
5	.8054	.8783	.9343	.9587	.9912
6	.7293	.8114	.8822	.9172	.9741
7	.6694	.7545	.8329	.8745	.9507
8	.6215	.7067	.7887	.8343	.9249
9	.5822	.6664	.7498	.7977	.8982
10	.5494	.6319	.7155	.7646	.8721
11	.5214	.6021	.6851	.7348	.8471
12	.4973	.5760	.6581	.7079	.8233
13	.4762	.5529	.6339	.6835	.8010
14	.4575	.5324	.6120	.6614	.7800
15	.4409	.5139	.5923	.6411	.7603
16	.4259	.4973	.5742	.6226	.7420
17	.4124	.4821	.5577	.6055	.7246
18	.4000	.4683	.5425	.5897	.7084
19	.3887	.4555	.5285	.5751	.6932
20	.3783	.4438	.5155	.5614	.6787
21	.3687	.4329	.5034	.5487	.6652
22	.3598	.4227	.4921	.5368	.6524
27	.3233	.3809	.4451	.4869	.5974
32	.2960	.3494	.4093	.4487	.5541
37	.2746	.3246	.3810	.4182	.5189
42	.2573	.3044	.3578	.3932	.4896
47	.2428	.2875	.3384	.3721	.4648
52	.2306	.2732	.3218	.3541	.4433
62	.2108	.2500	.2948	.3248	.4078
72	.1954	.2319	.2737	.3017	.3799
82	.1829	.2172	.2565	.2830	.3568
92	.1726	.2050	.2422	.2673	.3375
102	.1638	.1946	.2301	.2540	.3211

Source: From Table VII of R.A. Fisher and F. Yates, *Statistical Tables for Biological, Agricultural, and Medical Research*, published by Longman Group, Ltd., London (previously published by Oliver and Boyd, Ltd., Edinburgh) and by permission of the authors and publishers.

APPENDIX C Critical Values of χ^2

	Level of significance for a one-tailed test					
	.10	.05	.025	.01	.005	.0005
	Level of significance for a two-tailed test					
df	.20	.10	.05	.02	.01	.001
1	1.64	2.71	3.84	5.41	6.64	10.83
2	3.22	4.60	5.99	7.82	9.21	13.82
3	4.64	6.25	7.82	9.84	11.34	16.27
4	5.99	7.78	9.49	11.67	13.28	18.46
5	7.29	9.24	11.07	13.39	15.09	20.52
6	8.56	10.64	12.59	15.03	16.81	22.46
7	9.80	12.02	14.07	16.62	18.48	24.32
8	11.03	13.36	15.51	18.17	20.09	26.12
9	12.24	14.68	16.92	19.68	21.67	27.88
10	13.44	15.99	18.31	21.16	23.21	29.59
11	14.63	17.28	19.68	22.62	24.72	31.26
12	15.81	18.55	21.03	24.05	26.22	32.91
13	16.98	19.81	22.36	25.47	27.69	34.53
14	18.15	21.06	23.68	26.87	29.14	36.12
15	19.31	22.31	25.00	28.26	30.58	37.70
16	20.46	23.54	26.30	29.63	32.00	39.29
17	21.62	24.77	27.59	31.00	33.41	40.75
18	22.76	25.99	28.87	32.35	34.80	42.31
19	23.90	27.20	30.14	33.69	36.19	43.82
20	25.04	28.41	31.41	35.02	37.57	45.32
21	26.17	29.62	32.67	36.34	38.93	46.80
22	27.30	30.81	33.92	37.66	40.29	48.27
23	28.43	32.01	35.17	38.97	41.64	49.73
24	29.55	33.20	36.42	40.27	42.98	51.18
25	30.68	34.38	37.65	41.57	44.31	52.62
26	31.80	35.56	38.88	42.86	45.64	54.05
27	32.91	36.74	40.11	44.14	46.94	55.48
28	34.03	37.92	41.34	45.42	48.28	56.89
29	35.14	39.09	42.69	46.69	49.59	58.30
30	36.25	40.26	43.77	47.96	50.89	59.70
32	38.47	42.59	46.19	50.49	53.49	62.49
34	40.68	44.90	48.60	53.00	56.06	65.25
36	42.88	47.21	51.00	55.49	58.62	67.99
38	45.08	49.51	53.38	57.97	61.16	70.70
40	47.27	51.81	55.76	60.44	63.69	73.40
44	51.64	56.37	60.48	65.34	68.71	78.75
48	55.99	60.91	65.17	70.20	73.68	84.04
52	60.33	65.42	69.83	75.02	78.62	89.27
56	64.66	69.92	74.47	79.82	83.51	94.46
60	68.97	74.40	79.08	84.58	88.38	99.61

Source: From Table IV of R.A. Fisher and F. Yates, *Statistical Tables for Biological, Agricultural, and Medical Research*, published by Longman Group, Ltd., London (previously published by Oliver and Boyd, Ltd., Edinburgh) and by permission of the authors and publishers.

APPENDIX D Critical Values of *t*

	Level of significance for a one-tailed test					
	.10	.05	.025	.01	.005	.0005
	Level of significance for a two-tailed test					
df	.20	.10	.05	.02	.01	.001
1	3.078	6.314	12.706	31.821	63.657	636.619
2	1.886	2.920	4.303	6.965	9.925	31.598
3	1.638	2.353	3.182	4.541	5.841	12.941
4	1.533	2.132	2.776	3.747	4.604	8.610
5	1.476	2.015	2.571	3.365	4.032	6.859
6	1.440	1.943	2.447	3.143	3.707	5.959
7	1.415	1.895	2.365	2.998	3.499	5.405
8	1.397	1.860	2.306	2.896	3.355	5.041
9	1.383	1.833	2.262	2.821	3.250	4.781
10	1.372	1.812	2.228	2.764	3.169	4.587
11	1.363	1.796	2.201	2.718	3.106	4.437
12	1.356	1.782	2.179	2.681	3.055	4.318
13	1.350	1.771	2.160	2.650	3.012	4.221
14	1.345	1.761	2.145	2.624	2.977	4.140
15	1.341	1.753	2.131	2.602	2.947	4.073
16	1.337	1.746	2.120	2.583	2.921	4.015
17	1.333	1.740	2.110	2.567	2.898	3.965
18	1.330	1.734	2.101	2.552	2.878	3.922
19	1.328	1.729	2.093	2.539	2.861	3.883
20	1.325	1.725	2.086	2.528	2.845	3.850
21	1.323	1.721	2.080	2.518	2.831	3.819
22	1.321	1.717	2.074	2.508	2.819	3.792
23	1.319	1.714	2.069	2.500	2.807	3.767
24	1.318	1.711	2.064	2.492	2.797	3.745
25	1.316	1.708	2.060	2.485	2.787	3.725
26	1.315	1.706	2.056	2.479	2.779	3.707
27	1.314	1.703	2.052	2.473	2.771	3.690
28	1.313	1.701	2.048	2.467	2.763	3.674
29	1.311	1.699	2.045	2.462	2.756	3.659
30	1.310	1.697	2.042	2.457	2.750	3.646
40	1.303	1.684	2.021	2.423	2.704	3.551
60	1.296	1.671	2.000	2.390	2.660	3.460
120	1.289	1.658	1.980	2.358	2.617	3.373

Source: From Table III of R.A. Fisher and F. Yates, *Statistical Tables for Biological, Agricultural, and Medical Research*, published by Longman Group, Ltd., London (previously published by Oliver and Boyd, Ltd., Edinburgh) and by permission of the authors and publishers.

Index